Developing China's Capital Market

Also by Douglas Cumming

VENTURE CAPITAL AND PRIVATE EQUITY CONTRACTING: An International Perspective (*with S.A. Johan*)

OXFORD HANDBOOK OF ENTREPRENEURIAL FINANCE (*edited*)

OXFORD HANDBOOK OF VENTURE CAPITAL (*edited*)

OXFORD HANDBOOK OF PRIVATE EQUITY (*edited*)

VENTURE CAPITAL: Investment Strategies, Structures and Policies (*edited*)

PRIVATE EQUITY: Fund Types, Risks and Returns, and Regulation (*edited*)

Developing China's Capital Market

Experiences and Challenges

Edited by

Douglas Cumming
Schulich School of Business, York University, Toronto, Canada

Alessandra Guariglia
Department of Economics, University of Birmingham, UK

Wenxuan Hou
University of Edinburgh Business School, UK

and

Edward Lee
Manchester Business School, University of Manchester, UK

palgrave
macmillan

First published 2013 by
PALGRAVE MACMILLAN

Palgrave Macmillan in the UK is an imprint of Macmillan Publishers Limited, registered in England, company number 785998, of Houndmills, Basingstoke, Hampshire RG21 6XS.

Palgrave Macmillan in the US is a division of St Martin's Press LLC, 175 Fifth Avenue, New York, NY 10010.

Palgrave Macmillan is the global academic imprint of the above companies and has companies and representatives throughout the world.

Palgrave® and Macmillan® are registered trademarks in the United States, the United Kingdom, Europe and other countries

ISBN: 978–1–137–34156–3

This book is printed on paper suitable for recycling and made from fully managed and sustained forest sources. Logging, pulping and manufacturing processes are expected to conform to the environmental regulations of the country of origin.

A catalogue record for this book is available from the British Library.

A catalog record for this book is available from the Library of Congress.

Contents

List of Tables

List of Figures

Notes on Contributors

Chris Adcock is Professor of Financial Econometrics at the University of Sheffield and Visiting Professor of Quantitative Finance at the University of Southampton. He is the founding editor of *The European Journal of Finance* and sometime associate editor of several finance journals and Series C and D of the *Journal of the Royal Statistical Society*.

Martin Conyon is Professor of Finance at Lancaster University Management School in the U.K. and a Senior Fellow at the Wharton School, University of Pennsylvania. He has published more than 50 articles, books, or book chapters relating to corporate governance. He is an editorial board member of the *Strategic Management Journal*, *Strategic Organization*, and *Corporate Governance: An International Review*.

Douglas Cumming, J.D., Ph.D., CFA, is Professor of Finance and Entrepreneurship and the Ontario Research Chair at the Schulich School of Business, York University. His research interests include venture capital, private equity, hedge funds, entrepreneurship, and law and finance. He is Co-Editor of *Entrepreneurship Theory and Practice*, and has been a guest editor for 12 special issues of top journals. He has published over 90 articles in leading refereed academic journals in finance, management, and law and economics, such as the *Journal of Financial Economics*, *Review of Financial Studies*, *Journal of International Business Studies* and the *Journal of Empirical Legal Studies*. He is the coauthor of *Venture Capital and Private Equity Contracting* (2009), and *Hedge Fund Structure, Regulation and Performance around the World* (2013). He is the editor of the *Oxford Handbook of Entrepreneurial Finance* (2012), the *Oxford Handbook of Private Equity* (2012), and the *Oxford Handbook of Venture Capital* (2012). His work has been reviewed in numerous media outlets, including *The Economist*, *Canadian Business*, the *National Post*, and *The New Yorker*. He is a research associate with the Bocconi University Paolo Baffi Center for Central Banking and Financial Regulation (Milan), Groupe d'Economie Mondiale at Sciences Po (Paris), Capital Markets CRC (Sydney), Venture Capital Experts (New York), Cambridge University ESRC Center for Business Research (Cambridge UK), Center for Financial Studies (Frankfurt), Amsterdam Center for Research in International Finance, and the University of Calgary Van Horne Institute. He has also consulted for a variety of governmental and private organizations in Australasia, Europe and North America. Much of Cumming's work is online at SSRN: http://ssrn.com/author=75390.

Yizhe Dong is Lecturer in Finance at Aberystwyth University. He obtained his Ph.D. degree from Loughborough University. Previously, he worked as a post-doctoral fellow at Durham University Business School. Dong's research interests include efficiency and productivity analysis, bank governance, the structure and competition of banking markets and the design of banking regulation.

Michael Firth is Professor of Finance at Lingnan University. He has held university appointments in Scotland, New Zealand, the U.S., and Hong Kong. His research interests include financial accounting, auditing, governance, corporate finance, and investments.

Alessandra Guariglia received her Ph.D. from Boston University. She is currently a Professor of Financial Economics and Head of the Department of Economics at the University of Birmingham. Prior to that, she has worked at the Universities of Essex, Kent, Nottingham, and Durham. She is Associate Editor of the *Journal of Banking and Finance and the European Journal of Finance.* In 2011 and 2012, she has also served as a guest co-editor of two *European Journal of Finance* Special Issues on Chinese capital markets, and is currently co-editing an *International Small Business Journal* Special Issue also on Chinese capital markets. Her research interests are in the areas of financial economics and macroeconomics. Specifically, the focus of her research is on the links between macroeconomic activity and finance and on the economics of transition in China. She has published a range of papers including articles in the *Journal of Development Economics, Journal of International Economics, Journal of Banking and Finance, Journal of Comparative Economics, Economics Letters, Economica, Oxford Economic Papers, Oxford Bulletin of Economics and Statistics,* and *Econometrics Journal.*

Jiao Hanzhang received his master's degree at Durham University and served as a part-time research assistant. His research interests cover corporate governance and emerging markets. Since 2012, he worked at Bank of Communications in China.

Lerong He is Associate Professor of Management in the School of Business Administration and Economics at State University of New York at Brockport. Dr. He obtained her Ph.D. degree from the Wharton School, University of Pennsylvania and has published in the fields of corporate governance, entrepreneurship, and business ethics. Her recent research focus is on China.

Wenxuan Hou is Associate Professor of Finance at University of Edinburgh, and Associate Editor of European Journal of Finance. He received his Ph.D. from Manchester Business School and pursued executive training at Kellogg School of Management. His research interests include corporate governance, emerging markets, regulatory reform and business ethics. He has served as a guest editor for *Journal of Business, Business History, European Journal of Finance, International Small Business Journal, International Review of Financial Analysis,* and *Abacus*. He founded the China Development Research Centre and organized special issues conference in various countries. Prior to joining Edinburgh in 2012, he worked as Assistant Professor and then Associate Professor in Finance at Durham University. He has published papers in the *Journal of Business Ethics, British Accounting Review, European Journal of Finance Emerging Markets Review,* and *Journal of Multinational Financial Management.*

Xiuping Hua is Assistant Professor of Finance in Nottingham University Business School China. She obtained her Ph.D. degree in Finance from the University of Sheffield Management School (U.K.) and then joined the University of Nottingham Ningbo China in September 2010. Currently she also works work as a research fellow in both Bank of China and a prestigious Chinese think-tank in economics and finance, China Finance 40 Forum.

Man Jin is a Ph.D. candidate in the Department of Economics at State University of New York at Binghamton. She received her bachelor's degree in Finance from Zhejiang University, China. She also obtained her Master of Philosophy in Finance from Lingnan University, Hong Kong. Her research interests include corporate finance, information asymmetry and econometrics. She published her work in *The European Journal of Finance*.

Edward Lee is Associate Professor of Accounting and Finance at Manchester Business School, University of Manchester, UK. He received his Ph.D. from the University of Manchester. He served as a guest co-editor for *European Journal of Finance* 2011 and 2012 Special Issues and for *International Small Business Journal* 2012. She is currently co-editing *Journal of Business Ethics* 2013 Special Issues on Chinese capital market. He is currently on the editorial board of the *European Accounting Review* and has organized the joint London School of Economics and Manchester Business School annual accounting conference in the summer of 2012.

His research interests focuses on the interrelationship between corporate information disclosure, regulatory reforms, and the well-being of the capital market., He reviews papers for leading academic journals such as *Entrepreneurship Theory and Practice, Review of Accounting Studies, Journal of Business, Finance, and Accounting, Journal of Accounting and Public Policy, European Financial Management, Financial Review, Corporate Governance: An International Review, Review of Quantitative Finance and Accounting,* and *British Accounting Review.* He has published a range of papers in academic journals such as the *Journal of Accounting Research, Journal of Accounting and Public Policy, European Financial Management, International Journal of Accounting, Corporate Governance: An International Review,* and *Accounting and Business Research.* His paper in International Journal of Accounting is among the 10 most cited papers of this journal. He has also co-authored official reports for the Association of Chartered Certified Accountants (ACCA), which is one of the largest professional accounting organizations in the world. His work on has been cited by policy statements of the Accounting Standards Board (ASB), which is the main accounting regulating body of UK.

Ningyue Liu is a lecturer at School of Management and Economics, Beijing Institute of Technology. She holds Ph.D. degrees in Finance from University College Dublin and in Management from Renmin University of China respectively. Her research interests cover corporate governance and institutional investors in emerging markets.

Liming Wang is the Director of the Irish Institute for Chinese Studies at University College Dublin (UCD) and UCD Confucius Institute for Ireland. His research interests include comparative studies between Chinese and European economies, China's financial market and international trade, China's rural development and grain economy.

Shuo Wang is a master's candidate in the School of International Service at American University. He obtained his bachelor's degree in Economics from Zhejiang University, studied in Dublin and Barcelona, and researched in Edmonton, Canada. His current research concentrates on the politics and main institutions of the global economy.

Sheng Xiao is Assistant Professor of Finance at Bill and Vieve Gore School of Business of Westminster College in Salt Lake City, Utah, USA. He received his Ph.D. in Economics from Vanderbilt University. He has published papers in *Journal of International Money and Finance, European Journal of Finance, Emerging Markets Review, China Economic Review* and *Economics Letters.* His research interests include venture capital and innovations, empirical corporate finance, corporate governance and political economy.

Yuanyuan Zhang is Assistant Professor of Finance in the Department of Finance and Insurance, Lingnan University, Hong Kong. Dr. Zhang obtained her Ph.D. degree from the Department of Accounting and Finance, Lancaster University. Her research interests include corporate finance, derivatives and market microstructure.

Xiangyi Zhou is currently a Lecturer of Economics in Jinhe Center for Economic Research at Xi'an Jiaotong University, Shaanxi, China. He received his Ph.D. in Economics from Xi'an Jiaotong University. He has published papers in *Pacific-Basin Finance Journal, China Economic Quarterly, China Finance Review, Economic Science* and *Chinese Journal of Management*. His research interests include applied microeconomics and empirical corporate finance.

1

Introduction to the Experiences and Challenges in the Development of the Chinese Capital Market

Douglas Cumming, Alessandra Guariglia, Wenxuan Hou, and Edward Lee

Following the recent financial crisis and ongoing decline experienced by developed economies, the weight of global economic growth is shifting increasingly toward emerging economies. China is widely recognized as playing a leading role in spearheading this shift of economic power. Indeed, China, an increasingly influential emerging economy, is currently attracting worldwide attention from academics, business practitioners, policy makers, and also from the more mainstream media. According to the analyses of IHS Global Insight, which is the world's leading provider of economic research and intelligence, in 2010 China overtook the United States to become the largest manufacturing nation.[1] Based on the forecast of Pricewaterhouse Coopers (2011), China has the potential to surpass the United States, and become the world's largest economy by 2020.[2] China's growth has lifted millions of people out of poverty and has been hailed as one of the most important economic achievements in modern times. After three decades of transitioning from a centrally planned to a market-oriented economy, and as China's rise in prominence becomes ever more visible on the global stage, the importance of China's capital markets in this development process will only intensify.

The efficient allocation of financial resources is the primary objective of the capital market and a key determinant of economic growth in market-oriented economies. A well functioning capital market is crucial to promote investor confidence and facilitate capital acquisitions in order to convert growth opportunities into GDP. The knock on effects that spread from the banking sector difficulties into a global recession following the financial crisis of 2007–2008 demonstrates how capital markets can influence the well-being of the wider economy. As a result, the development of the capital market in China is set to play a crucial role in the country's ascension toward becoming one of the largest economies in the world. Since its inception in the early 1990s, the Chinese stock market has experienced unprecedented development. By the early 2000s, China's stock market was already the largest in the developing world, and, as of late 2010, the Shanghai Stock Exchange became the world's fifth largest in terms of market capitalization.[3] Given China's economic achievements so far, the development of its capital market is expected to have useful policy implications to other emerging economies. However, given China's economic ambition for the future, the challenges of its capital market development need to be identified to enable proper remedies to be formulated.

This book seeks to highlight some of the experiences and challenges pertaining to the development of China's capital market. As a result of its socio-political and culture background, the Chinese capital market is associated with many unique institutional factors that are distinct from those of the developed countries in the Western Hemisphere. Therefore, China offers a unique research setting that provides new insight to enrich academic literature in business, finance, and accounting. This book brings together a collection of cutting-edge empirical research findings contributed by researchers worldwide with expertise in Chinese capital market development. Among our contributors are Michael Firth, who is a world leading authority on China's financial market, as well as Martin Conyon, who is an internationally renowned expert in corporate governance. We group the topics into three themes ordered as follows: (I) asset valuation, (II) provision of capital, and (III) corporate governance. The two studies on asset valuation examine the impact of the information environment on the market value of Chinese listed firms (Chapter 2), and the effect of financial controls on the Chinese real estate market (Chapter 3). The three studies that deal with the provision of capital document the development of venture capitalism (Chapter 4), the growth of institutional investors (Chapter 5), and the impact of foreign bank entry (Chapter 6) in China. The corporate governance theme includes two studies: one explores executive remuneration issues (Chapter 7), and the second examines the association between independent director characteristics and firm performance (Chapter 8).

Chapter 2 by Michael Firth, Man Jin, and Yuanyuan Zhang, "Information Asymmetry and the Diversification Discount: Evidence from Listed Firms in China," examines the effect of corporate diversification and information asymmetry on the stock valuation of Chinese listed firms. The objective of this study is to analyze whether corporate diversification reduces the value of firms directly, or whether it does so indirectly through increased information asymmetry. The underlying research question of this study is important for China's fast growing economy. Diversification is an important but often controversial corporate strategy. If the firm value reduction associated with corporate diversification is not attributed to this strategy per se but due to the decline of transparency it invokes, then managers could alleviate the valuation effect of diversification through better corporate disclosure. In this study, the authors apply the probability of informed trading (PIN) as a measure of the degree of information asymmetry revealed through the trading process in the stock market. Over a sample period of 2003 to 2008, they reach the following conclusions. First, diversified firms have higher information asymmetry. Second, diversified firms have lower firm value. Third, after controlling for information asymmetry, the diversification strategy does not reduce firm value. In other words, managers that pursue a diversification strategy may not necessarily reduce shareholder wealth as long as they are able to enhance transparency. The policy implication of this evidence is that regulators of the Chinese capital market should try to strengthen corporate disclosure and reduce the adverse impact of information asymmetry induced by corporate diversification.

Chapter 3 by Xiuping Hua and Chris Adcock, "Asset Pricing under Financial Repression: Evidence from the Chinese Real Estate Boom during 1999 to 2010," examines whether financial policies such as tight control of interest rates, credit allocation, bank reserve requirements, and capital account influence the valuation of real estate at both national and big-city levels. The research question examined in this study is interesting for two reasons. First, the rapidly rising real estate prices represent a serious concern in China among both investors and authorities. Second, strict financial controls are common policies in developing economies and may have contributed to the growth of China's economy in its earlier stage. If an association is established between the real estate asset bubbles and the financial control policies, this would imply a need to promote policy reforms or to devise necessary solutions. The main findings of this study are as follows. First, the degree of financial control is positively associated with average housing prices. Second, this effect reduces the ability of direct interventions on the real estate market, such as transaction tax and minimum down payment ratio adjustments to control asset price rises. The main policy implication of this finding is that addressing China's existing real estate asset pricing bubble may require further reforms in the financial system beyond existing interventions in the real estate markets.

Chapter 4 by Shen Xiao and Xiangyi Zhou, "Venture capital investments in China: Reputation, Syndication, and Valuation," examines the multiple dimensions of venture capital (VC) development in China. These include the impact of VC firms' reputations on their investment, the comparison between syndicated VC investment and single VC firm investment, and the impact of capital inflows into VC funds on the valuation of these funds' new investments. These issues are important because, like in many Western developed economies, VCs have contributed to entrepreneurship, innovation, and economic growth in China. The main findings of this study are as follows. First, more reputable VC firms are associated with more successful investment exits and firms backed by more reputable VCs have higher asset productivity. Second, syndicated VC investments are associated with higher probability of successful exits. Third, when the VC fund inflows increase, the valuation of funds' new investment rises, and this supports the "money chasing deals" hypothesis. The overall policy implication of this study is that the expertise of VC firms matters and that authorities should continue to promote venture capitalism to further China's economic development.

Chapter 5 by Liming Wang, Ningyue Liu, and Shuo Wang, "Growth and Challenges in the Development in Institutional Investors in China," provides comprehensive discussion of the growth and expansion of institutional investors in China over the period 2003 to 2009. In emerging economies like China, the development of institutional investors is viewed as favorable because of the expertise such investors can bring to the capital market. The study also compares the preferences of local versus foreign institutional investors operating in the Chinese capital market. The main finding is that, unlike evidence from developed markets, foreign fund holdings in China are more influenced by firms' governance characteristics than financial indicators. One possible interpretation of this finding is that emerging countries have relatively less developed investor protection than Western developed economies, and this makes foreign investors more concerned about managerial expropriation. The main policy implication of this finding is that authorities should encourage further enhancement of corporate governance in order to widen the range of Chinese firms that will appeal to foreign investors. The study goes on to compare the development of China's institutional investors against other emerging countries. The authors conclude that, while the growth of institutional investors is common across many emerging economies, this development varies largely in structure and level of investment due to country-specific background such as regulations and market practices.

Chapter 6 by Yizhe Dong, Alessandra Guariglia, and Wenxuan Hou, "Impact of Foreign Bank Entry on the Performance of Chinese Banks," examines how competition from foreign banks affects Chinese local banks' profitability, efficiency, and level of risk. The banking sector plays an important role in the Chinese capital market for two reasons. First, due to limited bond market development, banks provide the primary source of debt capital. Second, due to limited investment options, bank deposits remain one of the most important investment channels for the average Chinese citizen. Based on a sample of 51 Chinese banks over the period 2002 to 2010, the study finds that increasing foreign banking presence enhanced the profitability and efficiency of the Chinese banking sector. However, there is no evidence of any effect on the non-interest activities and risk levels of the local banking market. The main implication of this study is that foreign bank entry is positively facilitating the development of the banking sector in China. The authors go on to suggest that policy makers should continue to reform the banking sector to facilitate foreign bank entry by reducing barriers, and could even encourage domestic banks to strengthen their expertise by forming partnership with foreign counterparts.

Chapter 7 by Martin Conyon and Lerong He, "Chinese Executive Compensation: Where Do We Stand?", examines the determinants of executive compensation in China. Since the financial crisis, managerial remuneration has been a topical and widely debated corporate governance issue in Western developed economies. As China evolves toward a market-oriented economy, the effect of executive compensation will become an increasingly visible issue as it affects both firm performance and investor confidence. This study first provides a thorough review on the institutional background and literature around the topic of executive compensation practices in China. It then explores empirically the characteristics of firms that issue incentives linked compensation such as stock options. The main finding is that equity incentives are more likely to be issued to executives of firms that are larger, better performing, and less risky. Firms that are privately controlled, have less ownership concentration, and have a compensation committee are also more likely to offer equity incentives to executives. The study then compares executive pay in China against other countries. It suggest that both the level of executive pay and the use of equity compensation are lower in China than in Western developed economies. The main policy implication of this study is that there could be room for further development or increase in the use of incentive-linked executive compensation in order to better align the interest of principal and agents.

Chapter 8 by Hanzhang Jiao, Yizhe Dong, Wenxuan Hou, and Edward Lee, "Independent Directors and Corporate Performance in China", explores the association between independent director characteristics and firm performance. The board of directors represents the interest of shareholders and serves as the primary internal governance mechanism to monitor managers against self-serving activities and expropriating investors. The experience and background of independent directors could also provide firms with external resources and expertise. This study first explores existing literature on the efficacy of independent directors in Western developed economies and suggests there are mixed results. It then classifies independent directors into seven groups, that is, academics, politicians, legal professionals, financial professionals, overseas returnees, and others. Academics and accountants make up the largest proportion of independent directors, which indicates that Chinese firms value the expertise of individuals who are highly educated or have a professional accountancy background. One of the main findings is that firms with academics or accountants serving on the board of directors are associated with higher corporate productivity. A policy implication which follows is that future reforms in China should not only regulate the number of independent directors but could also set guidelines to their characteristics.

In general, the eight chapters in this book consistently suggest that in order to appreciate the experiences and challenges of the development of the capital market in China, it is necessary to consider its unique institutional background, which arises from its transition from centrally planned to market-oriented economy. We encourage future research on Chinese capital markets to take into account institutional factors such as regulations, reforms, regional differences, ownership structure, and even business culture. By exploiting research settings that are different to those characterizing Western developed economies, such studies have the potential to make contributions to the academic literature in business, finance, and accounting. Another potential avenue that offers a wealth of opportunities is to conduct comparative research across the capital market of the Greater China region (that is, mainland China, Hong Kong, and Taiwan) or across the BRICs (Brazil, Russia, India, and China). Finally, we would like to express our gratitude to our contributors for their excellent input to this book.

Notes

1. http://www.londonstockexchange.com/news/specials/global-manufactoring/china-asia/china-manufacturing/china-manufacturing.htm
2. http://www.pwc.com/en_GX/gx/world-2050/pdf/world-in-2050-jan-2011.pdf
3. www.world-exchanges.org/statistics/ytd-monthly

2

Information Asymmetry and the Diversification Discount: Evidence from Listed Firms in China

Michael Firth, Man Jin, and Yuanyuan Zhang

2.1 Introduction

Some firms adopt a strategy of business diversification, with the aim of increasing profitability through greater sales obtained from new product lines and expansion into new markets. However, extensive literatures from the U.S. have shown that, on average, diversification is a value-decreasing activity and firms with multi-segment businesses sell at a discount to non-diversified firms[1] (see, for example, Gilson et al., 2001; Jensen, 1986; Myers and Majluf, 1984; Scharfstein, 1998). Although previous studies have examined differences in firm characteristics such as size, profitability, and leverage to explain the different valuations of diversified firms and focused firms, there is less empirical evidence on why this discount exists. One possible explanation for a discount is that corporate diversification is associated with a higher level of asymmetric information due to decreased transparency (Hadlock et al., 2001). We extend previous research by examining the relation between the diversification discount and the level of information asymmetry for firms listed in China's stock market. We argue that the accounting figures of diversified firms are less transparent and less informative than those of the focused firms because of the aggregated nature of diversified firms' consolidated accounting reports. Thus, investors tend to attach a lower level of credibility to the accounts of diversified firms.

We aim to answer the question of whether corporate diversification directly leads to a reduction in firm value or whether it does so indirectly through increased information asymmetry. We show that the increased information asymmetry in multi-segment firms is responsible for the diversification discount observed in China's stock market.

Prior empirical evidence shows that diversification activity can profoundly influence firm value, but it has shed less light on the process of how this has happened. Thomas (2002) claims that diversified firms are subject to larger asymmetric information problems and lower transparency than non-diversified firms. Thomas and Fee (2000), using data from the U.S. show that diversified firms with high levels of information asymmetry trade at a significant discount to firm value. Therefore, we directly examine the characteristics of diversified firms, especially the level of information asymmetry, and their effects on the firm value discount in China. We extend the work of Thomas (2002) and Thomas and Fee (2000) by examining, for the first time, the effect of information asymmetry on the diversification discount of firms listed in China.

China offers a unique economic and financial environment to address this issue. China's financial market is less developed than, and largely segmented from, markets in the rest of the world. Lin and Su (2008) suggest that China's financial market is characterized by a lack of reliable information and a high degree of information asymmetry. Information asymmetry increases the cost of external funds over internally generated funds in emerging markets where market imperfections are severe. At the same time, the state-owned banking environment of China makes it difficult for non-government-controlled firms to borrow from banks (Firth et al., 2008). Therefore, the diversification discount found in the U.S. or other countries with developed capital markets cannot be automatically generalized to countries where external capital is more constrained. For example, diversifications, allowing firms to create internal capital, might be beneficial for firms in China, especially for non-government-controlled firms. On the other hand, information asymmetry might reduce firm value because it increases the potential agency costs associated with corporate diversifications. With higher asymmetric information, management and large shareholders might more easily exploit the firm for their own interests by participating in different business segments. In addition, the Chinese government retains a lot of direct control over most listed firms. This political influence will have repercussions for a firm's strategies such as diversification, R&D expenditures, and the appointment of a CEO. As the relationships between diversification, firm value and information asymmetry are unclear, this chapter tests whether the diversified firms trade at a lower price or lower price-multiple than do non-diversified firms. If a diversification discount exists, we will further investigate if this stems from information asymmetry.

In this chapter, using data from 2003 to 2008, we construct a dummy variable (DIV), which indicates whether or not a firm is diversified, and the sales-based Herfindahl index (HI), which estimates the level of diversification. Our results provide evidence that diversified firms have lower value than non-diversified firms and the firm value, measured by Tobin's Q, decreases as the level of diversification increases. Our results are different from the findings of Lin and Su (2008), who find a diversification premium for firms in China from 2000 to 2002. However, our results on the diversification discount are overall consistent with the results for developed countries of the U.S. (Thomas, 2002; Thomas and Fee, 2000), Japan and the United Kingdom (Lins and Servaes, 1999), and some developing countries, including Hong Kong, India, Indonesia, Malaysia, Singapore, South Korea and Thailand (Lins and Servaes, 2002). Moreover, the diversification discount is more significant for the non-government-controlled firms. One possible explanation for this finding is that firms controlled by central or regional government or another state-owned enterprise might be influenced by political and country-wide strategic policies when making investment decisions, especially the decisions relating to multiple business segments. These firms, who work for the interests of central or regional governments, are more likely to receive governmental subsidies or other implicit cost-saving benefits.

To test the effect of information asymmetry on the diversification discount, we estimate the probability of informed trading (PIN) as the proxy for information asymmetry. The estimation method follows Easley et al. (1996, 1997a and 1997b). First, we show that diversified firms on average have higher information asymmetry, or PIN, than non-diversified firms. Hence our analysis is consistent with the transparency hypothesis, which states that multi-segment businesses result in an increase in asymmetric information, and is contrary to the information diversification hypothesis, which argues that insider information of different segments of a conglomerate can be diversified away. Second, the regression results show that corporate diversification is associated with lower firm values in China, mainly because these firms suffer from a higher level of information asymmetry or a lower level of transparency. After controlling for the measure of information asymmetry, the strategy of diversification itself does not reduce firm value. The results remain significant when we partition the sample into different subsamples and when we apply an alternative econometric model. We also find that diversified firms, on average, have smaller firm size, lower stock price volatility, lower growth of assets, lower return on assets, lower state ownership, lower institutional ownership, and lower ownership concentration, but have a longer firm listing history when compared with non-diversified or narrowly focused firms. Because many transitional economies have common features such as government-controlled firms and weakly enforced disclosure laws, our results for China may have resonance in other emerging markets.

The rest of this chapter proceeds as follows. Section 2.2 introduces the background literature and Section 2.3 describes the data sample and the variables. Section 2.4 shows some preliminary results and analysis on diversified firms. Section 2.5 provides the main results and Section 2.6 reports on a robustness test. Section 2.7 concludes with a summary of the findings.

2.2 Literature review

2.2.1 Diversification and firm value

There is an active debate on how diversification affects firm value. One argument is that conglomerates create value for the company; this argument proceeds as follows. Firstly, diversification can be a source of extra value resulting from an increase in the firm's debt capacity (Lewellen, 1971) and a decrease in the variation of cash flows (Amit and Livnat, 1988). Secondly, diversified firms have higher efficiency in resource allocation through competitive internal capital markets (Weston, 1969; Williamson, 1983). Thirdly, diversification may create shareholder value by mitigating risks in product, labor, and financial markets (Amihud and Lev, 1981; Martin and Sayrak, 2003). Finally, diversification is also beneficial in terms of economies of scope (Panzar and Willig, 1981; Teece, 1980; Teece 1982). The above theories have some empirical support. Villalonga (2004) finds that diversified firms in the U.S. trade at a significant premium using census data at the establishment level. Chronopoulos et al. (2011) find that diversified banks benefit from an efficient allocation of resources, debt coinsurance and scope economies, and are more likely to be cost- and profit-efficient.

In stark contrast to the above studies, other researchers claim that diversification is a value-destroying strategy resulting from inefficient external capital markets (Rajan et al., 2000; Scharfstein, 1998; Scharfstein and Stein, 2000), increased agency problems (Jensen, 1986), information asymmetry between the managers and outside investors (Myers and Majluf, 1984), and a lack of financial analyst specialization in conglomerates (Gilson et al., 2001). Early empirical studies support the diversification discount theory using samples from a number of countries. Lang and Stulz (1994) and Berger and Ofek (1995) find a valuation discount for U.S. diversified companies. Lins and Servaes (1999, 2002) find a significant discount for diversified firms in Japan, the United Kingdom, and a number of East Asian countries. In China, Zhang et al. (2005) and Hong and Xiong (2006) find that diversified firms have lower stock market valuations than focused firms, and the decrease in firm value becomes more severe after controlling for the endogeneity problem, while Lin and Su (2008) find a diversification premium for their sample of firms.

2.2.2 Information asymmetry

A large academic literature has explored extensively the information asymmetry revealed from the trading actions of investors. On one hand, some research focuses on the determinants of asymmetric information, both theoretically and empirically (for example, Aslan et al., 2008; Bardong et al., 2009; Easley et al., 1998). These studies show that information asymmetry measures in the U.S. are significantly and positively related to trading volumes and return on assets, and negatively related to firm size, firm age, and Tobin's Q. The estimated PINs are also shown to be higher for firms in the industries of Oil and Petroleum Products, Construction, Textiles, and Retail in the U.S. market (Aslan et al., 2008). In a search for factors that lead to information asymmetry, some studies focus on specific firm-level variables. In the U.S., Brown and Hillegeist (2007) find that information asymmetry decreases (increases) immediately following positive (negative) earnings surprises. Borisova and Yadav (2010) calculate measures of information asymmetry in the European Union and find that firms in which the government still retains a stake after privatization exhibit a lower level of information asymmetry than do the fully privatized peer firms.

Another stream of the literature relates informed trading to asset pricing. Easley et al. (2002) consider the effect of information asymmetry on a stock's required returns and find that stocks in the U.S. market with higher PINs consistently generate higher excess returns than those with lower PINs. The price risk of information asymmetry is also tested for stocks traded in China. Chan et al. (2008) show that the measures of information asymmetry explain a significant portion of the cross-sectional variation in the foreign share discounts. Therefore, foreign investors demand a higher rate of return as compensation for bearing a higher information risk when investing in stocks in China. Extending research on U.S. stocks to the A-shares traded on the Shanghai Stock Exchange, Copeland et al. (2009) find that PIN explains stock returns even after controlling for the Fama–French three factors.[2]

2.2.3 Information asymmetry and diversification

Some studies have directly tested the relationship between information asymmetry and diversification. Krishnaswami and Subramaniam (1999) find that firms that engage in spin-offs have a higher level of information asymmetry compared with their industry- and size-matched counterparts. Thomas (2002) examines the relation between corporate diversification and information asymmetry using analysts' forecasts and abnormal returns associated with earnings announcements as proxies of asymmetric information. He finds that greater diversification is not associated with increased asymmetric information in the U.S. market. Clarke et al. (2004) conclude that there are potential benefits from diversification since asymmetric information regarding each segment's performance is diversified away across segments. They also provide empirical evidence from U.S. data that supports the notion that the level of information asymmetry drops after diversification. Although there is no evidence of a direct positive relation between diversification and asymmetric information in Thomas and Fee (2000), they find that diversified firms with high levels of information asymmetry trade at a significant discount compared to firms with low levels of information asymmetry. Our study extends previous research by examining the relations between the diversification discount and the level of information asymmetry in China.

2.3 Data and variables

2.3.1 Data

A firm is required to disclose the results of its individual business segments if any segment contributes 10 percent or more of total sales. Following Lin and Su (2008), firms with two or more segments are considered to be diversified or multi-segment firms. Firms that have one business segment that accounts for more than 90 percent of its total sales are considered to be undiversified or a single-segment operation. The accounting information, industrial sector data, and stock returns data are collected from the Wind Financial Database (WindDB) and the China Stock Market and Accounting Research (CSMAR) database.

The intraday data used to estimate PIN are extracted from the high frequency database of SinoFin, and consist of all time-stamped trades and quotes from January 2002 to December 2008 for A-(local) and B-(foreign) shares traded on the Shanghai Stock Exchange (SHSE) and the Shenzhen Stock Exchange (SZSE). Following Chan et al. (2008), the days when trading was halted are excluded (that is, when shares reach the price limit of a 10 percent change with respect to the previous day's close price), as well as the trading days with less than 100 transactions, and the first and last fifteen minutes of each trading session during the day. Following Easley et al. (2002), we require a minimum of 60 trading days in one year for our estimations.

The sample of annual PIN estimates initially includes 1869 firms during the period from 2002 to 2008. We drop 30 financial firms because they are subject to very specific regulations and have very special characteristics that make them distinct from other firms. We also eliminate observations with no information about diversification and exclude observations from 2002 when data on corporate ownership concentration are not available. The final sample consists of 1131 firms with a total of 5377 firm-year observations from 2003 to 2008.

2.3.2 Measuring information asymmetry

Information asymmetry is estimated according to the microstructure model proposed in a series of papers by Easley et al. (1996, 1997a, 1997b), which provides a measure of PIN. In their model, market makers, through observing market data, update their beliefs of the probability of the trade being based on private information and then set the new price. Therefore, over time, stock prices converge to the true value of the asset (that is, the firm) and reflect full information. The model of PIN allows us to make inferences about unobservable informed trading using the observable trade and quotation data.

According to the setting of the model, a new information event occurs at the beginning of a trading day with a probability of α. If the event occurs, the probability of it being good news is $(1-\delta)$ and the probability of it being bad news is δ. Whether there is new information at the beginning of the trading day, and whether the news is good or bad, are chosen by nature. Throughout the trading day, trades are assumed to arrive following Poisson processes. Orders from informed traders arrive at a rate of μ (on information event days only). Informed traders buy if the event is good and otherwise sell. Buy orders from uninformed traders arrive at a rate of ε_b, and sell orders from uninformed traders arrive at a rate of ε_s. Easley et al. (1996, 1997a, 1997b) show that the unobservable parameter set, $\theta=(\alpha, \delta, \mu, \varepsilon_b, \varepsilon_s)$, reflecting the information structure of trades, can be estimated via maximum likelihood.

For a single trading day *i*, the likelihood function is:

$$L(\theta|B_i,S_i)=\alpha(1-\delta)e^{-(\mu+\varepsilon_b)}\frac{(\mu+\varepsilon_b)^{B_i}}{B_i!}e^{-\varepsilon_s}\frac{\varepsilon_s^{s}}{S_i!} + \alpha\delta e^{-\varepsilon_b}\frac{\varepsilon_b^{B_i}}{B_i!}e^{-(\mu+\varepsilon_s)}\frac{(\mu+\varepsilon_s)^{S_i}}{S_i!} + (1-\alpha)e^{-\varepsilon_b}\frac{\varepsilon_b^{B_i}}{B_i!}e^{-\varepsilon_s}\frac{\varepsilon_s^{S_i}}{S_i} \tag{1}$$

where B_i and S_i denote, respectively, the total number of buyer-initiated and seller-initiated trades for day *i* and $\theta=(\alpha, \delta, \mu, \varepsilon_b, \varepsilon_s)$ is the parameter vector.

Assuming that trading days are independent, Easley et al. (2002) give the likelihood function for a period of *I* trading days as follows:

$$L(\theta|M)=\prod_{i=1}^{I}L(\theta|B_i,S_i) \tag{2}$$

where $M=((B_i,S_i),...,(B_I,S_I))$ represents the dataset during the *I* trading days. Maximizing (2) by using the dataset *M* provide the estimates of the parameters.

The probability that the trade is information-based, PIN, is derived as follows:

$$PIN=\frac{\alpha\mu}{\alpha\mu+\varepsilon_b+\varepsilon_s} \tag{3}$$

where $\alpha\mu$ is the daily arrival of informed trades and $(\alpha\mu+\varepsilon_b+\varepsilon_s)$ is the arrival of both informed and uninformed trades. The PIN variables provide a direct measure of the risk derived from information-based trading and reflect the level of information asymmetry. PIN has been calculated for stocks in many different countries over different time periods and for various research questions.[3]

In order to estimate PIN, the daily number of buys (B_i) and sells (S_i) are required. However, the dataset records the intraday trades and quotations without showing whether each trade is initiated by a buy or a sell order. Following Easley et al. (2002), we use the standard Lee and Ready (1991) algorithm to classify the trades as buys or sells. The algorithm classifies any trade with a trading price higher (lower) than the midpoint of the bid as a buyer-initiated (seller-initiated) trade. For a trade at the midpoint, it is classified as a buy (sell) if its price is higher (lower) than the most recent but different trading price.[4] Following Lee and Ready (1991), we adopt a five-second lag of the recorded quotation time to adjust for the difference between the recording times of the trades and of the quotes.

The maximization of the likelihood function, (2), starts from self-selected starting values for the five parameters. Following Yan and Zhang (2010), Venter and Jongh (2004), and Borisova and Yadav (2010), we specify 125 sets of starting values for the five parameters. The maximization is performed based on each set of acceptable starting values and then the one that achieves convergence and generates the highest value of the likelihood function is adopted.

Table 2.1 provides the summary statistics of the annual estimates of PIN and its parameter measures for all shares traded on the SHSE and SZSE during the period from January 2002 to December 2008. Panel A presents the statistics of PIN. Overall, the mean (median) PIN is 0.23 (0.22) and the standard deviation is 0.08. The average PIN in the SZSE is significantly higher than the PIN for the SHSE at the 5 percent level. The mean estimate of PIN across all firms is 0.215 in 2002 and it remains at a relatively high level in the following four years. In 2007 and 2008, there is a substantial reduction in the mean PIN. One possible explanation is that starting from the bull market in 2006, more uninformed investors join the financial market. In that case, the arrival rates of uninformed investors (both buyers and sellers) would increase substantially. This explanation is supported by the statistics of the average arrival rates of uninformed buyers (ε_b) and sellers (ε_s), which are respectively 73.91 and 78.65 in 2006, and are almost tripled to 232.32 and 240.71 in 2007. The arrival rate of informed investors (μ) rises too but at a lower percentage rate from 2006 to 2007.

In addition to the stimulus from the bull market, the reform of non-tradable shares[5] could also attract individual investors to join the market and then raise the arrival rate of uninformed investors after 2006. By the end of 2006, 1301 listed companies have undergone or have already completed their non-tradable share reforms, accounting for 97 percent of the total companies that are required to be reformed. The aims of the reform are to change the situation where two kinds of stocks and pricings co-exist in the same market and to strengthen the common interests of all shareholders. In other words, it protects the interests of individual investors and makes the

Table 2.1 Summary statistics for PIN measure

Variables	mean	s.d.	median	25%	75%	Nobs
Panel A: Summary Statistics of PIN						
2002	0.215	0.068	0.214	0.177	0.251	1,247
2003	0.316	0.093	0.319	0.261	0.375	1,296
2004	0.234	0.067	0.248	0.192	0.283	1,444
2005	0.243	0.046	0.247	0.22	0.272	1,429
2006	0.227	0.05	0.231	0.201	0.261	1,489
2007	0.18	0.05	0.179	0.148	0.211	1,584
2008	0.176	0.057	0.170	0.136	0.218	1,663
SHSE	0.223	0.081	0.219	0.169	0.266	5,869
SZSE	0.227	0.068	0.230	0.181	0.270	4,283
Total	0.225	0.076	0.224	0.174	0.268	10,152
Panel B: Summary Statistics of PIN *parameters*						
α	0.287	0.137	0.266	0.182	0.372	10,152
δ	0.362	0.348	0.227	0.06	0.661	10,152
μ	130.611	88.341	109.726	62.653	187.891	10,152
ε_b	93.806	129.28	39.034	14.872	118.114	10,152
ε_s	99.482	129.612	46.375	17.489	127.598	10,152

The table shows the summary statistics of the annual PIN estimates and the parameters for 1869 firms listed on the SHSE and SZSE during the period from 2002 to 2008 with 10,152 firm-year observations. Panel A presents the summary statistics of PIN estimates by year and then by stock exchanges; Panel B shows the parameters that are used to calculate PIN.

financial markets more attractive to them. Therefore, the reform of non-tradable shares is probably responsible for the higher arrival rate of uninformed investors and results in a lower PIN in 2007 and 2008. However, since there are no data that precisely capture the reform procedure of each firm, we cannot empirically evaluate the effect of this reform on the results.

Panel B in Table 2.1 shows the statistics of the estimated parameters that are used to calculate PIN over the entire sample period. The mean (median) of α, the probability of an information event in a day, is 0.287 (0.266), and the mean (median) of δ is 0.362 (0.227), indicating that most of the information is good news.

According to Chan et al. (2008), the average PIN estimate is higher for the B-shares than for the A-shares due to the small amount of uninformed trades in the B-shares market. We analyze firms that have both A-shares and B-shares in one sample. In Table 2.2, the PIN statistics of B-shares versus the corresponding A-shares are presented. The differences in PIN between A-shares and B-shares are not consistently

Table 2.2 Comparison of PIN: B-shares versus the corresponding A-shares

		A-share		B-share		Diff PIN		
Year	**# of firms**	**mean**	**s.d.**	**mean**	**s.d.**	**mean**	**s.d.**	**t-stat**
Panel A: SHSE								
2002	19	0.204	0.035	0.213	0.220	–0.010	0.219	–0.194
2003	22	0.330	0.103	0.346	0.071	–0.016	0.004	-21.167
2004	34	0.241	0.069	0.223	0.052	0.018	0.090	1.158
2005	27	0.270	0.047	0.217	0.063	0.052	0.073	3.741
2006	44	0.247	0.050	0.254	0.052	–0.007	0.076	–0.629
2007	44	0.192	0.046	0.213	0.089	–0.020	0.087	–1.494
2008	44	0.200	0.051	0.227	0.046	–0.049	0.070	–4.687
Total	44	0.230	0.073	0.238	0.094	–0.008	0.107	–1.189
Panel A: SZSE								
2002	35	0.228	0.050	0.228	0.050	0.000	0.073	0.002
2003	34	0.304	0.040	0.318	0.070	–0.014	0.098	–0.827
2004	37	0.267	0.035	0.240	0.035	0.027	0.057	2.884
2005	30	0.255	0.044	0.222	0.054	0.033	0.083	2.164
2006	39	0.222	0.055	0.255	0.037	–0.033	0.069	–2.938
2007	40	0.172	0.047	0.215	0.070	–0.043	0.081	–3.341
2008	34	0.161	0.048	0.227	0.055	–0.065	0.064	–5.895
Total	42	0.229	0.069	0.243	0.063	–0.015	0.082	–2.847

The table shows the mean and standard deviation (s.d.) of the annual PIN estimates for the firms traded as both A-shares and B-shares during the period from 2002 to 2008. Panel A shows the statistics for stocks listed on the SHZE and Panel B for stocks listed on the SZSE. The annual difference between the PIN of A-shares and that of its corresponding B-shares is summarized under the columns of "Diff " (Diff PIN = PINA – PINB).

positive or negative over the sample period. In most years, the PIN estimate is higher for B-shares than for A-shares, because the PIN parameters, ε_b and ε_s, are significantly higher for A-shares than for B-shares. The difference in ε_b and ε_s between A-shares and B-shares are significantly and positively different from zero at the 1% level for all years in both exchanges. As pointed out by Chan et al. (2008), the higher information asymmetry in the B-shares market is attributed to the relatively low number of uninformed trades. However, the PIN estimate and its parameters in this chapter are not directly comparable to those in Chan et al. (2008). They focus on an event where Chinese citizens were allowed to trade B-shares in March 2001 using the monthly PIN from January 2000 to November 2001, while our data start from 2002.

Lin and Su (2008) claim that China's financial markets are characterized by a lack of reliable information and by a high degree of information asymmetry. Comparing China's PIN estimates with those in other regions, the Chinese listed firms are shown to have a higher level of information asymmetry. In Easley et al. (2002), the mean, median and maximum of PIN in the U.S. from 1983 to 1998, are respectively 0.191, 0.185, and 0.530. In Taiwan, the PIN statistics from 1997 to 2005, reported by Lu and Wong (2008), have a mean of 0.20 and a median of 0.18. In contrast to our study, Copeland et al. (2009) estimate the monthly PIN in the SHSE from 2001 to 2006 and find an average of 0.114.

2.3.3 Measuring diversification and firm value

We use two alternative proxies for firm diversification. The first one is the DIV, which is coded 1 for a multi-segment firm and 0 for a single-segment firm. The other measure for diversification is a sales-based HI defined as below:

$$HI_i = \sum_k \left(\frac{SALES_{k,I}}{Total(SALES)_i} \right)^2 \tag{4}$$

where $SALES_{k,i}$ refers to the annual sales revenue of sector k in firm i and $Total(SALES)_i$ represents the yearly total sales revenue of firm i. HI is inversely related to the degree of diversification.

To measure firm value, we use Tobin's Q (Q), defined as the sum of the market value of equity[6] and the book value of total debt divided by the book value of total assets. This definition follows the literature (Lang and Stulz, 1994; Lin and Su, 2008).

2.3.4 Control variables

A number of studies argue that the type of ownership structure can have an impact on firm performance in China because of complex agency problems and soft budget constraints (Chen et al., 2006; Wei et al., 2005). In light of this, we include the state ownership (*STATE*) of a firm as well as a *GOV* dummy variable to control for the state control effect. *STATE* is the percentage of shares held by the state while *GOV* is a dummy variable coded 1 if the firm is a state-owned enterprise and 0 otherwise. A distinct characteristic of Chinese firms is that they have one dominant shareholder whose ownership is much higher than the next largest shareholder (Chen et al., 2009; Firth et al., 2006). Hence, to control for the influence of ownership structure, we include a measure of ownership concentration (*SHRCR*), which is the percentage ownership of the largest shareholder, and the institutional ownership (*INS*), which is the institutional holdings expressed as a percentage of the total number of shares outstanding.

Because larger firms are more likely to diversify, we use the natural logarithm of the market value of equity (*SIZE*) to capture the effect of size. The annualized standard deviation of daily stock price returns (*VOLATILITY*) is included to capture the effect of return volatility (Clarke et al., 2004). As the growth opportunities of firms are positively related with firm value (Stowe and Xing, 2006), we control for this factor with two variables. Specifically, we use the percentage change in total assets (*TAGrow*) and the ratio of intangible assets to total assets (*INTANG*) to capture the growth rate of the firms. We use the dummy variable (*EXCHANGE*) to capture the variation across stock exchanges, which is coded 1 if the firm is listed on the SHSE and 0 if it is listed on the SZSE. In order to capture the variation across industries, we include industry dummy variables. According to the two-digit industry code of the China Securities Regulation Commission (CSRC), 13 industries are separately identified. In addition, we also include in the regression model the number of years after the firm went public (*AGE*), leverage (*LEVERAGE*) (Clarke et al., 2004; Doukas and Pantzalis, 2003), return on assets (*ROA*), and the year dummies.

2.3.5 Descriptive statistics

Table 2.3 presents the summary statistics of the annual estimates of diversification, firm value, and other firm-level and industry-level control variables over the period from January 2003 to December 2008. Within the total 1131 firms in the sample, the number of diversified firms increases from 379 in 2003 to 543 in 2008. Among all the 5377 firm-year observations, 2979 are multi-segment firms, which make up 55 percent of the total sample. On average, 70 percent of the total observations are controlled by the state and 54 percent of the total observations are listed on the SHSE.

2.4 Preliminary evidence on the effect of diversification on firm performance

Table 2.4 shows the correlation analysis of information asymmetry, PIN, and the explanatory variables. The results in Table 2.4 show that the stocks with higher information asymmetry (higher PIN) have significantly higher state ownership and ownership concentration, and have

Table 2.3 Summary statistics: diversification measures and firm-specific characteristics

Variables	Definition	mean	s.d.	median	25%	75%
DIV	Dummy variable for diversification	0.55	0.50	1.00	0.00	1.00
HI	Herfindahl Index for diversification	0.73	0.24	0.77	0.51	0.97
Q	Tobin's Q	1.35	0.51	1.15	1.00	1.49
ROA	Return on assets	0.05	0.06	0.05	0.03	0.08
SIZE	The logarithm of total assets	21.45	1.08	21.36	20.75	22.06
VOLATILITY	Annualized volatility of daily stock return	0.48	0.17	0.45	0.36	0.61
TAGrow	The percentage annual change in total assets	0.15	0.50	0.08	-0.01	0.21
INTANG	The ratio of intangible assets to total assets	0.04	0.06	0.02	0.01	0.05
LEVERAGE	The ratio of book value of debt to total assets	0.51	0.17	0.52	0.38	0.64
STATE	The percentage of shares held by State Agencies	30.54	24.37	31.73	2.00	51.46
GOV	A dummy variable that takes the value 1 if it is a state-owned firm	0.70	0.46	1.00	0.00	1.00
INS	The percentage of shares held by institutions	14.28	17.29	6.48	0.87	21.66
SHRCR	The percentage of shares held by the largest shareholder	38.62	16.31	36.27	25.7	51.11
AGE	The number of years after going public	8.03	3.50	8.00	6.00	11.00
EXCHANGE	A dummy variable that takes the value 1 if the firm is listed on the SHSE	0.54	0.50	1.00	0.00	1.00

The table presents the summary statistics of the annual estimates of diversification, firm values, and other firm-level control variables over the period from January 2003 to December 2008.

lower firm size, stock return volatility, growth opportunity (lower *TAGrow* and *INTANG*), institutional ownership, and number of years since going public. Table 2.4 also indicates that diversified firms have smaller size, volatility, growth of assets, state ownership, institutional ownership, and ownership concentration compared to focused firms. The correlation analysis shows that it is important to control for these variables when relating PIN to diversification and firm valuation.

Table 2.4 Correlation matrix

	PIN	DIV	HI	Q	ROA	SIZE	VOLATILITY	TAGrow	ITANG	LEVERAGE	STATE	GOV	INS	SHRCR
DIV	0.02*													
HI	0.01	–0.68***												
Q	–0.01	–0.01	0.00											
ROA	0.00	–0.01	0.00	0.61***										
SIZE	–0.17***	–0.03***	0.07***	–0.13***	–0.10***									
VOLATILITY	–0.26***	–0.04***	0.00	0.00	–0.01	–0.08***								
TAGrow	–0.05***	–0.07***	0.02	–0.01	–0.02**	0.13***	0.20***							
INTANG	–0.03***	0.05***	–0.06***	–0.01	–0.01	–0.15***	0.02***	–0.08***						
LEVERAGE	0.00	–0.02	–0.01	0.30***	0.08***	–0.15***	–0.01	–0.03***	–0.01					
STATE	0.08***	–0.06***	0.08***	–0.02*	–0.01	0.24***	–0.09***	0.00	–0.07***	–0.02				
GOV	–0.01	–0.07***	0.03**	0.00	–0.01	0.22***	–0.06***	0.04***	–0.07***	0.00	0.67***			
INS	–0.17***	–0.11***	0.04***	–0.01	–0.01	0.36***	0.08***	0.13***	–0.03***	–0.03**	–0.04***	0.04***		
SHRCR	0.08***	–0.12***	0.14***	–0.02*	–0.01	0.25***	–0.01	0.07***	–0.09***	–0.02**	0.55***	0.33***	0.05***	
AGE	–0.18***	0.11***	–0.08***	0.01	0.00	0.05***	0.13***	–0.06***	0.09***	0.05***	–0.15***	–0.05***	0.00	–0.20***

The table presents the correlations among all variables for PIN, diversification, and firm characteristics. These variables include the measure of information asymmetry (PIN), Tobin's Q (*Q*), return on assets (*ROA*), firm size (*SIZE*), stock return volatility (*VOLATILITY*), the change in total assets (*TAGrow*), the percentage of intangible assets (*INTANG*), leverage, state ownership (*STATE*), government-controlled dummy variable (*GOV*), institutional ownership (*INS*), ownership concentration (*SHRCR*) and the number of years after a firm went public (*AGE*). All the variables are annual measures during the period from January 2003 to December 2008. Significance at the 10%, 5% and 1% levels are shown by *, ** and ***, respectively.

Table 2.5 Comparison of diversified and non-diversified firms

	Diversified firms		Non-diversified firms		
Variable	**mean**	**s.d.**	**mean**	**s.d.**	**mean difference**
PIN	0.23	0.08	0.22	0.07	0.01** [1.81]
Q	1.34	0.51	1.36	0.50	-0.02* [1.38]
ROA	0.04	0.05	0.05	0.06	-0.01*** [-5.24]
SIZE	21.38	1.02	21.54	1.15	-0.16*** [-5.50]
VOLATILITY	0.50	0.44	0.54	0.46	-0.04*** [-4.00]
TAGrow	0.14	0.50	0.17	0.49	-0.03** [-2.22]
INTANG	0.05	0.06	0.04	0.06	0.01*** [4.41]
LEVERAGE	0.55	0.59	0.54	0.53	0.02 [1.02]
STATE	0.28	0.24	0.34	0.25	-0.06*** [- 8.42]
GOV	0.66	0.47	0.73	0.44	-0.07*** [-5.61]
INS	13.18	17.07	16.73	20.35	-3.55*** [-6.95]
SHRCR	36.53	15.98	41.21	16.33	-4.68*** [-10.57]
AGE	8.28	3.52	7.72	3.44	0.56*** [5.89]
Nobs	2,979		2,398		

The table shows the mean and standard deviation (s.d.) of PIN and other firm-specific variables when the sample is partitioned into two subsamples, diversified and non-diversified firm-year observations. The last column tests the difference in means. All the variables are annual measures during the period from January 2003 to December 2008. Significance at the 10%, 5% and 1% levels is shown by *, ** and ***, respectively.

Table 2.5 provides summary statistics for the sample divided into diversified and non-diversified firms. As shown in the table, the mean Tobin's Q of non-diversified firms is significantly higher than that of diversified firms, indicating that diversification is value-destroying. Moreover, the mean *ROA* for single-segment and multi-segment firms is 0.0525 and 0.044, respectively. The t-statistics for the difference in sample means is significant at the 1 percent level, indicating that diversified firms are less profitable. The statistics in Table 2.5 also show that diversified firms have higher information asymmetry than the non-diversified firms, consistent with the transparency hypothesis. The two samples also differ with respect to other variables. In particular, the diversified firms overall have significantly lower volatility, growth of assets, state ownership, institutional ownership, and ownership concentration. At the same time, diversified firms are older and smaller in terms of firm size than single-segment firms.

In China, most listed firms have a controlling shareholder that influences its strategies and policies and the central or regional government is most often the ultimate owner with the controlling stake. In other cases, the controlling shareholder is a state-owned enterprise or a private blockholder. Obviously, different types of controlling investor have different objectives and incentives, which will affect the corporate decision to diversify. Therefore, we explore the differences in ownership and assess their implications for diversification and firm valuation.

Table 2.6 partitions the sample along two dimensions: diversified versus non-diversified and government controlled versus non-government controlled. The means of the four subsamples are presented. For each variable of interest, the top two cells are for government-controlled firms, partitioned by whether the firms are diversified or not. The lower two cells are for non-government-controlled firms, also partitioned by diversification. Surrounding these four cells are the t-statistics that test for the differences in sample means of the rows and columns. Consistently with

Table 2.6 Comparison of government-controlled versus non-government-controlled and diversified versus non-diversified firms

		Diversified firms	**Non-diversified firms**	**Row Test**
PIN	Government-Controlled	0.22 (0.07)	0.22 (0. 07)	0.00 [0.60]
	Non-government	0.22 (0.07)	0.23 (0.07)	–0.00 [–0.63]
	Col Test	0.00 [0.05]	–0.00 [–1.08]	
Q	Government-Controlled	1.28 (0.47)	1.27 (0.45)	0.01 [0.70]
	Non-government	1.42 (0.57)	1.47 (0.60)	–0.05** [– 1.65]
	Col Test	–0.14*** [– 6.71]	–0.20*** [–8.37]	
ROA	Government-Controlled	0.04 (0.09)	0.05 (0.13)	–0.01*** [–3.49]
	Non-government	0.00 (0. 68)	0.03 (0.23)	–0.03 [–1.04]
	Col Test	–0.04 [–1.64]	0.02*** [3.34]	
SIZE	Government-Controlled	21.54 (1.03)	21.73 (1.14)	–0.20*** [–5.62]
	Non-government	21.07 (0.92)	21.01 (1.00)	0.06* [1.30]
	Col Test	0.47*** [12.03]	0.73*** [14.28]	
VOLATILITY	Government-Controlled	0.48 (0.18)	0.47 (0.16)	0.02*** [3.17]
	Non-government	0.50 (0.19)	0.51 (0.17)	–0.01 [–1.03]
	Col Test	–0.01* [–1.93]	–0.04***[–5.46]	
TAGrow	Government-Controlled	0.15 (0.57)	0.17 (0.39)	–0.02 [–1.22]
	Non-government	0.11 (0.32)	0.15 (0.69)	–0.05** [–1.86]
	Col Test	0.05*** [2.39]	0.02 [0.87]	
INTANG	Government-Controlled	0.05 (0.07)	0.04 (0.06)	0.01*** [4.86]
	Non-government	0.05 (0.06)	0.05 (0.07)	0.00 [0.19]
	Col Test	0.00 [0.01]	–0.01*** [–3.28]	

Continued

Table 2.6 Continued

		Diversified firms	Non-diversified firms	Row Test
LEVERAGE	Government-Controlled	0.52 (0.23)	0.51 (0.31)	0.00 [0.35]
	Non-government	0.63 (0.96)	0.61 (0.89)	0.02 [0.45]
	Col Test	-0.11*** [-4.86]	-0.11*** [-4.86]	
STATE	Government-Controlled	0.39 (0.20)	0.44 (0.44)	-0.04*** [-6.59]
	Non-government	0.06 (0.12)	0.06 (0.12)	-0.00 [-0.24]
	Col Test	0.34*** [49.61]	0.38*** [45.64]	
INS	Government-Controlled	13.63 (17.36)	17.56 (20.74)	-3.94*** [-6.31]
	Non-government	12.31 (16.45)	14.43 (19.08)	-2.13*** [-2.40]
	Col Test	1.32** [2.00]	3.13*** [3.33]	
SHRCR	Government-Controlled	39.94 (16.31)	44.45 (15.88)	-4.51*** [-8.54]
	Non-government	29.83 (12.93)	32.30 (14.11)	-2.47*** [-3.64]
	Col Test	10.11*** [17.10]	12.15*** [17.04]	
AGE	Government-Controlled	8.25 (3.54)	7.60 (3.40)	0.65*** [5.67]
	Non-government	8.35 (3.49)	8.04 (3.52)	0.31** [1.73]
	Col Test	-0.10 [-0.72]	-0.44*** [-2.75]	

The table shows the mean and standard deviation (s.d.) of PIN and other firm-specific variables when the sample is partitioned along two dimensions: diversified versus non-diversified and government controlled versus non-government controlled. The main figures are the sample means and the figures in parentheses are standard deviations. The null hypotheses that the differences in sample means across ownership type and across diversification type are zero are tested using a two-tailed two sample t-test. The differences in sample means across diversification type are reported in the row test, differences in sample means across ownership type are reported in the column test, and the figures in brackets are t-statistics. Significance levels of 1%, 5% and 10% are denoted by ***, ** and *, respectively.

Table 2.5, multi-segment firms have significantly lower Tobin's Q than single-segment firms for non-government-controlled firms and lower *ROA* for government-controlled firms. In comparison, non-government-controlled firms have significantly higher Tobin's Q than government-controlled firms no matter whether they are diversified or not. These results combined suggest that government control is an important factor when testing the effect of diversification on firm value. However, government control exerts a non-significant influence on the PIN variable.

Table 2.6 also shows that, after controlling for the identity of the ultimate owner, multi-segment firms have lower asset growth, institutional ownership, state ownership, ownership concentration, and a longer history, than single-segment firms. After controlling for diversification status, government-controlled firms have higher firm size, return on assets, institutional ownership, state ownership, asset growth and ownership concentration, but lower stock return volatility and leverage, than non-government-controlled firms.

2.5 Regression analysis and results

The summary statistics and comparisons show that diversified firms have lower firm values. However, the cause of the discount needs to be further investigated. In this section, we test whether information asymmetry can explain the diversification discount in firm value.

2.5.1 Econometric specification and hypotheses

We specify the regression models measuring the interaction between information asymmetry and firm diversification discount as follows:

$$\begin{aligned} Q_{i,t} = {} & \alpha_0 + \alpha_1 DIV_{i,t} + \alpha_2 SIZE_{i,t} + \alpha_3 VOLATILITY_{i,t} \\ & + \alpha_4 TAGrow_{i,t} + \alpha_5 INTANG_{i,t} + \alpha_6 LEVERAGE_{i,t} \\ & + \alpha_7 STATE_{i,t} + \alpha_8 GOV_{i,t} + \alpha_9 INS_{i,t} + \alpha_{10} SHRCR_{i,t} \\ & + \alpha_{11} AGE_{i,t} + \sum_k \varphi_k \, Industry\ Dummies + \sum_t \phi_t Year\ Dummies + \varepsilon_{i,t} \end{aligned} \tag{5}$$

$$\begin{aligned} Q_{i,t} = {} & \omega_0 + \omega_1 DIV_{i,t} + \omega_2 PIN_{i,t} + \omega_3 SIZE_{i,t} + \omega_4 VOLATILITY_{i,t} \\ & + \omega_5 TAGrow_{i,t} + \omega_6 INTANG_{i,t} + \omega_7 LEVERAGE_{i,t} + \omega_8 STATE_{i,t} \\ & + \omega_9 GOV_{i,t} + \omega_{10} INS_{i,t} + \omega_{11} SHRCR_{i,t} + \omega_{12} AGE_{i,t} \\ & + \sum_k \varphi_k \, Industry\ Dummies + \sum_t \phi_t \, Year\ Dummies + \varepsilon_{i,t} \end{aligned} \tag{6}$$

The definitions and the estimation details of the variables are discussed in Section 2.3. We also rerun the model by replacing the dummy variable, *DIV*, by *HI*, which is inversely related to the level of diversification. The two regressions together are used to test the effect of information asymmetry on the diversification discount.

According to the previous literature, diversification can destroy firm value for many reasons, such as the inefficient allocation of capital among divisions (Lamont, 1997; Shin and Stulz, 1998) and the insensitivity of CEO turnover to stock price performance (Berry et al., 2006). Therefore, in (5), a significantly negative α_1 indicates that a higher degree of diversification is related to a loss of firm value (that is, a lower Tobin's Q). According to Habib et al. (1997) and Nanda and Narayanan (1999), diversification could result in a higher level of asymmetric information problems, due to the lack of transparency. The increased information asymmetry could lead to a lower value for diversified firms. If this is true, we expect a significant negative estimate of α_1 in (5).

Based on the above analysis, PIN is included in (6) as our proxy of information asymmetry to test the effect of price informativeness on the diversification discount. If ω_2 is significantly and negatively related with Tobin's Q while ω_1 is no longer significant, we can conclude that information asymmetry leads directly to diversification discount. In other words, diversification does not affect firm value directly but does so indirectly through the channel of information asymmetry. Conglomerates suffer from a higher level of asymmetric information that leads to a reduction in firm value. Specifically, using the econometric specification in (5) and (6), we test the following hypotheses:

H_0: $\alpha_1 = 0$, $\omega_1 \neq 0$, or $\omega_2 = 0$.
H_1: $\alpha_1 \neq 0$, $\omega_1 = 0$ and $\omega_2 = 0$.

2.5.2 Regression results

Table 2.7 shows the regression results defined by (5) and (6). The regression results in columns [1] and [4] are based on (5), where the diversification is measured by *DIV* in column [1] and by *HI* in column [4]. The results in columns [2] and [5] are based on (6), using two different proxies of diversification, *DIV* and *HI*, respectively. Additionally, the interaction terms in columns [3] and [6], *DIV*×PIN and *HI*×PIN, measure the effects of the interplay between diversification and information asymmetry on firm value. Moreover, to control for the causality problem, one-year ahead Tobin's Q is used as the dependent variable in columns [7] and [8]. According to the regression results, multi-segment firms have lower Tobin's Q than do single-segment firms, as the coefficient estimates for *DIV* are significantly negative at the 1 percent level and the coefficient estimates for *HI* are significantly positive at the 5 percent level. The results of firm value discount are consistent with the findings for U.S. firms reported in previous studies (for example, Gilson et al., 2001; Jensen, 1986; Myers and Majluf, 1984).

We next test whether the effect of diversification on firm value is subsumed by information asymmetry through the regression equation specified in (6). The results are shown in columns [2], [3], [5], and [6], where diversification is measured by *DIV* in columns [2] and [3] and by *HI* in columns [5] and [6]. After adding PIN as an explanatory variable for Tobin's Q, the coefficient estimates for *DIV* and *HI*

Table 2.7 Panel data regressions of the effect of PIN and diversification on firm value

	Q						Q_{t+1}	
	[1]	[2]	[3]	[4]	[5]	[6]	[7]	[8]
DIV	–0.02***	–0.01	0.04				–0.05***	–0.03
	[–2.60]	[–1.13]	[1.24]				[–3.45]	[–0.73]
HI				0.04**	0.02	–0.09		
				[2.13]	[0.91]	[–1.46]		
PIN		–0.53***	–0.22**		–0.52***	–0.80***		–0.53***
		[–6.54]	[–2.04]		[–6.55]	[–3.88]		[–3.50]
*DIV**PIN			–0.27**					–0.00
			[–2.17]					[–0.01]
*HI**PIN						0.59**		
						[2.25]		
SIZE	–0.17***	–0.19***	–0.17***	–0.17***	–0.19***	–0.17***	–0.23***	–0.26***
	[–33.33]	[–38.82]	[–33.44]	[–33.32]	[–38.83]	[–33.46]	[–32.84]	[–36.46]
VOLATILITY	0.06	0.07*	0.03	0.06	0.07*	0.03	–0.04	–0.02
	[1.32]	[1.69]	[0.77]	[1.28]	[1.67]	[0.76]	[–0.61]	[–0.31]
TAGrow	–0.04***	–0.05***	–0.04***	–0.04***	–0.05***	–0.04***	–0.07***	–0.08***
	[–4.42]	[–5.52]	[–4.13]	[–4.40]	[–5.52]	[–4.10]	[–4.94]	[–5.81]
INTANG	–0.07	–0.05	–0.07	–0.06	–0.05	–0.07	–0.07	–0.05
	[–0.89]	[–0.7]	p–0.93]	[–0.85]	[–0.68]	[–0.89]	[–0.64]	[–0.46]
LEVERAGE	0.05***	0.05***	0.05***	0.05***	0.05***	0.05***	0.03***	0.03***
	[6.35]	[6.44]	[6.36]	[6.36]	[6.45]	[6.38]	[2.76]	[2.69]
STATE	0.03	–0.06**	0.03	0.03	–0.06*	0.03	0.08	0.11***
	[0.97]	[–1.97]	[0.87]	[0.94]	[–1.96]	[0.82]	[1.80]	[2.62]

GOV	−0.07***	−0.07***	−0.07***	−0.07***	−0.07***	−0.07***	−0.12***	−0.13***
	[−4.82]	[−5.28]	[−4.82]	[−4.75]	[−5.25]	[−4.47]	[−6.17]	[−6.54]
INS	0.02***	0.01***	0.02***	0.02***	0.01***	0.02***	0.03***	0.01***
	[23.66]	[34.22]	[23.90]	[23.69]	[34.27]	[8.27]	[17.75]	[25.90]
SHRCR	−0.00	−0.01**	−0.00	−0.00*	−0.00**	−0.00	−0.00***	−0.00***
	[−1.81]	[−2.36]	[−1.64]	[−1.79]	[−2.35]	[−1.57]	[−2.74]	[−3.21]
AGE	0.01***	0.01***	0.01***	0.01***	0.01**	0.01***	0.02***	0.02***
	[8.43]	[9.82]	[8.26]	[8.43]	[9.82]	[8.27]	[7.71]	[8.71]
CONSTANT	4.60***	5.37***	4.80***	4.56***	5.35***	4.88***	6.04***	6.87***
	[41.86]	[45.53]	[39.00]	[41.46]	[45.28]	[38.25]	[38.92]	[39.98]
INDUSTRY	Yes	Yes	Yes	Yes	Yes	Yes	Yes	Yes
YEAR	Yes	Yes	Yes	Yes	Yes	Yes	Yes	Yes
R^2	0.565	0.6063	0.5668	0.5648	0.6063	0.5667	0.5503	0.5571
Obs	5,377	5,377	5,377	5,377	5,377	5,377	5,377	5,377

The table contains regression results following (5) and (6), with 5377 firm-year observations. The dependent variable is Tobin's Q (Q) in year *t* in columns [1] to [6] and Tobin's Q in year *t+1* in columns [7] and [8]. *DIV* is the dummy variable for diversification, *HI* is the sales-based Herfindahl index and PIN is the estimate of information asymmetry. The interaction terms, *DIV*×PIN and *HI*×PIN, measure the effects of the interplay between diversification and information asymmetry on the firm value. *SIZE* is the logarithm of total assets, *VOLATILITY* is the annualized volatility of daily stock returns, *TAGrow* is the percentage change in total assets, *INTANG* is the percentage of intangible assets, *LEVERAGE* is the ratio of book value of debt to total assets, *STATE* is the percentage of shares held by the state agency, *GOV* is the dummy variable that takes the value 1 if the firm is state controlled, *SHRCR* is the ownership concentration measure, *INS* is the percentage of shares held by institutions, *AGE* is the number of years after going public, and *INDUSTRY* and *YEAR* are respectively the industry dummies and year dummies. Figures in brackets are t-statistics. Significance levels of 1%, 5% and 10% are denoted by ***, **, and * denote.

become insignificant while the coefficient estimates of PIN are all significantly negative at the 1 percent or 5 percent levels. This suggests that the increased information asymmetry is directly responsible for the diversification discount, but the diversification strategy itself does not destroy firm value. In column [3] (respectively [6]), the interaction term, $DIV \times$ PIN (respectively $HI \times$ PIN), is negatively (respectively positively) significant, implying that the effect of information asymmetry (PIN) on firm value (Q) varies with the degree of diversification. More specifically, the negative effect of PIN on Q is enhanced as the firm's diversification increases. In other words, the more diversified the firm is, the greater the damage to firm value due to increased information asymmetry. At the same time, the sign and significance of the other variables are consistent overall with those in columns [1] and [4].

To control for the problem of causality, we lag all the independent variables one year in the last two columns and use Q_{t+1} as the dependent variable. The results are consistent with the previous results, as the coefficient estimate on *DIV* is negatively significant with Q but becomes insignificant after adding PIN as the proxy of information asymmetry. The results suggest that the increased information asymmetry is responsible for the diversification discount even after considering the problem of causality.

The regression results show that government control reduces a firm's Tobin's Q, because the coefficient estimates for *GOV* are all significantly negative. These results are consistent with the prediction that political influence will detract from firm value, and is consistent with the analysis in Table 2.6. On average, firms that are smaller in size, older in corporate history, have higher institutional ownership, higher leverage and lower ownership concentration are found to have higher Tobin's Q.

To examine the influence of the stock exchanges, we divide the sample into two categories, firms listed on the SHSE and firms listed on the SZSE, and rerun the tests. The regression results in columns [1] and [3] of Table 2.8 are based on (5). According to the results, diversified firms have lower Tobin's Q than non-diversified firms, as the coefficient estimates for *DIV* are significantly negative. This conclusion is consistent with the results in Table 2.7, where the sample includes the whole market.

The regression results in columns [2] and [4] are based on (6), using data from the two stock exchanges separately. After including PIN as an explanatory variable for Tobin's Q, the coefficient estimates of *DIV* become insignificant while the coefficient estimates of PIN are all significantly negative at the 1% level. The results suggest that the increased information

Table 2.8 Regression of the effect of PIN on diversification discount: subsamples

Independent Variables	SHSE		SZSE		A-shares		Gov-Controlled		Non-Gov-Controlled	
	[1]	[2]	[3]	[4]	[5]	[6]	[7]	[8]	[9]	[10]
DIV	−0.02*	−0.00	−0.04***	−0.02	−0.03***	−0.01	−0.02	−0.02	−0.03*	−0.03
	[−1.82]	[−0.11]	[−2.61]	[−1.37]	[−2.70]	[−1.15]	[−1.60]	[−1.48]	[−1.73]	[−1.00]
PIN		−0.45***		−0.63***		−0.52***		−0.46***		−0.49**
		[−4.47]		[−4.62]		[−6.34]		[−4.86]		[−2.48]
SIZE	−0.13***	−0.18***	−0.18***	−0.22***	−0.17***	−0.20***	−0.14***	−0.15***	−0.22***	−0.23***
	[−19.52]	[−28.24]	[−21.72]	[−25.92]	[−33.94]	[−39.11]	[−25.43]	[−25.93]	[−19.99]	[−16.16]
VOLATILITY	0.04	0.12**	−0.01	−0.02	0.04	0.04	0.07	0.04	0.12*	0.51***
	[0.68]	[2.39]	[−0.10]	[−0.27]	[1.56]	[1.46]	[1.31]	[0.76]	[1.68]	[6.46]
TAGrow	−0.03**	−0.05***	−0.05**	−0.05***	−0.05***	−0.06***	−0.04***	−0.03***	−0.04**	0.04
	[−2.42]	[−4.54]	[−2.53]	[−2.78]	[−3.54]	[−4.52]	[−3.26]	[−3.01]	[−2.07]	[1.45]
INTANG	−0.31***	−0.23**	0.06	0.00	−0.08	−0.07	−0.06	−0.07	−0.03	0.04
	[−2.75]	[−2.00]	[0.50]	[0.28]	[−1.03]	[−0.96]	[−0.73]	[−0.80]	[−0.18]	[0.21]
LEVERAGE	0.05***	0.05	0.06***	0.06***	0.01***	0.05***	−0.04**	−0.04**	0.06***	0.05***
	[4.80]	[0.01]	[3.50]	[3.67]	[6.70]	[6.75]	[−2.12]	[−1.97]	[5.43]	[3.55]
STATE	−0.05	0.04	0.02	0.07	0.03	0.05	−0.04	−0.04	−0.09	−0.26**
	[−1.00]	[0.87]	[0.46]	[1.47]	[1.02]	[1.71]	[−0.99]	[−1.05]	[−1.17]	[−2.43]
GOV	−0.05***	−0.06***	−0.06***	−0.01***	−0.07***	−0.06***				
	[−2.65]	[−3.32]	[−2.95]	[−3.58]	[−4.60]	[−4.70]				
INS	0.02***	0.01***	0.02***	0.00***	0.02***	0.01***	0.02***	0.02***	0.03***	0.03***
	[18.00]	[26.18]	[15.20]	[21.91]	[24.54]	[33.28]	[19.65]	[19.92]	[12.51]	[14.12]
SHRCR	−0.00	−0.01*	−0.00	−0.00*	−0.00*	−0.00**	0.00	0.00	−0.00***	−0.00***
	[−0.68]	[−1.80]	[−0.98]	[−1.65]	[−1.68]	[−2.17]	[0.41]	[0.56]	[−3.84]	[−4.11]

Continued

Table 2.8 Continued

Independent Variables	SHSE		SHSE		A-shares		Gov-Controlled		Non-Gov-Controlled	
	[1]	[2]	[3]	[4]	[5]	[6]	[7]	[8]	[9]	[10]
AGE	0.01***	0.01***	0.02***	0.02***	0.01***	0.01***	0.01***	0.01***	0.01***	0.02***
	[3.97]	[6.79]	[6.12]	[5.76]	[8.45]	[9.65]	[6.78]	[6.70]	[4.05]	[4.69]
CONSTANT	3.95***	5.11***	4.80***	5.82***	4.70***	5.45***	4.06***	4.35***	5.71***	5.91***
	[27.51]	[34.16]	[25.67]	[28.83]	[42.95]	[46.41]	[32.73]	[31.69]	[23.90]	[17.80]
INDUSTRY	Yes	Yes	Yes	Yes	Yes	Yes	Yes	Yes	Yes	Yes
YEAR	Yes	Yes	Yes	Yes	Yes	Yes	Yes	Yes	Yes	Yes
R^2	0.5196	0.6064	0.5710	0.6116	0.5689	0.6079	0.5342	0.537	0.6116	0.6177
Obs	3,139	3,139	2,238	2,238	5,126	5,126	3,736	3,736	1,641	1,641

The table contains regression results following (5) and (6) when the sample is partitioned into different subsamples. The dependent variable is Tobin's Q (Q) in year *t* in columns [1] to [6] and Tobin's Q (Q) in year *t+1* in columns [7] and [8]. *DIV* is the dummy variable for diversification, *HI* is the sales-based Herfindahl index and PIN is the estimate of information asymmetry. The interaction terms, *DIV*×PIN and *HI*×PIN, measure the effects of the interplay between diversification and information asymmetry on the firm value. *SIZE* is the logarithm of total assets, *VOLATILITY* is the annualized volatility of daily stock returns, *TAGrow* is the percentage change in total assets, *INTANG* is the percentage of intangible assets, *LEVERAGE* is the ratio of book value of debt to total assets, *STATE* is the percentage of shares held by the state agency, *GOV* is the dummy variable that takes the value 1 if the firm is state controlled, *SHRCR* is the ownership concentration measure, *INS* is the percentage of shares held by institutions, *AGE* is the number of years after going public, and *INDUSTRY* and *YEAR* are respectively the industry dummies and year dummies. Figures in brackets are t-statistics. Significance levels of 1%, 5% and 10% are denoted by ***, **, and *, respectively.

asymmetry level is responsible for the diversification discount, which is consistent with the conclusion in Table 2.7. We note that the adjusted R-square is higher in the SZSE regression than that in the SHSE regression.

Next, we exclude 251 observations that relate to B-shares and investigate the relation between information asymmetry and the diversification discount using A-shares only. The regression results are shown in columns [5] and [6] of Table 2.8 and the same conclusion is derived from this subsample, that is, that the multi-segment firms have lower value due to a higher level of information asymmetry. Therefore, the same conclusion is achieved regardless of the stock exchange and the share type (domestic shares or foreign shares).

Finally, regarding the political influence on the effect of diversification, we divide the sample into government-controlled firms versus non-government-controlled firms and check the effect of information asymmetry on the diversification discount. The regression results are shown in columns [7] to [10] of Table 2.8 and are consistent with the previous results shown in Table 2.6 that indicate that government control is an important factor when testing for the effect of diversification on firm value. As to non-government-controlled firms, the coefficient estimate of *DIV* is significant in column [9], but loses its significance after adding PIN in column [10]. The result is consistent with our previous tests. For the government-controlled firms, the effect of diversification is not as strong as in the non-government-controlled firms while information asymmetry is still significantly negatively related to firm value. Our results show that the government-controlled firms have smaller firm value discounts associated with the corporate diversification than do the non-government-controlled firms. One possible explanation for this finding is that the firms controlled by the central or regional government or another state-owned enterprise might be influenced by political and country-wide strategic policies when making investment decisions, especially the decisions relating to multiple business segments. These firms, who work for the interests of central or regional governments, are more likely to get governmental subsidies or other implicit cost-saving benefits. The coefficient estimates of other control variables in Table 2.8 are similar to those in Table 2.7.

2.6 Robustness checks

To test the robustness of the results, we use a three-step approach to evaluate the effect of information asymmetry on the diversification discount and report the results in this section.

2.6.1 Econometric Specification

Three combined regressions are used here to test whether, after controlling for information asymmetry, diversification has any effect on the firm value discount. In the first step, the diversification dummy variable (*DIV*) is estimated as a function of information asymmetry (PIN) along with a set of firm-specific and industry-specific characteristics, using the following Logit model and a sample of 5377 firm-year observations:

$$\begin{aligned} DIV_{i,t} = {} & \beta_0 + \beta_1 PIN_{i,t} + \beta_2 SIZE_{i,t} + \beta_3 VOLATILITY_{i,t} + \beta_4 TAGrow_{i,t} \\ & + \beta_5 INTANG_{i,t} + \beta_6 LEVERAGE_{i,t} + \beta_7 STATE_{i,t} + \beta_8 SHRCR_{i,t} \\ & + \beta_9 AGE_{i,t} + \beta_{10} EXCHANGE_{i,t} + \sum_k \varphi_k \, Industry\ Dummies \\ & + \sum_t \phi_t \, Year\ Dummies + \varepsilon_{i,t}. \end{aligned} \tag{7}$$

The predicted diversification variable $\widehat{DIV}_{i,t}$ and the regression residual $\widehat{Resid}_{i,t}$ are estimated by the Logit regression in (7). The models use the mapping method to project *DIV* into the space with PIN and other explanatory variables in the first step. The predicted $\widehat{DIV}_{i,t}$ from (6) represents the part of the original *DIV* explained by PIN and other variables, while the residual, $\widehat{Resid}_{i,t}$, orthogonal to the space of information asymmetry, reflects the part of *DIV* that is not explained by the regression model of (7). In the second step, we use $\widehat{DIV}_{i,t}$ and $\widehat{Resid}_{i,t}$, to explain the firm value discount in the regressions. The regression model with $\widehat{DIV}_{i,t}$ as the explanatory variable is as follows:

$$\begin{aligned} Q_{i,t} = {} & \gamma_0 + \gamma_1 \widehat{DIV}_{i,t} + \gamma_2 SIZE_{i,t} + \gamma_3 VOLATILITY_{i,t} + \gamma_4 TAGrow_{i,t} \\ & + \gamma_5 INTANG_{i,t} + \gamma_6 LEVERAGE_{i,t} + \gamma_7 STATE_{i,t} + \gamma_8 SHRCR_{i,t} \\ & + \gamma_9 AGE_{i,t} + \gamma_{10} EXCHANGE_{i,t} + \sum_k \varphi_k \, Industry\ Dummies \\ & + \sum_t \phi_t \, Year\ Dummies + \varepsilon_{i,t}. \end{aligned} \tag{8}$$

The regression model with $\widehat{Resid}_{i,t}$ as the explanatory variable is as follows:

$$\begin{aligned} Q_{i,t} = {} & \theta_0 + \theta_1 \widehat{Resid}_{i,t} + \theta_2 SIZE_{i,t} + \theta_3 VOLATILITY_{i,t} + \theta_4 TAGrow_{i,t} \\ & + \theta_5 INTANG_{i,t} + \theta_6 LEVERAGE_{i,t} + \theta_7 STATE_{i,t} + \theta_8 SHRCR_{i,t} \\ & + \theta_9 AGE_{i,t} + \sum_k \varphi_k \, Industry\ Dummies + \sum_t \phi_t \, Year\ Dummies + \varepsilon_{i,t} \end{aligned} \tag{9}$$

where Tobin's Q and all the other variables are as specified in Section 2.3.

The primary coefficient of interest in (7) is the coefficient on PIN, β_1, which captures the relation between stock price informativeness and the firm's diversification. In (8), the primary coefficient of interest is the coefficient on predicted diversification, γ_1, which indicates the influence on firm valuation exerted by the projection of diversification as explained by (7). If γ_1 is significantly different from 0, the information asymmetry of the diversified firm is responsible for the discount in firm value. At the same time, an insignificant coefficient on the residual θ_1 in (9), indicates that without the effect of PIN, the remaining part of diversification does not influence firm value. So the hypothesis is as follows:

$$H_0: \beta_1 = 0, \gamma_1 = 0 \quad \text{or} \quad \theta_1 \neq 0$$

$$H_1: \beta_1 \neq 0, \gamma_1 \neq 0 \quad \text{and} \quad \theta_1 = 0.$$

2.6.2 Regression results

Table 2.9 presents the regression results of (7), (8) and (9). From columns [1] (respectively [4]), the PIN variable is positively (respectively negatively) related with *DIV* (respectively *HI*) indicating that diversified firms have higher information asymmetry compared with single-focus firms. As shown in the table, the coefficient estimates for $\widehat{DIV}_{i,t}$ are significantly negative (positive) at the 1 percent level in column [2] (column [5]), providing convincing evidence that the lower firm value stems from the higher information asymmetry level after diversification. The more diversified the firms are, the higher the level of information asymmetry they will suffer and, in turn, the lower the value placed on the firm by investors due to the lower transparency implied by higher PIN. At the same time, the coefficient estimates, $\widehat{Resid}_{i,t}$, are not significant no matter whether the diversification is estimated by *DIV* or *HI*, as shown in columns [3] and [6]. So diversification cannot affect the value of the firms without the involvement of information asymmetry.

When it comes to the other explanatory variables, on average, firms with a higher ratio of intangible assets, lower institutional ownership and lower ownership concentration are more diversified. Listed firms on the SHSE are more diversified compared with those listed on the SZSE as the coefficient estimate on *EXCHANGE* is significantly positive (negative) at the 1 percent level in column [1] (column [4]). Firms that are smaller in size, older in corporate history, have higher institutional ownership, higher leverage, and lower ownership concentration

Table 2.9 Robustness test of the effect of PIN on the diversification discount

	DIV			HI		
	[1]	[2]	[3]	[4]	[5]	[6]
Independent Variables	**First-stage**	**Second-stage**	**Residual**	**First-stage**	**Second-stage**	**Residual**
PDIV		−2.60***				
		[−8.39]				
PHI					6.35***	
					[9.58]	
Residual			−0.00			0.01
			[−0.85]			[0.49]
PIN	0.94**			−0.10**		
	[2.02]			[−2.00]		
SIZE	−0.06*	−0.17***	−0.19***	0.00	−0.20***	−0.19***
	[−1.89]	[−24.42]	[−30.24]	[0.39]	[−31.23]	[−30.41]
VOLATILITY	0.10	0.33***	0.33***	−0.00	0.25***	0.33***
	[0.64]	[12.37]	[12.38]	[−0.05]	[9.03]	[12.39]
TAGrow	−0.02	0.03*	0.03*	0.00	0.02	0.03*
	[−0.23]	[1.68]	[1.94]	[0.27]	[1.38]	[1.95]
INTANG	1.03**	0.46***	−0.07	−0.18***	1.07***	−0.07
	[2.08]	[4.01]	[−0.78]	[−3.60]	[7.06]	[−0.78]
LEVERAGE	−0.03	0.03***	0.04***	0.00	0.04***	0.04***
	[−0.51]	[2.88]	[4.28]	[0.00]	[4.33]	[4.28]
STATE	−0.15	−0.12***	−0.03	0.01	−0.07**	−0.03
	[−0.99]	[−3.80]	[−1.12]	[0.53]	[−2.47]	[−1.13]
INS	−0.01***	0.01***	0.01**	0.77**	0.01***	0.01***
	[−6.84]	[4.92]	[33.82]	[2.45]	[23.88]	[33.75]
SHRCR	−0.01***	−0.01***	−0.00***	0.00***	−0.01***	−0.00***
	[−5.09]	[−9.44]	[−4.23]	[5.39]	[−10.50]	[−4.32]
AGE	0.06***	0.05***	0.02***	−0.01***	0.07***	0.02***
	[7.16]	[11.73]	[10.43]	[−8.46]	[12.47]	[10.43]
EXCHANGE	0.52***	0.30***	−0.00	−0.05***	0.31***	−0.00
	[8.79]	[7.96]	[−0.06]	[−7.74]	[8.98]	[−0.06]
CONSTANT	−0.18	6.56***	5.04***	−4.89**	0.36***	5.04***
	[−0.25]	[29.04]	[37.17]	[−2.17]	[3.34]	[37.15]
INDUSTRY	Yes	Yes	Yes	Yes	Yes	Yes
YEAR	Yes	Yes	Yes	Yes	Yes	Yes
R^2	0.1028	0.3262	0.3176	0.1032	0.3288	0.3175
Obs	5,377	5,377	5,377	5,377	5,377	5,377

The table shows the regression results following (7), (8) and (9). Column [1] ([4]) presents first-stage logit regression estimates with *DIV* (*HI*) as the dependent variable. Column [2] ([5]) presents the second-stage regression estimates with Tobin's Q (Q) as dependent variable, and the predicted *DIV* (*HI*) as the major independent variable. Column [3] ([6]) shows the regression estimations with Tobin's Q (Q) as the dependent variable, and the residuals from the first-stage regression as the main independent variable. The sample consists of listed firms in China from 2003 to 2008 with 5377 firm-year observations. Regressions include industry dummies and year dummies. Figures in brackets are t-statistics. Significance levels of 1%, 5% and 10% are denoted by ***, **, and *, respectively.

are associated with higher Tobin's Q based on the evidence provided in columns [2], [3], [5], and [6].

2.7 Conclusion

This chapter analyzes the relation between corporate diversification and information asymmetry and their effects on firm value, using data from China from 2003 to 2008. We estimate PIN and use it as a proxy of information asymmetry for 1869 firms traded on the two stock exchanges in China. As predicted, the PIN estimates are higher in China than those found in the U.S. and European countries. Diversified firms exhibit higher levels of asymmetric information than focused firms. This finding is consistent with the transparency theory suggested by Thomas (2002) and the discount is higher for the non-government-controlled firms than for the government-controlled firms.

Compared with single-focus firms, multi-segment firms have lower Tobin's Q after controlling for other firm-specific factors, including firm size, stock price volatility, growth opportunities, ownership structures and others. Therefore, Chinese firms exhibit a diversification discount.

The main question of the study is to determine whether diversification affects firm value directly, or indirectly through information asymmetry. Consistent with our hypothesis, it is the information asymmetry resulting from corporate diversification that leads to a firm value discount. The rationale behind this relation is that corporate diversification results in a higher level of asymmetric information, and therefore the loss of firm value for diversified firms is attributed to the more severe asymmetric information problems. After controlling for PIN, the remaining part of diversification does not explain the fluctuations in firm value. If asymmetric information problems are well controlled or managed, the cost of diversification will be reduced significantly. We expect that further studies will investigate how to control or reduce the asymmetric information to lower the negative effect of diversification on firm value.

Notes

1. There is an active debate in the literature on how diversification affects firm value. Some studies argue that diversification is value-destroying and will lead to a loss in firm value. In contrast, other studies argue that diversification is a value-enhancing activity. In China, Lin and Su (2008) find that diversified firms have significantly higher *Tobin's Q* than non-diversified firms, although the value of diversification depends on government control. We will explicitly discuss these arguments in the chapter.

2. A similar study by Lu and Wong (2008) finds that information risk is priced for the stocks traded on the Taiwan stock exchange.
3. The PIN estimates have been applied to stocks listed on the New York Stock Exchange (NYSE) that operates with a specialist system (see Easley et al. (2002), Bardong et al. (2009) and others). It has also been applied by other researchers to stock markets that are order-driven without market makers. For example, Borisova and Yadav (2008) use PIN for stocks in European countries; Copeland et al. (2009) and Chan et al. (2008) use PIN for stocks in mainland China; and Lu and Wong (2008) use PIN for stocks in the Taiwan stock market. In an order-driven market, the uninformed trader, similar to a market maker in the specialist system, serves as the liquidity provider to the liquidity demander who is an informed trader.
4. If the trading price equals the previous trading price, we will revert to additional lags. The maximum number of lags is two in our study.
5. Not all the shares in a listed company are freely tradable. The split share structure of the Chinese public securities market refers to the existence of a large number of non-tradable shares, including state-owned shares and legal person shares of a listed Chinese company. Only about one-third of the shares in a listed Chinese company are freely tradable. The CSRC published guidance notes in 2005 on the split share structure reform of listed companies or the reform of non-tradable shares. The reform is designed to float the non-tradable legal person shares through the open market. Such legal person shares could, under the reform program, be converted to tradable A-shares. The converted A-shares are subject to a lockup period.
6. A large percentage of total outstanding shares are non-tradable shares in China. We use the sum of the net asset value of non-tradable shares and the market capitalization of tradable shares, as the market value of equity.

References

Amihud, Y., and Lev, B. 1981. Risk Reduction as a Managerial Motive for Conglomerate Mergers. *The Bell Journal of Economics* 12(2): 605–617.

Amit, R., and Livnat, J. 1988. A Concept of Conglomerate Diversification. *Journal of Management* 14(4): 593–604.

Aslan, H., Easley, D., Hvidkjaer, S., and O'Hara, M. 2008. The Charateristics of Informed Trading: Implications for Asset Pricing. *Journal of Empirical Finance* 18(5): 782–801.

Bardong, F., Bartram, S. M., and Yadav, P. K. 2009. Informed Trading, Information Asymmetry, and Pricing of Information Risk: Empirical Evidence from the NYSE. Working Paper, Oklahoma University.

Berger, P. G., and Ofek, E. 1995. Diversification's Effect on Firm Value. *Journal of Financial Economics* 37(1): 39–65.

Berry, T. K., Bizjak, J. M., Lemmon, M. L., and Naveen, L. 2006. Organizational Complexity and CEO Labor Markets: Evidence from Diversified Firms. *Journal of Corporate Finance* 12(4): 797–817.

Borisova, G., and Yadav, P. K.. 2010. How does Privatization affect Information asymmetry? Evidence from the European Union. Working Paper, Iowa State University and Oklahoma University.

Brown, S., and Hillegeist, S. A. 2007. How Disclosure Quality Affects the Level of Information Asymmetry. *Review of Accounting Studies* 12(2–3): 443–477.

Chan, K., Albert J. Menkveld, A. J., and Zhishu, Y. 2008. Information Asymmetry and Asset Prices: Evidence from the China Foreign Share Discount. *The Journal of Finance* 63(1): 159–196.

Chen, G., Firth, M., Gao, D. N., and Rui, O. M. 2006. Have China's Enterprise Reforms Led to Improved Efficiency and Profitability? *Emerging Markets Review* 7: 82–109.

Chen, G., Firth, M., and Xu, L. 2009. Does the Type of Ownership Control Matter? Evidence from China's Listed Companies. *Journal of Banking and Finance* 33: 171–181.

Chronopoulos, D.K, Girardone, C. and Nankervis, J. C. 2011. Are There Any Cost and Profit Efficiency Gains in Financial Conglomeration? Evidence from the Accession Countries. *The European Journal of Finance* 17(8): 603–621.

Clarke, J. E., Fee, C. E., and Thomas, S. 2004. Corporate Diversification and Asymmetric Information: Evidence from Stock Market Trading Characteristics. *Journal of Corporate Finance* 10(1): 105–129.

Copeland, L., Wong, W. K., and Zeng, Y. 2009. Information-based Trade in the Shanghai Stock Market. *Global Finance Journal* 20(2): 180–190.

Doukas, J. A., and Pantzalis, C. 2003. Geographic Diversification and Agency Costs of Debt of Multinational Firms. *Journal of Corporate Finance* 9(1): 59–92.

Easley, D., Hvidkjaer, S., and O'Hara, M. 2002. Is Information Risk a Determinant of Asset Returns? *The Journal of Finance* 57(5): 2185–2221.

Easley, D., Kiefer, N. M., and O'Hara, M. 1996. Cream-Skimming or Profit-Sharing? The Curious Role of Purchased Order Flow. *Journal of Finance* 51(3): 811–33.

Easley, D., Kiefer, N. M., and O'Hara, M. 1997a. The Information Content of the Trading Process. *Journal of Empirical Finance* 4(2–3): 159–186.

Easley, D., Kiefer, N. M. and O'Hara, M. 1997b. One Day in the Life of a Very Common Stock. *Review of Financial Studies* 10(3): 805–835.

Easley, D., O'Hara, M., and Paperman, J. 1998. Financial Analysts and Information-based Trade. *Journal of Financial Markets* 1(2): 175–201.

Firth, M., Fung, P. M. Y., and Rui, O. M.. 2006. Corporate Performance and CEO Compensation in China. *Journal of Corporate Finance* 12(4): 693–714.

Firth, M., Lin, C. and Wong, S. M. 2008. Leverage and Investment under a State-Owned Bank Lending Environment: Evidence from China. *Journal of Corporate Finance*, 14: 642–653.

Gilson, S. C, Healy, P. M., Noe, C. F. and Palepu, K. G. 2001. Analyst Specialization and Conglomerate Stock Breakups. *Journal of Accounting Research* 39(3): 565–582.

Habib, M. A., Johnson, D. B. and Naik, N. Y. 1997. Spinoffs and Information. *Journal of Financial Intermediation* 6(2): 153–176.

Hadlock, C. J., Ryngaert, M. and Thomas, S. 2001. Corporate Structure and Equity Offerings: Are There Benefits to Diversification? *Journal of Business* 74(4): 613–35.

Hong, D. and Xiong, D. 2006. The Analysis of Diversification and Performance of Listed Companies in China. *Journal of Financial Research*, no. 11: 33–43.

Jensen, M. C. 1986. Agency Costs of Free Cash Flow, Corporate Finance, and Takeovers. *The American Economic Review* 76(2): 323–329.

Krishnaswami, S., and Subramaniam, V. 1999. Information Asymmetry, Valuation, and the Corporate Spin-off Decision. *Journal of Financial Economics* 53(1): 73–112.

Lamont, O. 1997. Cash Flow and Investment: Evidence from Internal Capital Markets. *The Journal of Finance* 52(1): 83–109.

Lang, L. H. P., and Stulz, R. M. 1994. Tobin's q, Corporate Diversification, and Firm Performance. *Journal of Political Economy* 102(6): 1248–80.

Lee, C. M. C., and Ready, M. J. 1991. Inferring Trade Direction from Intraday Data. *Journal of Finance* 46(2): 733–46.

Lewellen, W. G. 1971. A Pure Financial Rationale for the Conglomerate Merger. *Journal of Finance* 26(2): 521–37.

Lin, C., and Su, D. 2008. Industrial Diversification, Partial Privatization and Firm Valuation: Evidence from Publicly Listed Firms in China. *Journal of Corporate Finance* 14(4): 405–417.

Lins, K. and Servaes, H. 1999. International Evidence on the Value of Corporate Diversification. *Journal of Finance* 54(6): 2215–2239.

Lins, K. and Servaes, H. 2002. Is Corporate Diversification Beneficial in Emerging Markets? *Financial Management* 31(2): 5.

Lu, R. C., and Wong, W. K. 2008. Probability of Information-Based Trading as a Pricing Factor in Taiwan Stock Market. Working Paper, Ming Chuan University.

Martin, J. D., and Sayrak, A. 2003. Corporate Diversification and Shareholder Value: A Survey of Recent Literature. *Journal of Corporate Finance* 9(1): 37–57.

Myers, S. C., and Majluf, N. S. 1984. Corporate Financing and Investment Decisions when Firms Have Information that Investors do not Have. *Journal of Financial Economics* 13(2): 187–221.

Nanda, V., and Narayanan, M. P. 1999. Disentangling Value: Financing Needs, Firm Scope, and Divestitures. *Journal of Financial Intermediation* 8(3): 174–204.

Panzar, J. C., and Willig, R. D. 1981. Economies of Scope. *The American Economic Review* 71(2): 268–272.

Rajan, R., Servaes, H. and Zingales, L. 2000. The Cost of Diversity: The Diversification Discount and Inefficient Investment. *The Journal of Finance* 55(1): 35–80.

Scharfstein, D. S. 1998. The Dark Side of Internal Capital Markets II: Evidence from Diversified Conglomerates. Working Paper, Harvard Business School.

Scharfstein, D. S. and Stein, J. C. 2000. The Dark Side of Internal Capital Markets: Divisional Rent-Seeking and Inefficient Investment. *Journal of Finance* 55(6): 2537–2564.

Shin, H.-H., and Stulz, R. M. 1998. Are Internal Capital Markets Efficient?. *Quarterly Journal of Economics* 113(2): 531–552.

Stowe, J. D., and Xing, X. 2006. Can Growth Opportunities Explain the Diversification Discount? *Journal of Corporate Finance* 12(4): 783–796.

Teece, D. J. 1980. Economies of Scope and the Scope of the Enterprise. *Journal of Economic Behavior & Organization* 1(3): 223–247.

Teece, D. J. 1982. Towards an Economic Theory of the Multiproduct Firm. *Journal of Economic Behavior & Organization* 3(1): 39–63.

Thomas, S. E., and Fee, C. E. 2000. Corporate Diversification, Asymmetric Information, and Firm Value: Evidence from Stock Market Trading Characteristics. Working Paper, University of Pittsburgh and Michigan State University.

Thomas, S. 2002. Firm Diversification and Asymmetric Information: Evidence from Analysts' Forecasts and Earnings Announcements. *Journal of Financial Economics* 64(3): 373–396.

Venter, J. H., and De Jongh, D. C. J. 2004. Extending the EKOP Model to Estimate the Probability of Informed Trading. Working Paper, North-west University.

Villalonga, B. 2004. Diversification Discount or Premium? New Evidence from the Business Information Tracking Series. *The Journal of Finance* 59(2): 479–506.

Wei, Z., Xie, F. and Zhang, S. 2005. Ownership Structure and Firm Value in China's Privatized Firms: 1991–2001. *Journal of Financial and Quantitative Analysis* 40(1): 87–108.

Weston, J. F. 1969. The Nature and Significance of Conglomerate Firms. *St. John's Law Review* 44: 66.

Williamson, O. E. 1983. *Markets and Hierarchies: Analysis and Antitrust Implications*. Free Press, January 1.

Yan, Y., and Zhang, S. 2010. An Improved Estimation Method and Empirical Properties of the Probability of Informed Trading. Working Paper, University of Pennsylvania and Nanyang Technological University.

Zhang, Y., Liu, W. and Gong, L. 2005. An Empirical Study on Diversification and Firm Performance. *Journal of Financial Research*, no. 09: 122–136.

3

Asset Pricing under Financial Repression: Evidence from the Chinese Real Estate Boom during 1999–2010

Xiuping Hua and Chris Adcock

3.1 Introduction

China is well known for having adopted financial repression policies to achieve faster economic growth (Huang, 2010; Lin, Cai and Li, 1995). The term "financial repression" refers to government policies which regulated interest rates, set high reserve requirements on bank deposits and mandatorily allocated financial resources (MaKinnon, 1973). Such policies are common in developing countries. Despite more than 30 years of economic reform, the Chinese economy still exhibits characteristics typical of financial repression: heavily regulated interest rates, state-influenced credit allocation, frequently adjusted reserve requirements and tightly controlled capital account (Huang and Wang, 2011).

In the early reform and development years immediately after 1978, mild financial repression helped China to maintain financial stability. This in turn had a favorable effect on growth performance (Li, 2001). China has been one of the fastest growing economies of the world in the last thirty years and has had an average annual gross domestic product (GDP) growth rate of 9 to 10 percent. In the 1980s and 1990s this remarkable growth rate was a consequence, at least in part, of the government's financial repression policies. Huang and Wang (2011) find that repressive financial policies markets did not seriously jeopardize growth performance and helped Chinese economic growth for the first twenty years after 1978. However, financial repression did have negative consequences, such as a distorted economic structure, inefficient financial markets, inflation pressure and asset price bubbles.

The central argument of this chapter is that financial repression helps to explain rapid price rises or asset bubbles in the Chinese urban real estate markets in the last decade. Since 1998, when the Chinese government deemed the free market to be the main channel for allocating housing among its citizens, residential real estate construction and prices in all of China's major metropolitan areas have experienced explosive growth. By the end of 2009, the total market value of China's residential real estate market reached 91.5 trillion Yuan (US$13.4 trillion at the January 2010 exchange rate); nearly three times China's GDP for the same year.[1] Urban real estate prices also increased at a high rate in the last decade. Based on the house prices indices used in this chapter, in the period 1999–2010 overall property prices in 70 cities approximately doubled (see also Ahuja *et al.*, 2010), while the average price growth for 12 big cities was almost fourfold.

Many papers have investigated the nature and determinants of residential real estate values in China (Ahuja et al., 2010; Chen, Guo and Wu, 2011; Du, Ma and An, 2010; Hou, 2010; Hui and Yue, 2006; Ito, 2010; Liang and Cao, 2007; Liu, Yun and Zheng, 2002; Sato, 2006; Wu, Gyourko, and Deng, 2011; Xu and Chen, 2012). From the demand side, rapid GDP or disposable income growth, user costs-push, bank lending, rural-urban migration and urbanization, are among the important determining factors (Chen et al., 2011; Liang and Cao, 2007). From the supply side, central-local fiscal relations and land developmentalism, land price, and insufficient economic housing supply are considered to be the key factors (Ahuja et al., 2010; Du et al., 2010; Liu et al., 2002; Su and Tao, 2010). However, the analyses in these papers suffer from potential analytical shortcomings and a dependence on data which is acknowledged as not very reliable. Most previous studies of Chinese residential real estate prices have relied on the official data as the source for real estate pricing information. Methodologically, previous research about the determinants of China's residential real estate market has not included factors unique to China's real estate price dynamics.

We argue that China's repressive financial policies have had very significant effects on real estate prices. The mechanism of financial repression works largely because household savers have few alternative financial assets to bank deposits. Equity investment is an option, but as Lardy (2008) pointed out, the extreme price volatility in the Chinese stock market in recent years may inhibit investors who demonstrate a high degree of risk-aversion. Due to government policy the rates of returns on real assets, notably property, are higher than those of stocks and show lower volatility. They thus become an attractive investment for Chinese households. Due to the negative real returns on bank deposits and high volatility in stock returns, many households have chosen to buy multiple residential properties. We also hypothesize that the main reasons for and economic consequences of financial repression policies have meant that the policy is behind price rises in the real estate market. Correspondingly, we propose several testable hypotheses regarding the relationship between financial repression and real estate pricing.

Our chapter stands out among related literature by explicitly linking the recent real estate boom to China's financial repression policies. It contributes to the literature in three ways. First, many papers have examined the impacts of repressive financial policies on economic growth and efficiency (for a literature review, see Huang and Wang, 2011), but there have been relatively few studies examining the effects of financial repression on asset pricing. To the best of our knowledge, this is the first work to explore this topic within the Chinese context. Secondly, in addition to employing official data published by the National Bureau of Statistics (NBS) and the former National Development and Reform Commission (NDRC), we contribute to the current China-related house pricing literature by adopting a unique set of monthly residential real estate price data for 12 major Chinese cities during the period from 1999 to 2010. Thirdly, we control our tests using a comprehensive set of macroeconomic and financial variables, including income, land prices, user costs and government intervention policies.

The chapter is organized as follows. Section 3.2 reviews the existing literature and develops the main hypotheses that we test. Section 3.3 presents the data and summarizes data construction methods. Section 3.4 describes the models used and reports the empirical results. Section 3.5 concludes and discusses policy implications.

3.2 Hypothesis development

This section has three parts. The first contains a review of related literature. The second summarizes the policies of financial repression and their consequences. These lead naturally to the third part, which describes the five hypotheses which are investigated in this chapter.

3.2.1 Limitations of previous literature

As discussed in the introduction, residential real estate construction and prices in China's major metropolitan areas have experienced tremendous growth. At present, housing assets constitute the largest single source of household wealth in China,[2] comprising around half of the total wealth. In view of its magnitude, the future value of that wealth may have important implications for the Chinese economy in particular and the global economy in general.[3] Numerous papers have explored the fundamental determinants of house prices in a number of countries. Demand fundamentals include income measures (affordability), user or occupancy costs, population growth or structure, interest rates, monetary policy and demographic developments (Costello *et al.*, 2011; Goodman, 1989; Holly and Jones, 1997; Iacoviello, 2005; Iacoviello and Minetti, 2003; Negro and Otrok, 2007; OECD), 2005; Wheaton and Nechayev, 2008; Tsatsaronis and Zhu, 2004). Supply fundamentals consist of rising land values and construction or house structure costs (Davis and Heathcote, 2007, 2008; OECD, 2005). Among relevant literature, a strand of papers has investigated determinants of residential real estate values in China. Identified determinants include rapid GDP or disposable income growth, user costs-push, credit expansion or bank lending, inflation, rural-urban migration and urbanization, central-local fiscal relations and land developmentalism, land price, inefficient economic housing supply, exports and RMB appreciation. (Zhang *et al.*, 2012). However, these papers suffer from the acknowledged unreliable Chinese housing price data as well as potential analytical limitations.

With respect to data, most previous studies of Chinese residential real estate prices have relied on the NBS and the NDRC as the sources for real estate pricing information. In 1998, the NDRC and the NBS began to jointly issue quarterly real estate price indices for the entire country and for 35 major cities.[4] The NDRC and NBS data consisted of published home sales price indices. Three types of index were available: Home Sales Price Index, Housing Lease Price Index and Land Transaction Price Index. These data were collected by independent survey and calculated as year-on-year (YoY) percentage growth rates. From July 2005, 35 other Chinese cities were included in the list. Official property data covered 70 large and medium-sized cities and constituted the famous 70-city index. Because the data is based on YoY growth rates at quarterly frequency, we use cubic spline interpolation to transform YoY growth rates into month-on-month (MoM) percentage growth rates.[5]

Recently this official data has been criticized for significantly underestimating real residential real estate price increases in these major cities (Ahuja *et al.*, 2010; Ito, 2010; Wu *et al.*, 2012). As a result of this criticism, in early 2011 the NBS abandoned the 70-city index and now publishes price changes in individual cities without any reference to a nationwide average.[6] Importantly, the criticism and subsequent abandonment of the 70-city index raises questions about the reliability of the results of previous research on China's property markets which used this data for analysis. This chapter tackles the issue of data reliability and contributes to the literature by constructing a quarterly housing price series for 12 of China's largest cities for the period 1999 to 2010. This uses three sources of data: the official Home Sales Price Index from the NBS, yearly data available from the China Real Estate Information Corporation (CRIC), and monthly data from CRIC.

Analytically, previous research about the determinants of China's residential real estate market also has some limitations. Perhaps most importantly, previous studies fail to consider key factors unique to China's real estate price dynamics, notably financial repression policies. As stated in the introduction, the objective of this chapter is to fill this gap by analyzing the effects of financial repression on house pricing in China. This study is the first to employ financial repression proxies to explain real estate prices at both national and big-city levels after controlling for key fundamental factors and other macroeconomic variables.

3.2.2 Financial repression policies and their consequences

Financial repression has been seen as an intrinsic characteristic of China's financial system (Lu and Yao, 2009). Most of China's financially repressive policies were introduced in the pre-reform period and in the early stages of reform to promote economic growth and maintain financial stability (Huang and Wang, 2011). After China adopted open-up and reform policies in 1978, the financial system remained repressive. First, the interest rate, controlled by the central bank, is much lower than the market rate. This has led to negative real returns on bank deposits, particularly in recent years as inflation has risen. Garnaut *et al.* (2001) point out that official interest rates have been consistently lower than the rates found in the informal credit market by 50 to 100 percent. Secondly, the banking sector is overwhelmingly dominated by four large state-owned banks (Lu and Yao, 2009). In the early 1990s, credits issued by these four state-owned banks consisted of more than 90 percent of the total. In 2005, their share of the credits was still 60 percent. These banks suffer from serious problems caused by large non-performing loans and inefficient operations. Thirdly, the government adopted strict capital controls. It imposed ownership restrictions on foreigners seeking to acquire shares in domestic firms and also restricted the amount of shares available to domestic investors (Gordon and Li, 2003; Kang *et al.*, 2002; Wang and Iorio, 2007). In addition to restricting share purchases, the government also imposed outward capital controls, in principle preventing domestic investors from investing abroad (Gordon and Li, 2003).

Based on the literature, there are probably three important reasons for China's financial repression policies. First and foremost, these measures were used to mobilize resources for economic development at times when the financial system was underdeveloped. The purpose of interest rate controls was not only to lower the cost of capital for investment but also to avoid interest rate competition among financial institutions, while state-influenced credit allocation ensured that scarce financial resources were channeled to priority areas as identified by the government (Huang and Wang, 2011).

Secondly, the policy is associated with reducing the costs of heavy exchange rate intervention. Following the models used by Japan, Germany, and South Korea, China's economic growth since 1978 has been export-led and foreign direct investment (FDI) driven. The government designed policies to create favorable business environments for producers and exporters, including a favorable exchange rate. Since 1978, the exchange rate regime has been either fixed or heavily managed. Government policy has maintained a relatively undervalued RMB to promote economic growth. The persistent trade surplus of China in recent times had necessitated rapid accumulation of foreign reserves. Since the late 1990s, China has been stockpiling international reserves and has surpassed Japan to become the largest reserve holder in the world (Ouyang *et al.*, 2010). All these have put upward pressure on the RMB exchange rate. Financial repression policies have helped to reduce the cost to the government of intervention to sustain China's undervalued exchange rate. In particular, since February 2002, financial repression appears to be the consequence of the government's policy of maintaining an undervalued exchange rate (Lardy, 2008).

Thirdly, it is related to the government's revenue extraction behavior, namely by imposing an implicit tax on business and household income. McKinnon and Mathieson (1981) point out that governments exact revenue via forced sales of government bonds to the system through high reserve requirements. Feldman and Gang (1987) state that rates of monetary growth inconsistent with stable prices interact with high reserve requirements and usury laws to create an inflation tax that further enhances government revenues. Roubini and Sara-i-Martin

(1992, 1995) show that financial repression helps the government make the financial sector the source of easy resources for the public budget. They argue that in countries where tax evasion is large the government will optimally choose to repress the financial sector in order to increase seignorage taxation. Gordon and Li (2003) also argue that all of these financial repression policies can be consistent with a government choosing regulations that maximize a standard type of social welfare function. The observed regulations all aid the government in collecting revenue from both foreign and domestic investors.

What are the economic consequences of China's financial repression policies? We may summarize them as three main effects, namely growth efficiency loss, credit expansion and inflation effect. First, although China's financial repression did not seriously jeopardize its growth performance in the early years, it increasingly became a burden for economic performance (Huang and Wang, 2011; Li, 2001). It is widely recognized that financial development is an important determinant of economic growth and financial repression policies would eventually have adverse effects on growth (Beck *et al.*, 2000; Levine, 1997; Roubini and Sala-i-Martin, 1995). The literature on financial repression and its effects on the growth of developing countries is quite voluminous, see Gupta and Lensink (1997), Huang and Wang (2011) for a review. Developing countries may be more able to manage money supply and financial stability under repressive financial policies at the early state of economic growth (Li, 2001; Stiglitz, 1994). In China's case, Huang and Wang (2011) also show that the impact turned from positive in the 1980s and the 1990s to negative in the 2000s.

Secondly, financial repression policies resulted in efficiency loss. It is generally accepted in the literature that financial repression may discourage the development of financial institutions and instruments and hence may impede financial deepening and hinder efficiency of the financial system (King and Levine, 1993; Pagano, 1993). We take China's stock market as an example. Although China's stock market has developed rapidly since the early 1990s, with the establishment of the Shanghai and Shenzhen stock exchanges, it is famous for having a very high stock price synchronicity and low firm-specific return variation because of poor investor protection and special ownership structure (Gul *et al.*, 2010; Morck *et al.*, 2000).

Thirdly, it increases money demand and hence inflationary pressure. Due to the underdevelopment of and efficiency loss in the financial system, the monetary system itself is the most important intermediary between savers and borrowers. Roubini and Sala-i-Martin (1992) present a model to suggest that financial repression policies increase the demand for money and deliver easy inflationary revenues. China's experience provides a good empirical case for this argument. On the one hand, the government has the strong incentive to expand the money supply; on the other hand, trade surplus and hot money generated by RMB appreciation result in a tremendous foreign exchange reserve build-up and hence an excessive domestic credit expansion. In fact, China's broad money supply (M2) has expanded at an average rate of 18.8 percent a year during 1999 to 2010. Both China's international reserve and M2-to-GDP ratio are now the highest in the world.

More importantly, financial repression is self-sustaining. It has contributed to the expansion of underground finance as well as a more seriously distorted structure of demand. This makes it less likely that China will be able to develop a fully and efficiently functioning capital market (Huang and Wang, 2011; Lardy, 2008). By modifying the price structure and allocation mechanisms of real and financial resources, financial repression transforms the decision making process on almost every level of the economy (Cebenoyan *et al.*, 1995), and hence has important implications for asset pricing.

3.2.3 Testable hypotheses

The central hypothesis of this chapter is that the rapid rise in real estate prices in urban Chinese cities in recent years is at least partly due to financial repression policies. This is simply because these have made real estate the main investment tool of most households in China. Financial repression policies have led to an expansion in market demand for real estate assets, and hence generate positive feedback to housing prices.

Hypothesis 1: Financial repression is positively related to real estate price growth.

We also raise the prospect that the mechanism of financial repression of asset returns works through interactions with several key macroeconomic variables. In particular, economic growth and rises in personal disposable income have helped produce an increase in consumption and investment demand. Hence, these may greatly impact real estate asset prices as well. Thus, we propose the following hypothesis.

Hypothesis 2: Economic growth is positively related to real estate price growth.

Due to the efficiency loss in the financial system, China's stock market suffers from very high stock price synchronicity and low firm-specific return variation. The very high level of volatility in the stock market makes equity investment less attractive to investors. When the stock market's volatility is high, investors are more willing to invest in China's real estate market. Thus, our third hypothesis is as follows.

Hypothesis 3: China's housing prices are positively associated with stock market volatility.

The amount of money and credit available is an important factor in the determination of asset prices. Loose monetary policy may help to fuel a rapid rise in equity, housing and land prices, as in Japan in the late 1980s (IMF, 2010). The effects of China's credit expansion on real estate prices have been discussed by some recent studies, such as Xu and Chen (2012) and Zhang *et al.* (2012). Empirical results consistently demonstrate that lower interest rates, faster money supply growth and loosening mortgage down payment requirements tend to accelerate the subsequent home price growth, and vice versa. Thus, we have our fourth hypothesis.

Hypothesis 4: China's real estate asset prices are positively associated with excessive domestic credit expansion.

In the last decade, RMB appreciation expectations have made foreign investors around the world channel hot money into China. Loose monetary policy may produce positive shocks to output and inflation, resulting in rising user costs such as house rents (Ahuja *et al.*, 2010; OECD, 2005). However, despite rising inflation in the last decade, the Chinese government was reluctant to raise interest rates for fear of attracting even larger speculative inflows, which would have compounded the challenge of controlling the pace of appreciation and the growth of monetary aggregates (Lardy, 2008). A positive impact on house pricing is generated by either currency appreciation or speculative cash inflow.

Hypothesis 5: Currency appreciation expectations are positively associated with financial repression.

3.3 Measurement of variables and data construction

The period studied in this chapter covers the twelve-year period, 1999–2010. All variables described below are collected or constructed at monthly frequency. Hence, each time series comprises 144 monthly observations. This section describes the dependent variables used in the model, measures of financial repression and pricing indicators. To save space, the construction of pricing indicators is described in Appendix A. The control variables used in the model are described in Appendix B. These appendices are available from the corresponding author on request. All variables are listed and briefly described in Tables 3.1 and 3.2.

Table 3.1 Variable definitions and sources

Code	Description	Source
(I) Dependent variables		
ACH	Average 12-city housing pricing index	CRIC; NBS; City Yearbook; Authors' calculation
NH	70-city home sales price index at national level	NBS; NDRC;
(ii) Financial repression variables		
BR	Bank reserve ratio	Peoples Bank of China (PBoC) ; NBS;
BRD	Bank reserve ratio dummy	PBoC ; NBS; Authors' calculation
RI	Real interest rate	PBoC ; NBS;
RID	Real interest rate dummy	PBoC ; NBS; Authors' calculation
(iii) Pricing and rents		
ACL	Average 12-city land pricing index	China's Ministry of Land and Resources; NBS; Authors' calculation
ACR	Average 12-city implicit rent	NBS; NDRC; City Yearbook; OECD (2005); Authors' calculation
NL	70-city land sales price index at national level	NBS; NDRC
NR	70-city rent index at national level	NBS; NDRC

Table 3.2 Variable definitions and sources

Code	Description	Source
(iv) Control variables		
ACP	Average growth rate of 12 big-city populations based on Household Registration System (Hukou)	NBS; NDRC; City Yearbook; China data online
BL	Total RMB bank loans	PBoC
CA	Current account balance, namely trade and service balance	NBS; Authors' calculation
CI	Capital inflows, namely the sum of hot money and foreign direct investment	PBoC; NBS; Authors' calculation
CPI	Consumer price index	NBS

Continued

Table 3.2 Continued

Code	Description	Source
DPD	Down payment dummy variable that equals 1 if there is an increase in the minimum down payment percentage requirement, –1 if there is a decrease, 0 otherwise	The State Council; public media; Authors' calculation
DR	Demand rate	PBoC
DX	The nominal USD/RMB spot exchange rate	PBoC
FR	Foreign exchange reserves	PBoC
GDP	Real GDP output	NBS
HM	Hot money, calculated by change in FR minus (trade and service balance) minus (foreign direct investment)	PBoC; NBS; Authors' calculation
HTD	Housing transaction tax dummy variable that equals 1 if there is an increase in the housing transaction tax requirement, –1 if there is a decrease, 0 otherwise.	The State Council; public media; Authors' calculation
M2	Broad money supply	PBoC
MR	Mortgage rate of bank loans for five years' or above	PBoC
NDF	12-Month RMB/dollar non-deliverable forward contracts	Wind; Bloomberg
NEER	Nominal effective exchange rate	BIS (Bank for International Settlements)
ODR	One year deposit rate	PBoC
PPI	Producer price index	NBS
PY	Average personal disposable income	NBS
REER	Real effective exchange rate	BIS
SP	Shanghai Stock Exchange Composite Index	Shanghai stock exchange
SRV	Conditional GARCH of Shanghai Stock Exchange composite index returns	Shanghai stock exchange; Authors' calculation
TD	Total international trade	NBS
UX	The unexpected RMB appreciation calculated by spot exchange rate minus lagged NDF rate	PBoC ; Wind; Bloomberg
VAI	Value-added industrial output	NBS

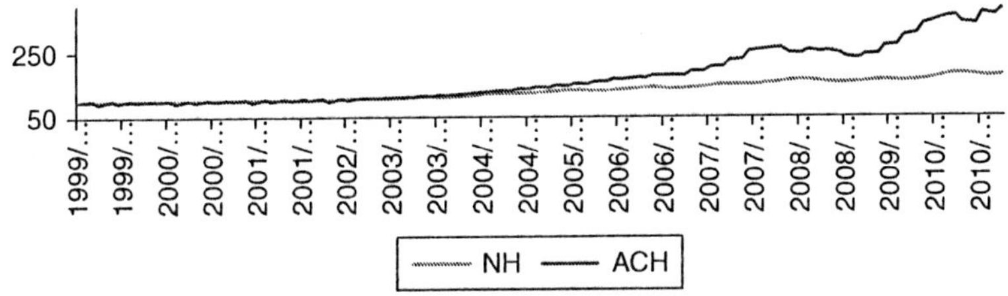

Figure 3.1 Official 70-city home sales price index (NH) vs. constructed average 12 big-city price index (ACH)

Sources: NBS, NDRC, CRIC, Authors' calculation

3.3.1 Dependent variable: average housing prices at national and big-city levels

We take the official 70-city monthly home sales price index (NH) published jointly by the NDRC and the NBS at national level as our proxy of average housing prices. The YoY growth rates are transformed into MoM rates as described above. To deal with the issue of data reliability, already noted above, we construct monthly average housing price series for 12 of China's largest cities[7] for the period 1999–2010 using three sources of data: the CRIC,[8] the official Home Sales Price Index from the NBS and official city statistics. Figure 3.1 depicts the two housing price indices constructed. In comparison with the official NH index, the constructed ACH index is more volatile and exhibits a stronger upward trend after quarter 1 of 2004.

3.3.2 Financial repression variables

We adopt a definition of financial repression which comprises four indicators in two areas. The first variable is real interest rate (RI), which is defined as the nominal demand deposit rate minus the rate of consumer price inflation (CPI) according to Lardy (2008). The second indicator (RID) is based on the difference between demand rate and the CPI rate. Following Agarwala (1983) and Huang and Wang (2011), RID is defined as follows

$$RID = \begin{cases} 0 & if\ RI > 0, \\ 0.5 & if\ 0 \geq RI > -5\%, \\ 1 & if\ RI \leq -5\%. \end{cases}$$

Figure 3.2 shows these variables. There are two points to note. First, there was a substantial decrease in the RI after October 2003, indicating

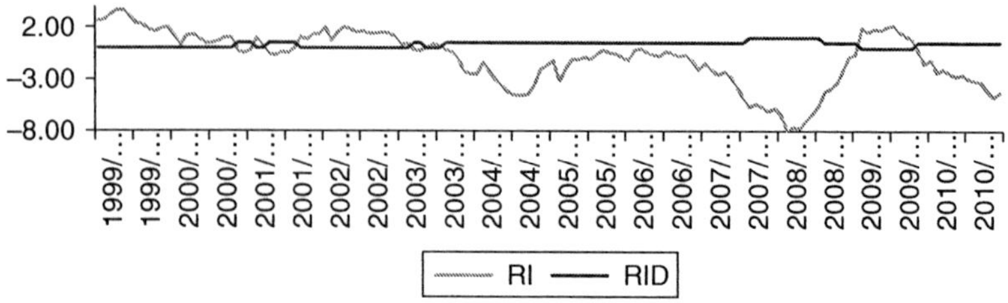

Figure 3.2 Financial repression measured by real interest rate (RI) and real interest rate dummy (RID)

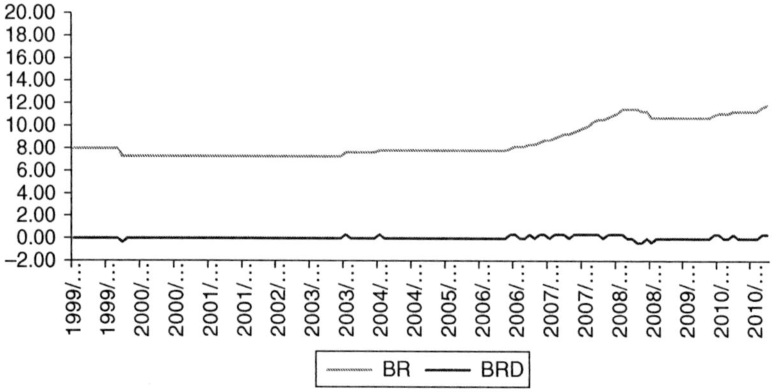

Figure 3.3 Financial repression measured by bank reserve requirement ratio (BR) and bank reserve requirement ratio dummy (BRD)

an increased degree of financial repression. Second, real interest rates were less than –5 percent between August 2007 and July 2008, but then started to increase.

The third variable is the bank reserve requirement ratio for big financial institutions (BR). The fourth variable is a dummy variable (BRD) based on the required bank reserve ratio. BRD is set to –1 if the People's Bank of China reduced the required bank reserve ratio, to 0 if there was no change, and to 1 if BR was increased. Figure 3.3 depicts these two variables. Based on this definition, the degree of financial repression started to increase after August 2006.

3.3.3 Land pricing and rents

With respect to land pricing data, we use the official 70-city Land Transaction Price Index at national level (NL) as our first proxy. For

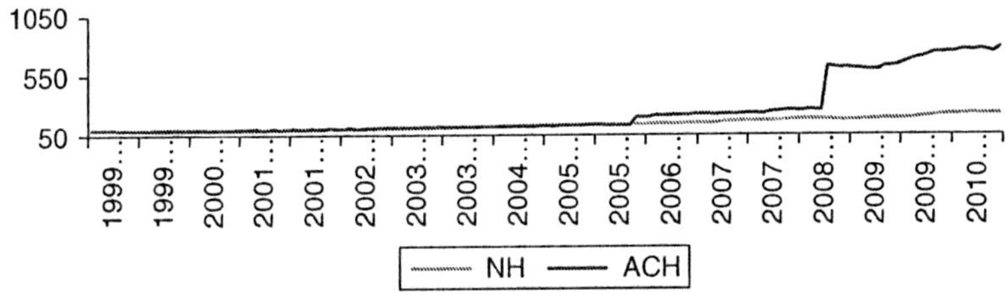

Figure 3.4 Official 70-city land transaction price index (NL) vs. average 12 big-city price index (ACL)

Sources: China's Ministry of Land and Resources, NBS, NDRC, Authors' calculation.

average land price at 12 big-city level, we use the official data on average Residential Land Price (Yuan per square meter) published by China's Ministry of Land and Resources and the NBS. An average big-city land price index (ACL) is computed using methods which are similar to those used for housing price indices. Figure 3.4 shows the two housing price indices. The official 70-city Land Transaction Price Index is relatively stable compared with those for the 12 big cities.

For the rent index at national and big-city levels, we take the 70-city Housing Lease Price Index at national level (NR) as our first proxy. Following Poterba (1992), we construct the user costs for a housing asset in 12 big cities in China by the equation $UC_t = P_t(i + \tau + f - \pi)$, where i is the published nominal mortgage interest rate, τ is the property tax rate, f is the recurring holding costs consisting of depreciation, maintenance and the risk premium on residential property, and π is the expected capital gains (or losses). In equilibrium, the expected cost of owning a house should equal the cost of renting, and hence the constructed user costs are the implicit rents. In China, land and property taxes are levied on transactions rather than asset holdings during the period 1999–2010. The income tax rate levied on the average annual income on a rental property in China is around 5 percent, but most landlords chose not to pay it. Hence we assume $\tau = 0$. Following OECD (2005), holding costs consisting of depreciation, maintenance and the risk premium on residential property in China are assumed to be constant at 4 percent, while the expected capital gains π may be defined as a moving average of consumer price inflation at city levels. We define this newly constructed variable as the average city rent index (ACR). Figure 3.5 shows the two housing rent indices. The official 70-city Housing Lease Price Index is relatively stable compared with the average implicit 12 big cities rent index.

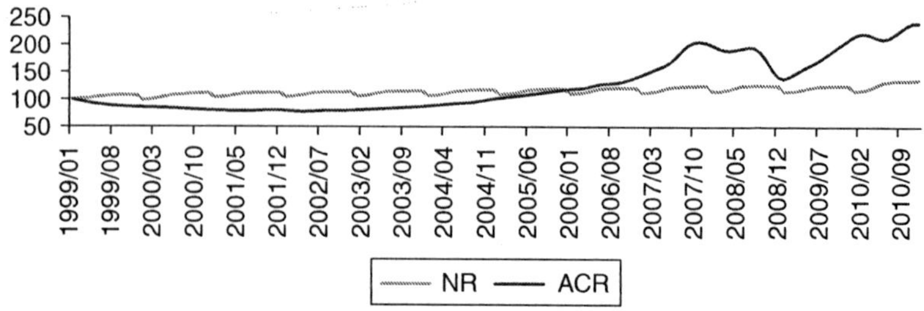

Figure 3.5 Official 70-city housing lease price index (NR) vs. average 12 big-city rent index (ACR)

sources: NBS, NDRC, City Yearbook, OECD (2005), Authors' calculation.

3.4 Model specification and empirical results

This section is in two parts. There is a brief description of the models in Section 3.4.1. The main empirical results are presented in Sections 3.4.2 to 3.4.4.

3.4.1 Empirical models for hypothesis testing

To test for the effects of financial repression and other economic factors on housing prices, we estimate the following specification

$$HP_t = \beta_0 + \beta_1 FRP_t + \beta_2 X_t + \varepsilon_t \tag{1}$$

where HP_t is the average housing price at either national level or big-city level at month t, namely NH_t or ACH_t ,FRP_t is one of four proxies for financial repression at month *t*, including *RI, RID, BR* and *BRD*, X_t is a set of other control variables, *NL, ACL, NR, ACR, GDP, PY, SRV, ACP, M2* and *NDF*. The residual ε_t is assumed to be a normal distribution. Unit root tests for stationarity of both level values and first differences of the individual time series reveal that most of them are integrated at order 1 or 2. Thus we employ two methods, namely the ordinary least squares (OLS) regressions and co-integrating regressions with fully modified OLS (FMOLS) as proposed by Phillips and Hansen (1990). The latter method modifies least squares to account for serial correlation effects and for the endogeneity in the regressors that results from the existence of a co-integrating relationship when both dependent and control variables have unit roots.

One of the other popular econometric frameworks for dealing with unit roots in multiple time series is the vector-autoregressive/error-correction

Table 3.3 Correlation matrix of average housing prices and key control variables

	NH	*ACH*	*RI*	*RID*	*BR*	*BRD*	*NL*	*ACL*	*NR*	*ACR*	*GDP*	*PY*	*SRV*	*M2*	*NEER*	*NDF*
NH	1															
ACH	0.964	1														
RI	−0.584	−0.523	1													
RID	0.546	0.461	−0.880	1												
BR	0.916	0.937	−0.497	0.416	1											
BRD	0.333	0.326	−0.449	0.459	0.259	1										
NL	0.987	0.985	−0.546	0.490	0.929	0.311	1									
ACL	0.846	0.910	−0.224	0.158	0.882	0.077	0.893	1								
NR	0.855	0.829	−0.571	0.519	0.759	0.245	0.850	0.716	1							
ACR	0.945	0.974	−0.599	0.540	0.935	0.409	0.955	0.821	0.809	1						
GDP	0.925	0.933	−0.511	0.447	0.890	0.243	0.930	0.860	0.915	0.905	1					
PY	0.935	0.941	−0.471	0.426	0.907	0.297	0.947	0.885	0.716	0.901	0.834	1				
SRV	0.413	0.405	−0.263	0.219	0.558	0.225	0.379	0.324	0.281	0.493	0.385	0.423	1			
M2	0.971	0.982	−0.467	0.410	0.919	0.271	0.989	0.933	0.844	0.930	0.937	0.951	0.351	1		
NEER	0.273	0.403	0.160	−0.253	0.520	−0.148	0.339	0.610	0.213	0.335	0.375	0.405	0.248	0.398	1	
NDF	−0.959	−0.924	0.637	−0.577	−0.895	−0.362	−0.942	−0.789	−0.832	−0.912	−0.898	−0.916	−0.405	−0.933	−0.288	1

Notes: NH and ACH are average housing prices at national level or big-city level. The four proxies for financial repression are real interest rate (RI), real interest rate dummy (RID), bank reserve requirement ratio (BR) and bank reserve requirement ratio dummy (BRD). NL and ACL are the average land prices at national level or big-city level. NR and ACR are the average implicit rents at national level or big-city level. ACP is average city population growth. PY is personal disposable income. SRV is the conditional GARCH variance of stock market index returns. M2 is broad money supply. NEER is nominal effective exchange rate index. NDF is 12-month RMB/dollar non-deliverable forward contracts.

model (VAR/VECM). This is a reduced-form linear dynamic simultaneous equation model in which all variables are treated as endogenous. It has proved to be a convenient method of summarizing the dynamic relationships among macroeconomic variables. In this chapter it is used to test the interaction between housing price, financial repression, stock market volatility, money supply, and RMB appreciation expectations. Many other authors have used it to include various combinations of variables, for example Bernanke and Gertler (1995) and Iacoviello (2005) to name but a few. A p-dimensional vector time series Z_t is considered and modeled as an unrestricted vector autoregression (VAR) involving up to k-lags

$$\boldsymbol{Z}_t = \sum_{i=1}^{k} \mathbf{A}_i \boldsymbol{Z}_{t-i} + \boldsymbol{\mu} + \boldsymbol{\varepsilon}_t, \quad \boldsymbol{\varepsilon}_t \sim IID\ N_p\,(0, \Sigma), \tag{2}$$

where the $\mathbf{A}_i$ are $p \times r$ matrices of parameters. This equation can be reformulated as a vector error correction model (VECM) as follows

$$\Delta \boldsymbol{Z}_t = \sum_{i=1}^{k-1} {}_i \Delta \boldsymbol{Z}_{t-1} + \Pi \boldsymbol{Z}_{t-1} + \boldsymbol{\mu} + \boldsymbol{\varepsilon}_t, \quad t = 1, \ldots, T, \tag{3}$$

where Δ is the first difference operator and $\boldsymbol{Z}_t$ is now a set of $I(1)$ variables, $\boldsymbol{\mu}$ is the drift parameter, and Π is a $p \times p$ matrix of the form $\Pi = \boldsymbol{\alpha}\boldsymbol{\beta}^{\mathrm{T}}$, where $\boldsymbol{\alpha}$ and $\boldsymbol{\beta}$ are $p \times r$ matrices of full rank, with $\boldsymbol{\beta}$ containing the r co-integrating vectors and $\boldsymbol{\alpha}$ including the corresponding adjustment coefficient in each of the r vectors

As a first step, in Table 3.3 we report the correlation coefficients between average housing prices, financial repression indicators and the key explanatory variables. Average housing prices at both national and big-city levels have high correlations with bank reserve requirements. The correlations of real interest rate and its dummy are significantly different from zero. Their signs are also as expected, indicating that the degree of financial repression is positively correlated with average housing prices.

3.4.2 Test of H1: Direct impact of financial repression on housing prices

Tables 3.4 and 3.5 report the estimation results for NH and ACH, showing estimation results from the OLS and FMOLS regressions of equation (4.1). The R^2 values indicate that the models fit the data well. All four measures of financial repression generate consistent results at

Table 3.4 Test of H1: *Dependent variable HP = NH*

	OLS				FMOLS			
Variables	Model 1	Model 2	Model 3	Model 4	Model 5	Model 6	Model 7	Model 8
Constant	−244.5***	−229.7***	−286.2***	−254.9***	239.34***	49.74***	321.67***	282.08***
	(−10.252)	(−9.634)	(−11.150)	(−10.091)	(−5.510)	(10.902)	(−7.226)	(−5.926)
RI	−0.438***	–	–	–	−0.438**	–	–	–
	(−3.965)				(−2.280)			
RID	–	4.246***	–	–	0.346***	9.627***	–	–
		(4.824)			(6.898)	(4.729)		
BR	–	–	0.532***	–	–	–	0.739***	–
			(3.300)				(2.657)	
BRD	–	–	–	1.118*	–	–	–	1.349
				(1.863)				(1.311)
NL	0.333***	0.349***	0.268***	0.333***	0.346***	0.485***	0.254***	0.390***
	(12.804)	(13.561)	(7.690)	(11.538)	(6.898)	(6.774)	(4.180)	(6.470)
NR	−0.136**	−0.128**	–	–	–	–	–	–
	(−2.378)	(−2.306)						
ACP	3.244***	3.065***	3.549***	3.202***	3.044***	–	3.919***	3.438***
	(11.932)	(11.298)	(12.797)	(11.817)	(6.569)		(8.161)	(6.878)
GDP	–	–	−0.000	−0.000	–	0.000	–	−0.000
			(−1.751)	(−0.555)		(1.460)		(−1.123)
PY	–	–	–	–	−0.015	0.058	−0.058**	−0.036
					(−0.648)	(1.710)	(−2.356)	(−1.343)
No. of obs.	144	144	144	144	143	143	143	143
R^2	0.989	0.990	0.989	0.989	0.989	0.980	0.989	0.988

This table shows the estimation results from the OLS or FMOLS regressions of equation (4.1). HP = NH, FRP is one of four proxies for financial repression. X is a set of control variables; average land prices at national level (NL), average implicit rents at national level (NR), average city population growth (ACP), GDP and personal disposable income (PY). Numbers in parentheses are *t*-statistics. Statistical significance at the 1 percent and 5 percent significance levels is denoted by *** and ** respectively. Variable acronyms are as defined in Tables 3.1 and 3.2.

Table 3.5 Test of H1: *Dependent variable HP = ACH*

	OLS				FMOLS			
Variables	**Model 1**	**Model 2**	**Model 3**	**Model 4**	**Model 5**	**Model 6**	**Model 7**	**Model 8**
Constant	−297.1***	−304.6***	−770.6***	−695.2***	−396.9*	27.139***	649.99***	307.2)
	(−6.375)	(−6.222)	(−7.835)	(−6.958)	(−1.940)	(3.872)	(−3.398)	(1.172
RI	−1.198***	–	–	–	−5.962***	–	–	–
	(−2.836)				(−4.148)			
RID	–	7.284**	–	–	–	33.760***	–	–
		(2.033)				(2.903)		
BR	–	–	5.390***	–	–	–	5.439***	–
			(5.959)				(3.247)	
BRD	–	–	–	24.251***	–	–	–	26.879***
				(6.405)				(4.389)
ACL	0.121***	0.118***	0.082***	0.153***	0.190***	0.111***	0.114***	0.077**
	(16.386)	(15.094)	(5.571)	(11.135)	(6.639)	(3.172)	(4.107)	(2.505)
ACR	0.898***	0.917***	–	–	–	–	–	–
	(23.789)	(24.832)						
ACP	3.091***	3.132***	8.039***	7.511***	4.582**	–	6.866***	−2.853
	(6.615)	(6.334)	(8.070)	(7.501)	(2.238)		(3.531)	(−1.062)
GDP	–	–	0.000**	0.001***	–	0.001***	–	0.002***
			(2.489)	(4.116)		(4.960)		(5.112)
PY	–	–	–	–	0.304*	0.525***	0.135	0.677***
					(1.978)	(4.578)	(0.803)	(3.884)
No. of obs.	144	144	144	144	143	143	143	143
R^2	0.991	0.991	0.957	0.959	0.957	0.963	0.953	0.963

This table shows the estimation results from the OLS or FMOLS regressions of equation (4.1). HP = ACH, FRP is one of four proxies for financial repression. X is a set of other control variables, such as the average land prices at big-city level (ACL), average implicit rents at big-city level (ACR), average city population growth (ACP), GDP, personal disposable income (PY), and so on. Statistical significance at the 1 percent and 5 percent significance levels is denoted by *** and ** respectively. Numbers in parentheses are *t*-statistics. Variable acronyms are as defined in Tables 3.1 and 3.2.

both national and big-city price levels. The regression coefficients are all significant at the 5 percent level, except that of BRD in model 8 in Table 3.4.

In both tables, average land price is always a significant explanatory variable with consistent positive signs at the 5 percent level. Land price rises (NL) are strong indicators of house price dynamics at both the national and big-city level. In comparison, the rent variable displays mixed results, with a negative (positive) coefficient entering the fitted regression equation for NH (ACH). This is consistent with findings in previous literature, such as Ahuja *et al.* (2010) and Wu *et al.* (2012). They argued that the house price boom in China was partly a result of local governments' dependence on land financing; namely that local governments have both the strong incentive and capability to generate significant revenue from the sale of "land use rights." Rural-urban migration and urbanization, which is proxied by average household registration system population increase at big-city level (ACP), is another important factor driving the average housing price. In all the regression models, it enters with a significant positive sign. This finding provides supportive evidence for the arguments in Chen *et al.* (2011) and Wu *et al.* (2012), who find that the different processes of provincial urbanization and the migration situation have significant effects on urban house prices in China. Overall, the results from all the OLS and FMOLS regressions strongly suggest that higher degrees of financial repression are associated with higher than average housing prices.

3.4.3 Tests of H1 to H5: interactions of housing prices, financial repression, and other factors

Tables 3.6 and 3.7 report regression results for average housing prices at national and big-city levels, respectively. As the empirical evidence from all four financial repression measures are very similar, we report models based on the real interest dummy (RID) in Table 3.6 and the bank reserve requirement ratio dummy (BRD) in Table 3.7. In general, the empirical evidence is consistent across the OLS and FMOLS methods.

The economic growth measurement (GDP) is a significant explanatory variable at the big-city level and has positive coefficient. The same variable displays mixed or insignificant results at the national level. Hypothesis H2 is only partly verified. By contrast, stock market volatility, measured by the conditional GARCH variance of China stock market index returns, has a significant effect on the average housing prices. Furthermore, this finding is consistent across different models and regression estimation methods. When stock market volatility is

Table 3.6 Test of H1–H5: *Dependent variable HP = NH*

	OLS				FMOLS			
Variables	**Model 1**	**Model 2**	**Model 3**	**Model 4**	**Model 5**	**Model 6**	**Model 7**	**Model 8**
Constant	84.861***	84.179***	82.62***	137.45***	80.756***	83.930***	81.914***	119.95***
	(51.941)	(103.512)	(100.111)	(9.570)	(34.516)	(56.527)	(57.360)	(4.555)
RID	13.980***	14.744***	14.44***	11.045***	14.031***	18.289***	17.470***	14.435***
	(5.016)	(10.634)	(11.327)	(7.336)	(3.550)	(7.293)	(7.948)	(5.312)
GDP	0.001***	0.000	–	–	0.001***	0.000	–	–
	(25.757)	(0.747)			(20.016)	(0.174)		
M2	–	0.000***	0.000***	0.000***	–	0.000***	0.000***	0.000***
		(20.737)	(55.749)	(18.079)		(11.429)	(31.465)	(10.326)
SRV	–	–	358.3***	293.72***	–	–	443.277***	365.75***
			(4.604)	(3.854)			(3.306)	(2.654)
NDF	–	–	–	–6.004***	–	–	–	–4.151
				(–3.823)				(–1.440)
No. of obs.	144	144	144	144	143	143	143	143
R^2	0.877	0.970	0.974	0.976	0.868	0.968	0.972	0.975

This table shows the estimation results from the OLS or FMOLS regressions of equation (4.1). HP = NH, FRP = RID, X is a set of other control variables GDP, M2, SRV, NDF, and so on. Statistical significance at the 1 percent and 5 percent significance levels is denoted by *** and ** respectively. Numbers in parentheses are *t*-statistics. Variable acronyms are as defined in Tables 3.1 and 3.2.

Table 3.7 Test of H1–H5: *Dependent variable HP = ACH*

	OLS				FMOLS			
Variables	**Model 1**	**Model 2**	**Model 3**	**Model 4**	**Model 5**	**Model 6**	**Model 7**	**Model 8**
Constant	33.358***	31.107***	26.901***	–5.443	19.267***	29.813***	25.273***	–16.846
	(6.626)	(12.270)	(9.947)	(–0.278)	(2.716)	(6.131)	(5.030)	(–0.502)
BRD	20.189***	12.634***	11.09***	12.656***	20.430**	19.494***	17.251***	19.212***
	(3.495)	(4.313)	(3.897)	(4.247)	(2.535)	(3.503)	(3.280)	(3.764)
GDP	0.003***	0.000***	0.000**	0.000**	0.003***	0.001*	0.000	0.000
	(30.342)	(2.733)	(2.170)	(2.241)	(23.858)	(1.942)	(1.389)	(1.102)
M2	–	0.000***	0.000***	0.000***	–	0.000***	0.000***	0.000***
		(20.422)	(21.409)	(20.792)		(10.308)	(11.348)	(12.217)
SRV	–	–	924.3***	845.51***	–	–	1160.59**	951.450**
			(3.574)	(3.236)			(2.426)	(2.124)
NEER	–	–	–	0.315	–	–	–	0.425
				(1.666)				(1.312)
No. of obs.	144	144	144	144	143	143	143	143
R^2	0.881	0.970	0.973	0.973	0.872	0.968	0.971	0.972

This table shows the estimation results from the OLS or FMOLS regressions of equation (4.1). HP = ACH, FRP = BRD, X is a set of other control variables GDP, M2, SRV, NDF, and so on. Statistical significance at the 1 percent and 5 percent significance levels is denoted by *** and ** respectively. Numbers in parentheses are *t*-statistics. Variable acronyms are as defined in Tables 3.1 and 3.2.

high, average housing prices will generally increase as well. These results thus provide supportive empirical evidence for H3. To the best of our knowledge, this finding has not been reported in the literature before. Credit expansion, measured by M2, displays consistent and significant results across all the models. As indicated by Tables 3.6 and 3.7, it enters all sixteen models with a positive coefficient at the 1 percent significance level. It suggests that the credit expansion is one of the key driving forces behind the change of real estate price growth in China, thus verifying hypothesis H4.

To check the robustness of our regression results, Tables 3.8 and 3.9 report the results of OLS and FMOLS regressions of NH and ACH in which the control variables are different from those used above. In these two tables, we include the one-month lagged value of the dependent variable and lagged values of the housing transaction tax dummy variable (HTD) and down payment dummy (DPD). These are to check for the effectiveness of the government's intervention policies in affecting housing prices. We also used other macroeconomic variables, including hot money (HM) and inflation (CPI and PPI) among others.

We find that the financial repression measures BR and BRD are still significant at the 5 percent level. The credit expansion measurement (BL) impacts the average housing price positively, but mortgage rate (MR) affects housing price negatively. Total international trade (TD) and the real effective exchange rate (REER) also have some positive effects on the housing price. One particularly interesting finding based on Tables 3.8 and 3.9 is that the government intervention policies on the housing market, such as increasing transaction tax or minimum down payment dummy variables, do not work well in our sample period, namely 1999–2010. Theoretically, we expect that the coefficients of two dummy variables, namely housing transaction tax dummy and down payment ratio dummy, should be negative. However, regression results show that most coefficients were not significant at all or entered the models with positive signs. In more detail, in most models for the average prices at national level, the coefficients of the two dummy variables are not significant, which means that such intervention policies did not work well. In the case of the average housing prices at big-city level, the coefficients of these two dummy variables became more significant, but were wrongly signed. This indicates that after the government adopted tougher regulation over the real house market with an expectation of slowing down the boom, the average prices in big cities have increased rather than decreased.

Table 3.8 Test of H1 to H5: *Dependent variable HP = NH*

	OLS				FMOLS			
Variables	**Model 1**	**Model 2**	**Model 3**	**Model 4**	**Model 5**	**Model 6**	**Model 7**	**Model 8**
Constant	0.308	83.493***	126.5***	–92.34***	0.233	82.935***	124.5***	–132.8***
	(0.533)	(68.767)	(59.513)	(–8.351)	(0.375)	(34.578)	(27.778)	(–11.001)
BR	–	–	–	1.211***	–	–	–	–0.801
				(3.942)				(–0.296)
BRD	0.940***	5.441***	16.246***	–	0.759***	8.754***	22.348**	–
	(3.516)	(3.965)	(3.391)		(2.656)	(3.253)	(2.220)	
NH(–1)	1.001***	–	–	–	0.999***	–	–	–
	(223.988)				(208.257)			
BL	–	0.000***	–	–	–	0.000***	–	–
		(41.347)				(21.077)		
HM	–	–	0.004***	–	–	–	0.006*	–
			(2.788)				(1.950)	
PPI	–	–	–	1.922***	–	–	–	2.395***
				(15.440)				(21.670)
HTD(–1)	–0.231	–1.274	1.636	2.750	–0.189	–2.064	1.691	3.805
	(–0.563)	(–0.595)	(0.214)	(1.385)	(–0.432)	(–0.492)	(0.105)	(0.921)
DPD(–1)	0.236	–4.055	27.931**	1.736	0.065	–6.333	41.974*	0.826
	(0.391)	(–1.274)	(2.540)	(0.599)	(0.101)	(–1.015)	(1.818)	(0.136)
No. of obs.	143	143	143	143	142	142	142	142
R^2	0.998	0.937	0.195	0.946	0.997	0.933	0.150	0.938

This table shows the estimation results from the OLS or FMOLS regressions of equation (4.1). HP = NH, FRP is one of four proxies for financial repression RI, RID, BR and BRD. X is a set of other control variables, such as bank loans (BL), hot money (HM), inflation measure (PPI), one-month lags of dependent variable (NH) as well as housing transaction tax dummy (HTD) and down payment dummy (DPD). Statistical significance at the 1 percent and 5 percent significance levels is denoted by *** and ** respectively. Numbers in parentheses are *t*-statistics. Variable acronyms are as defined in Tables 3.1 and 3.2.

Table 3.9 Test of H1 to H5: *Dependent variable HP = ACH*

	OLS				FMOLS			
Variables	**Model 1**	**Model 2**	**Model 3**	**Model 4**	**Model 5**	**Model 6**	**Model 7**	**Model 8**
Constant	2.455***	6.434	–79.411**	117.44***	1.714	4.234	–102.393	123.95***
	(1.149)	(1.615)	(–2.343)	(8.212)	(1.097)	(0.555)	(–1.647)	(4.714)
BR	–	5.830***	7.429***	10.080***	–	5.784***	6.905***	11.070***
		(6.788)	(6.811)	(12.972)		(3.460)	(3.407)	(7.829)
BRD	2.908*	–	–	–	3.077**	–	–	–
	(1.656)				(2.406)			
ACH(-1)	0.973***	–	–	–	0.978***	–	–	–
	(43.602)				(60.088)			
ACL	0.015**	–	–	–	0.012**	–	–	–
	(2.026)				(2.169)			
REER	–	–	0.995***	–	–	–	1.215*	–
			(2.922)				(1.945)	
MR	–	–	–	–17.01***	–	–	–	–18.48***
				(–7.154)				(–4.222)
TD	–	0.019***	0.063***	0.057***	–	0.010	0.066***	0.051***
		(3.112)	(10.936)	(12.742)		(0.843)	(6.129)	(6.156)
VAI	–	0.330***	–	–	–	0.375***	–	–
		(8.095)				(4.795)		
HTD(-1)	0.436	10.212*	14.179**	12.664**	0.801	14.653	18.761	15.693
	(0.191)	(1.919)	(2.267)	(2.302)	(0.481)	(1.437)	(1.655)	(1.580)
DPD(-1)	0.390	30.601***	28.2***	27.332***	–0.370	42.558***	33.325**	32.798**
	(0.114)	(3.952)	(3.086)	(3.401)	(–0.149)	(2.871)	(2.012)	(2.264)
No. of obs.	143	143	143	143	142	142	142	142
R^2	0.993	0.962	0.948	0.959	0.993	0.961	0.947	0.958

This table shows the estimation results from the OLS or FMOLS regressions of equation (4.1). HP = ACH, FRP is one of four proxies for financial repression RI, RID, BR and BRD. X is a set of other control variables, such as bank loans (BL), hot money (HM), inflation measure (PPI), one-month lags of dependent variable (NH) as well as housing transaction tax dummy (HTD) and down payment dummy (DPD). Statistical significance at the 1 percent and 5 percent significance levels is denoted by *** and ** respectively. Numbers in parentheses are *t*-statistics. Variable acronyms are as defined in Tables 3.1 and 3.2.

3.4.4 VAR/VECM evidence for interactions among housing prices and key explanatory factors

We run VAR/VECM models to evaluate the robustness of the results of the OLS and FMOLS regressions and to examine the interactions between key factors. To avoid over fitting, we do not include all explanatory variables in the VAR model. Based on the results in Table 3.6, we do not need to include both GDP and M2 in our vector Z_t specified in equations (4.2) and (4.3). The VAR model for NH only consists of five variables: housing price (NH), financial repression (RID), stock market volatility (SRV), broad money (M2) and RMB appreciation expectations (NDF). Based on Table 3.7, the VAR model for ACH includes housing price (ACH), financial repression (BRD), economic growth (GDP), broad money (M2), and stock market volatility (SRV). Figure 3.6 presents impulse responses of average housing price at national level (NH) from the VAR model. The results are generally consistent with our expectations. They suggest that the interactions between housing prices at national level and other key explanatory variables are as follows: (1) housing price is found to show a positive response to disturbances in financial repression (RID), stock market volatility (SRV) and broad money supply (M2). However, the impact of a disturbance in financial repression (RID) is the most significant one. (2) A significant negative

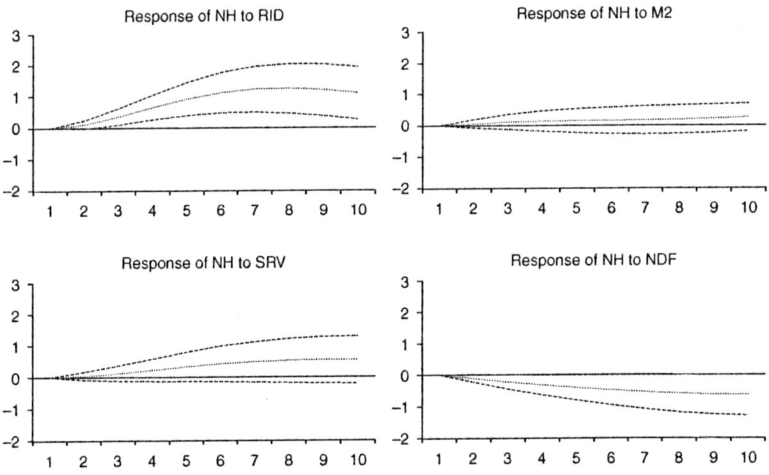

Figure 3.6 Impulse responses of average housing price at national level (NH) to Cholesky one S.D. innovation

Notes: Dashed line shows 95 percent confidence interval.

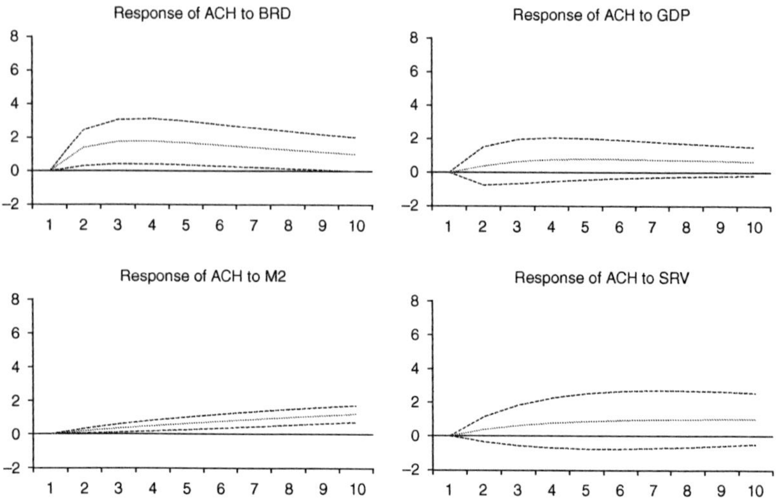

Figure 3.7 Impulse responses of average housing price at big-city level (ACH) to Cholesky one S.D. innovation

Notes: Dashed line shows 95 percent confidence interval.

response of housing price to NDF is found as well, which means a positive response to an RMB appreciation disturbance. Figure 3.7 presents impulse responses of average housing price at big-city level (ACH) from the VAR model. The results are not very different from those from housing price at national level. Generally we find that (1) housing price is found to show a positive response to disturbances in financial repression (BRD), economic growth (GDP), stock market volatility (SRV) and broad money supply (M2). (2) This time, significant responses are found for both financial repression and broad money supply, while GDP and SRV have less significant lagged effects.

Clearly, the effects of a one standard deviation shock of financial repression on the average housing prices at both national and big-city levels are always positive and might generally last over the first 10 month period. The VAR/VECM model provides robust evidence to support H1 too. However, the VAR/VECM models lend mixed support to other hypotheses. Although the directions of responses are all as expected, the movements of the average housing price in response to a disturbance of one standard deviation in other explanatory factors such as economic growth, broad money supply and RMB appreciation is generally less significant than that of financial repression. This is partly because some of the effects have already been incorporated in that of financial repression.

3.5 Conclusions

Limited financial development is a characteristic of many developing countries. In this chapter, we argue that financial repression is a very important variable in determining real estate prices in China. There are three main findings based on our econometric models of the relationship between housing price and financial repression. First, the degree of financial repression is positively associated with the average housing price. The higher the degree of financial repression, the higher the average housing price at both national and big-city level in China. Secondly, financial repression in China has some key economic consequences, such as economic growth, high stock market volatility, credit expansion and currency appreciation, and they are also positively associated with the average housing price. Thirdly, because financial repression is one of the key reasons behind fast housing price growth during our sample period, direct intervention policies on the real estate market, such as transaction tax and minimum down payment ratio adjustments, have not worked very well.

Our research has an important policy implication as well. Concerns about potential risks of a bubble-burst in the housing market prompted China's policymakers to take a number of actions to contain the housing bubble. In recent years the government has adopted several policy packages for this purpose. The most dramatic tightening measures were introduced in April 2010 and were focused mainly on transaction tax, down payment ratio or administrative matters. This chapter reveals, however, that such intervention policies were not very effective
AQ2 during 1999–2000. We argue that the real estate bubble may be due to the hidden costs of financial repression policies, and that those direct intervention measures may not be sufficiently effective. Further reform of China's financial system may be necessary to curb recent and future real estate bubbles.

Notes

1. China Securities Journal, July 15, 2010; B. Powell, China's Property: Bubble, Bubble, Toil and Trouble, Time Magazine, March 22, 2010.
2. T. Chen (2009) Housing assets are the largest single source of household wealth in China, *Southern Weekend* (Nanfang zhoumo), October 8, 2009.

3. See J. Anderlini, China revives property tax to avert bubble. Financial Times. December 11, 2009; S. MufsonIn, China, fear of a real estate bubble. The Washington Post, January 11, 2010. Y. Chen, et al., China's real estate bubble, a heated debate, Xinhua news, January 14, 2010.
4. The 35 cities are: Beijing; Changchun; Changsha; Chengdu; Chongqing; Fuzhou; Guangzhou; Guiyang; Ha'erbin; Haikou; Hangzhou; Hefei; Huhehaote; Jinan; Kunming; Lanzhou; Nanchang; Nanjing; Nanning; Ningbo; Qingdao; Shanghai; Shenzhen; Shenyang; Shijiazhuang; Taiyuan; Tianjin; Wulumuqi;. Wuhan; Xi'an; Xiamen; Yinchuan; Zhengzhou; Xining; Dalian.
5. The transformation is made by adopting a relatively simple assumption that the monthly changes in 1998 were average rates of those in the years 1999–2010. We admit it may incur some inaccuracy. However, given the fact that price changes in the 1990s were not huge, it is a pragmatic solution.
6. See Aaron Back and Esther Fung, "China Scraps Property Data, Clouding View," The Wall Street Journal Online, February 17, 2011. Accessed February 21, 2012. http://online.wsj.com/article/SB10001424052748703373404576147792827651116.html.
7. The 12 big cities are Beijing, Shanghai, Hangzhou, Shenzhen, Guangzhou, Tianjin, Nanjing, Wuhan, Chongqing, Chengdu, Xi'an, and Shenyang.
8. The CRIC is a leading provider of real estate information, consulting, and online services in China. They began operations in 2006 as E-House (China) Holdings Limited's real estate information and consulting business unit, and in October 2009, merged with SINA Corporation's online real estate business following the completion of our initial public offering on the NASDAQ Global Select Market under the symbol "CRIC." Initially created as an internal resource to support E-House's real estate services, the CRIC system is an advanced and comprehensive real estate information database and analysis system that we have been operating in-house since 2001. As of September 30, 2011, we provided real estate data through CRIC system in over 80 cities across China. Its official website is http://ir.cric.com/.

References

Agarwala, R. 1983. *Price Distortions and Growth in Developing Countries*, World Bank, Washington, DC.

Ahuja, A., Cheung L., Han G., Porter N., and Zhang W. 2010. Are house prices rising too fast in China? *IMF working paper*, WP/10/274.

Bayoumi, T., Tong, H. and Wei, S-J., 2010, The Chinese Corporate savings Puzzle: A Firm-level Cross-country Perspective, *IMF Working Paper*, International Monetary Fund.

Beck, T., Levine, R. and Loayza, N. 2000. Finance and the sources of growth. *Journal of Financial Economics*, 58(1–2): 261–300.

Bernanke, B. S. and Gertler M. 1995. Inside the black box: the credit channel of monetary policy transmission, *Journal of Economic Perspectives*, 9: 27–48.

Cebenoyan, A. S., Fischer, K. P. and Papaioannou, G. J. 1995. Corporate financial structure under inflation and financial repression: a comparative study of north American and emerging markets firms, *Global Finance Journal*, 6: 25–45.

Chen, J., Guo, F., and Wu, Y. 2011. One decade of urban housing reform in China: Urban housing price dynamics and the role of migration and urbanization, 1995–2005, *Habitat International*, 35: 1–8.

Chen, R. and Dao, M. 2011. The real exchange rate and employment in China, *IMF working paper* WP/11/148.

Cochrane, J. H. 2005. *Asset Pricing* (Revised Edition), Princeton, New Jersey, Princeton University Press.

Costello, G., Fraser P. and Groenewold, N. 2011. House prices, non-fundamental components and interstate spillovers: the Australian experience. *Working Paper*.

Davis, M., and Heathcote J. 2007. The price and quantity of residential land in the United States, *Journal of Monetary Economics*, 54: 2595–2620.

Davis, M.A. and Palumbo, M. G. 2008. The price of residential land in large US cities. *Journal of Urban Economics*, 63: 352–384.

Du, H., Ma, Y. and An, Y. 2010. The impact of land policy on the relation between housing and land prices: evidence from China, *Quarterly Review of Economics and Finance*, doi:10.1016/j.qref.2010.09.004.

Feldman, D. H. and Gang, I. N. 1987. Financial repression and the relative price of non-traded goods, *Economics Letters*, 25: 31–34.

Garnaut, R., Song, L., Tenev, S., and Yao, Y. 2003. *Study on restructured SOEs (Gaizhi) in China*, World Bank, Washington, DC.

Goodman, A. 1989. Topics in empirical housing research. In: Muth, R.F. and Goodman, A.C. (eds), *The Economics of Housing Markets*. Harwood Academic Publishers, Melbourne.

Gordon, R. H. and Li, W. 2003. Government as a discriminating monopolist in the financial market: the case of China, *Journal of Public Economics*, 87: 283–312.

Gul, F. A., Kim, J., Qiu, A. A. 2010. Ownership concentration, foreign shareholding, audit quality, and stock price synchronicity: Evidence from China, *Journal of Financial Economics*, 95: 425–442.

Guo, F. and Huang, Y. S. 2010. Does "hot money" drive China's real estate and stock markets? *International Review of Economics and Finance*, 19: 452–466.

Huang, Y. and Wang, X. 2011. Does Financial Repression Inhibit or Facilitate Economic Growth? A case Study of Chinese Reform Experience, *Oxford Bulletin of Economics and Statistics*, 73: 833–855.

Hallwood, C. P. and MacDonald, R. 2000. *International Money and Finance*, 3rd Edition, Blackwell, Oxford UK and Cambridge US.

Holly, S. and Jones, N. 1997. House prices since the 1940s: cointegration, demography and asymmetries, *Economic Modelling*, 14: 549–565.

Hou, Y. 2010. Housing price bubbles in Beijing and Shanghai? A multi-indicator analysis, *International Journal of Housing Markets and Analysis*, 3: 17–37.

Huang, Y. 2010. Dissecting the China puzzle: asymmetric liberalization and cost distortion, *Asia Economic Policy Review*, 5: 281–295.

Hui, E. and Yue, S. 2006. Housing Price Bubbles in Hong Kong, Beijing and Shanghai: A Comparative Study, *Journal of Real Estate Finance and Economics*, 33: 299–327.

Kang, J, Liu, M and Ni, X. 2002. Contrarian and momentum strategies in the China stock market: 1993–2000, *Pacific-Basin Finance Journal*, 10: 243–265.

King, R. G. and Levine, R. 1993. Finance, entrepreneurship, and growth: theory and evidence, *Journal of Monetary Economics*, 32: 513–542.

Iacoviello, M. 2005. House prices, borrowing constraints, and monetary policy in the business cycle, *American Economic Review*, 95: 739–764.

IMF. 2010. People's Republic of China: 2010 Article IV Consultation-Staff Report, IMF Country Report, No. 10/238.

Ito, T. 2010. China's property bubble, VOX, 15 April 2010, available at http://www.voxeu.org/index.php?q=node/4885.

Lardy, N. R. 2008. Financial Repression in China, Policy Brief No. 8, Peterson Institute of International Economics, Washington, DC.

Li, D. 2001. Beating the trap of financial repression in China, *Cato Journal*, 21: 77–90.

Liang, Q. and Cao, H. 2007. Property prices and bank lending in China, *Journal of Asian Economics*, 18: 63–75.

Lin, J. Y., Cai, F. and Li, Z. 1995. *The China Miracle: Development Strategy and Economic Reform*, The Chinese University of Hong Kong Press, Hong Kong.

Liu, H., Yun, W. P. and Zheng, S. 2002. The interaction between housing investment and economic growth in China, *International Real Estate Review*, 5: 40–60.

Lu, S. F. and Yao, Y. 2009. The effectiveness of law, financial development, and economic growth in an economy of financial repression: evidence from China. *World Development*, 37: 763–777.

McKinnon, R. I. 1973. *Money and Capital in Economic Development*, The Brookings Institution, Washington, DC.

McKinnon, R. and Mathieson, D. 1981. *How to manage a repressed economy, Essays in International Finance no. 145*. Princeton University, Princeton, NJ.

Morck, R., Yeung, B. and Yu, W. 2000. The information content of stock markets: why do emerging markets have synchronous stock price movements? *Journal of Financial Economics*, 58: 215–260.

Negro, M. D. and Otrok, C. 2007. 99 Luftballons: Monetary policy and the house price boom across U.S. states, *Journal of Monetary Economics*, 54: 1962–1985.

OECD. 2005. Recent house price developments: The role of fundamentals. *OECD Economic Outlook*, 78: 123–155.

Ouyang, A. Y., Ramkishen, S. R. and Willett, T. D. 2010. China as a reserve sink: the evidence from offset and sterilization coefficients, *Journal of International Money and Finance*, 29: 951–972.

Pagano, M. 1993. Financial markets and growth: an overview, *European Economic Review*, 37: 613–622.

Phillips, P. C. B. and Hansen, B. E. 1990. Statistical inference in instrumental variables, *Review of Economic Studies*, 53: 473–496.

Phylaktis, K., and Ravazzolo, F. 2005. Stock prices and exchange rate dynamics. *Journal of International Money and Finance*, 24: 1031–1053.

Poterba, J. 1992. Taxation and housing: Old questions, new answers, *American Economic Review*, 82: 237–242.

Roubini, N. and Sala-i-Martin, X. 1992. Financial repression and economic growth, *Journal of Development Economics*, 39: 5–30.

Roubini, N. and Sala-i-Martin X. 1995. A growth model of inflation, tax evasion, and financial repression, *Journal of Monetary Economics*, 35: 275–301.

Sato, H. 2006. Housing inequality and housing poverty in urban China in the late 1990s, *China Economic Review*, 17: 37–50.

Stiglitz, J. E. 1994. The role of the state in financial markets, in Bruno M. and Pleskovic B. (eds), *Proceeding of the World Bank Annual Conference on Development Economics, 1993*: Supplement to the World Bank Economic Review and the World Bank Research Observer, Washington, DC: World Bank, 19–61.

Stiglitz, J. E. 2000. Capital market liberalization, economic growth and instability, *World Development*, 28: 1075–1086.

Su, F. and Tao, R. 2010. *Visible Hand or Crippled Hand: Stimulation and Stabilization in China's Real Estate Markets, 2008–2010*, East Asia workshop, University of Chicago.

Wang, Y. and Iorio, A. D. 2007. Are the China-related stock markets segmented with both world and regional stock markets, *International Financial Markets, Institutions & Money*, 17: 277–290.

Wheaton, W. C. and Nechayev, G. 2008. The 1998–2005 housing "bubble" and the current "correction": what is different this time? *Journal of Real Estate Research*, 30: 1–26.

Wu, J., Gyourko. J., and Deng, Y. 2012. Evaluating conditions in major Chinese housing markets, *Regional Science and Urban Economics*, 42: 531–543.

Xu, X. E., and Chen, T. 2012. The effect of Monetary Policy on real estate price growth in China, *Pacific-Basin Finance Journal*, 20: 62–77.

Zhang, Y., Hua, X., and Zhao, L. 2011. Exploring Determinants of Housing Prices: A Case Study of Chinese Experience in 1999–2010, Economic Modelling, revision and resubmission. Also see BOFIT Discussion Papers No. 17. Available at SSRN: http://ssrn.com/abstract=1914290.

4
Venture Capital Investments in China: Reputation, Syndication, and Valuation

*Sheng Xiao and Xiangyi Zhou**

4.1 Introduction

Since the 1950s, venture capital (VC) has become a unique, dynamic, and fast-growing financial intermediary. Since the establishment of the world's first VC firm, American Research and Development, in 1947 in Boston, VC firms have fostered many highly successful companies such as Apple, Google, Microsoft, Intel, Cisco, Amazon, Federal Express, Starbucks, and Staples. VC investments spur firm innovation, cultivate new firms, and promote local economic development. For example, Kortum and Lerner (2000) examine an exogenous policy shift in the United States in 1979 that spurred VC fundraising and find that VC investments indeed caused more firm innovation in the United States. They find that a dollar of VC was 3.1 times more likely to lead to a patent than was a corporate R&D dollar. Samila and Sorenson (2011) find that greater supply of VC is associated with significantly more firm starts, higher employment, and higher aggregate income in American cities.

VC firms are similar to traditional financial intermediaries (for example, banks and stock markets) in that they connect investors with promising projects. Therefore, like banks, they systematically screen potential projects to identify the most promising ones. However, they are very different from traditional financial intermediaries because they usually make equity investments exclusively in early-stage, high-

* Corresponding author: Xiangyi Zhou works at Xi'an Jiaotong University. Jinhe Center for Economic Research, No.28 Xian Ning West Road, Xi'an, Shaanxi Province, PR China. Email: marton@mail.xjtu.edu.cn

potential, and high-risk startup companies. They add value to these startup companies by improving their strategies, corporate governance, management, and efficiency, and so on (see, for example, Chemmanur, Krishnan, and Nandy, 2011; Bottazzi, Da Rin, and Hellmann, 2008). In return, they usually make huge profits when they sell their equity holdings in these companies at the initial public offerings (IPOs) or mergers and acquisition (M&A) deals, which are regarded as successful exits of VC investments. For example, Cochrane (2005, p. 3) finds that even after adjusting for selection bias, VC investments around the world generated an enormous arithmetic average return of 59 percent per year and a large arithmetic alpha of 32 percent per year between 1987 and 2000.

In China, VC investments have grown rapidly in the period 1985–2012. In 1985, China's first VC firm, China New Technology Venture Capital Company was established. It was fully funded by the Chinese government. However, China's VC investments did not take off until 1998, when the Chinese People's Political Consultative Conference (CPPCC) proposed that the Chinese government should support and accelerate the development of China's VC investments. The Chinese government adopted this proposal and implemented a series of policies to promote the development of the VC sector in China. As a result, 1998 was a "turning point" for VC investments in China. The growth rate of the total amount of VC investments in China surged from 7.5 percent in 1996 to 76.2 percent in 1998, 74.3 percent in 1999, and 70.1 percent in 2000. From a very low level of 556 million USD in 1994 to 12,765 million USD in 2011 (Ministry of Science and Technology of China, 2003; Zero2IPO.com, 2012), the total amount of VC investments in China grew at a staggering average rate of 20 percent per year during that 17 year period. In fact, since 2003, China has emerged as the world's largest net importer of VC deals (Aizenman and Kendall, 2008).

Similarly to VC firms in the United States, VCs in China have contributed to firm innovations and economic development. VCs have fostered successful Chinese companies such as Tencent (publicly listed at the Hong Kong Stock Exchange, with a market capitalization of 54 billion USD in June 2012) and Baidu (publicly listed at NASDAQ with a market capitalization of 42 billion USD in June 2012). In 2010, VC-backed firms in China increased their R&D expenditure by an average growth rate of 30.25 percent, much higher than the average growth rate of 20.3 percent for all firms in China. The sales of VC-backed firms increased by 35.21 percent, much faster than the gross domestic product (GDP) growth at 10.3 percent. The value-added of VC-backed firms increased by 36.63 percent, much faster than the average growth rate of 10.85 percent for the value-added of all firms in China (Ministry of Science and Technology of China, 2011).

This chapter will first examine two main features of VC development in China in the global context and then summarize previous studies on VC investments in China. After these qualitative discussions, we will systematically explore the following important quantitative research questions related to VC investments in China:

(1) How does VC reputation affect their investments in China? Specifically, how does VC reputation affect the exit of VC investments? How does VC reputation affect the asset productivity (sales to assets) of VC-backed portfolio companies at IPOs?
(2) How do VC firms in China establish their reputation? Particularly, how do young VC firms signal their high quality and establish a good reputation?
(3) What are the differences between the investments made in China by a group of VC firms ('syndicated VC investment') and the investments made by a single VC firm?
(4) What are the effects of capital inflows into venture funds on the valuation of these funds' new investments in China?

4.2 VC development in China in the global context

The first prominent feature of VC development in China is the heavy involvement of the government, which includes the government's direct investment and the government's indirect promotion through policies. For example, according to Ahlstrom, Bruton, and Yeh (2007), there was a proliferation of VC firms backed by provincial and local governments in China in the 1990s. Unfortunately, these efforts usually failed due to lack of experience among the government officials and the entrepreneurs (Oster, 2001). In addition to these direct investments, provincial and local governments in China indirectly promoted VC development by providing tax rebates and subsidies for VC firms. Kenney, Han, and Tanaka (2004, 2007) compare the degree of government involvement in VC development in mainland China, Taiwan, Hong Kong, the United States, Israel, India, Japan, Korea, and Singapore. They find that, except for Hong Kong, governments in the above economies have all played important roles in their VC development. However, they also find that, in contrast with the Chinese government, the US government has not recently invested directly in VC.

Despite the prevalence of government involvement in VC development in many countries, cross-country studies by Armour and Cumming (2006) and Lerner (2009) show that direct government investments in VC are rarely effective in promoting VC development. On the other hand, Armour and Cumming (2006) examine data from 15 countries and find that liberal bankruptcy laws stimulate entrepreneurial demand for VC. Da Rin, Di Giacomo, and Sembenelli (2011) examine data from 17 European countries and find that lowering the corporate income tax rate would significantly stimulate the entry of new companies. Klapper, Laeven, and Rajan (2006) examine data from 23 European countries and find that lowering the entry costs would significantly increase the entry rate of new firms, while raising the entry costs would significantly decrease the entry rate, especially in industries that should naturally have a high entry rate. Given the above evidence, we think the Chinese government may more effectively promote VC development in China by indirect intervention such as implementing favorable policies (for example, implementing more liberal bankruptcy laws, lowering corporate taxes, and/or entry barriers) instead of direct investments in VC firms.

The second prominent feature of VC development in China is its underdeveloped institutional environment, such as the lack of property rights protection, rule of law, and investor protection. Cross-country studies by Armour and Cumming (2006) and Li and Zahra (2012) show that the institutional environment has positive and significant effects on VC development around the world. Even though China's institutional environment is currently underdeveloped, it is quickly improving (Hasan, Wachtel, and Zhou, 2009; Berkman, Cole, and Fu, 2011). Therefore, we are cautiously optimistic that VC development in China will keep its accelerating pace.

4.3 Review of the literature on VC investments in China

In contrast with the rapid development of VC investments in China, research on this topic is still scarce. One strand of literature focuses on the outcomes of investments by heterogeneous VCs in China. For example, Qian and Zhang (2007) find that non-government-backed VCs generate significantly higher returns than government-backed VCs. Similarly, Zhang and Liao (2011) find that government-backed VCs are associated with higher IPO underpricing, and government-backed VCs tend to have lower cumulative abnormal returns from their investments. Zhang and Liao (2011) find that foreign-VC-backed IPOs are less underpriced, and foreign VCs reap larger cumulative abnormal returns from their investments. They show that foreign-VC-backed IPOs have superior performance because foreign VCs adopt conservative investment strategies and improve the portfolio companies' corporate governance and accounting performance. Wang and Wang (2011) show that in determining cross-border VC investment and portfolio company performance in China, domestic entrepreneurs' experience matters much more than foreign VC firms' human capital.

Another strand of research on VC investments in China focuses on the systematic differences in the institutional backgrounds between China and the west. For example, Bruton and Ahlstrom (2003); Ahlstrom, Bruton, and Yeh (2007); Batjargal (2007); and Batjargal and Liu (2004) all emphasize the important roles of personal relationships (*guanxi*), social networks, and social capital in VC investments in China. This is consistent with Allen, Qian, and Qian's (2005) observation that in China, informal institutions such as personal relationships substitute for the formal legal system, and *guanxi* is a crucial foundation for business success there.

4.4 VC reputation in China

4.4.1 Literature review

The reputation of financial intermediaries, such as investment banks, auditors, and VCs, is an important determinant of financial outcomes. For example, the reputation of underwriters (investment banks) affects the probability of IPO, the IPO pricing, post-IPO long-run issuer performance, and perceived seasoned equity offering (SEO) quality (see, for example, Sorensen, 2007; Carter and Manaster, 1990; Megginson and Weiss, 1991; Carter, Dark, and Singh, 1998; Chemmanur and Fulghieri, 1994). Balvers, McDonald, and Millier (1988) and Titman and Trueman (1986) show that reputable auditors and investment banks lead to lower IPO underpricing and better post-IPO stock performance.

Compared with the reputation of investment banks and auditors, the reputation of VC appears to be even more important because the information asymmetries between VCs and investors are more severe than those between other financial intermediaries and investors. These information asymmetries may be more severe in China than in other countries because China is an emerging market with less developed disclosure rules. We therefore hypothesize that in China, more reputable VCs tend to have more successful exits and the time to exit will be shorter. Furthermore, we hypothesize that in China, the asset productivity (sales to assets) of more reputable VC-backed portfolio companies will be higher.

4.4.2 Data and methodology

To examine the effects of VC reputation on the outcomes of VC investments, we collect data from a newly available data set, the CVSource data set developed by ChinaVenture Group. Yixiong Li at Xi'an Jiaotong University in China conducted the raw data collection and initial data analysis.

Our research methodology is similar to that of Nahata (2008). Specifically, if a portfolio company that the VC has invested in goes public or is acquired, then we would define this VC investment as a successful one. For VC reputation, we use the IPO capitalization rate, which is the cumulative market capitalization of IPOs backed by the VC firm in the IPO market, as a proxy. The market capitalization of IPOs is computed by multiplying the closing price of the portfolio company on the IPO day by the total number of shares outstanding. The higher the IPO capitalization rate, the higher the VC reputation. Nahata (2008) finds that in the US context, this VC reputation measure is the most powerful one in predicting the exit success and asset productivity at IPOs. We would like to see if this conclusion also holds true for VC investments in China.

Similarly to Nahata (2008), to see how VC reputation affects its exit success, we estimate the Cox hazard model. We use the log of time to exit as the dependent variable. The time to exit of a successful VC is the calendar time taken to exit from the date of the VC's first investment in that portfolio company. The time to exit of VCs yet to exit successfully by the beginning of 2012 is right censored at the end of calendar year 2011. The Cox hazard model, as a semi-parametric model, has been widely used in finance. For example, Lane, Looney, and Wansley (1986) use the Cox hazard model to study bank failures in the United States.

Specifically, the regression specification of the Cox hazard model is

$$h(t|X)=h(t)\exp(X_1\beta_1+\cdots+X_p\beta_p$$

where $h(t|X)$ is the hazard function, which is assumed to be arbitrary, and $h(t)$ is the "baseline" hazard function. No distributional assumptions of the hazard function are required to carry out the estimation of this regression. In this regression, a positive coefficient would indicate that the independent variable increases the hazard of a successful exit and shortens the expectation duration (the time to exit). The main advantage of using the Cox hazard model is that it accounts for the right-censored feature of the data. In other words, if companies had not successfully exited by the end of 2011, then they would be treated as unsuccessful exits, though they may still exit successfully in the future. The Cox hazard model can tackle this technical issue.

Similarly to Nahata (2008), to study the effect of VC reputation on the VC-backed portfolio company's asset productivity at IPO, we estimate the Tobit model. The asset productivity is defined as the log of one plus the sales-to-book assets ratio of the VC-backed portfolio company. The Tobit model is estimated here because asset productivity is censored at 0 on the left.

4.4.3 Estimation results

Table 4.1 reports the year-wise distribution of VC investments between 1997 and 2007, in companies that received their first round of VC funding beginning in 1997, and for which relevant data are available. VC-backed companies that went public or were acquired between 1997 and 2011, inclusive, are classified as "Successful" exits, and otherwise denoted as "Unsuccessful" exits. We start our research with 1997 because, as mentioned in the introduction section of this chapter, China's VC investments started to take off around 1997. Table 4.1 shows that during the sample period, about 29 percent of VC investment exits

Table 4.1 Year-wise distribution of VC investments in China (1997–2007)

	VC investments at the beginning of 2012		
Funding year	**Successful**	**Unsuccessful**	**Success rate (%)**
1997	1	3	25.00
1998	3	5	37.50
1999	8	14	36.36
2000	37	41	47.43
2001	32	52	38.10
2002	11	30	26.83
2003	31	67	31.63
2004	48	103	31.79
2005	33	139	19.19
2006	66	182	26.61
2007	183	497	26.91
Total	453	1133	28.56

This table presents the year-wise distribution of VC investments in China between 1997 and 2007, in companies that received their first round of VC funding beginning in 1997, and for which relevant data are available. VC-backed companies that went public or were acquired between 1997 and 2012, inclusive, are classified as "Successful" exits, and otherwise denoted as "Unsuccessful" exits.

Table 4.2 Hazard analysis of VC-backed portfolio companies at the beginning of year 2012

	Log(time to exit)	
	(1)	(2)
IPO Capitalization share (Lead VC reputation)	0.280 [0.00]***	0.285 [0.00]***
Lead VC connectedness		-0.023 [0.18]
VC syndicate size	0.267 [0.00]***	0.271 [0.00]***
Total VC funding across all rounds	-0.0001 [0.85]	-0.00002 [0.95]
Median market-to-book ratio in the high-tech industry in the year	0.127 [0.00]***	0.123 [0.00]***
Log(aggregate fund inflows in the VC industry in the year prior to first VC investment in the portfolio company)	-0.021 [0.83]	0.027 [0.80]
Log(number of IPOs in the previous quarter)	4.111 [0.00]***	4.174 [0.00]***
Log(number of M&A deals in the previous quarter)	-11.96 [0.00]***	-12.11 [0.00]***
Chinese VC dummy	0.373 [0.02]**	0.318 [0.04]**
Indicator = 1 if lead VC investment is at an early/seed stage	0.029 [0.93]	0.042 [0.90]
Log(lead VC's age)	0.038 [0.82]	0.08 [0.63]
-Log likelihood	1926	1925
Observations	1203	1203

The sample in the regression consists of VC investments in China between 1997 and 2007, in companies that received their first round of VC funding beginning in 1997, and for which relevant data are available. The Cox hazard model is estimated with log of time to exit being the dependent variable. The time to exit of a successful VC is the calendar time taken to exit from the date of the VC's first investment in that portfolio company. For definitions of control variables, please see Section 4.4.2 of the chapter. Robust p-values are in brackets. Significance at the 1 percent, 5 percent, and 10 percent levels is denoted by ***, **, and *, respectively.

in China were successful. This success rate is slightly lower than the one reported by Nahata (2008) in the US context (about 34 percent).

Table 4.2 reports the results from the Cox hazard model. The coefficient on the IPO capitalization rate is positive and significant, which implies the higher the VC reputation, the more likely this VC investment will have a successful exit, and the time to exit will be shorter. This key result is consistent with Nahata (2008) and shows that VC reputation has significant and positive effects on VC exits, not only in the United States – a well-developed market with a reasonably long history of VC and stock markets – but also in China, an emerging market with a very young VC sector and stock markets.

Among the control variables, lead VC's connectedness is measured by the number of unique VCs each VC has syndicated within five years on a rolling basis and normalizing it by the number of relationships possible during those five years. VC experience is measured by the age of the VC firm. The quality of the portfolio company is measured by the total VC investment in the portfolio company across all financing rounds. To measure the stage of VC investment, we include a dummy variable that equals 1 if lead VC investment is at an early/seed stage. We also include the size of the VC syndicate, because Brander, Amit, and Antweiler (2002) report that syndicated VC deals have higher returns. In addition to the above control variables for the VC firm and the portfolio company, we also control for the aggregate market conditions by including control variables such as the median market-to-book ratio in the high-tech industry in the year, aggregate fund inflows in the VC industry, the number of IPOs in the previous quarter, and the number of M&A deals in the previous quarter. These aggregate market conditions are used to measure the timing market effects. In addition, we include a Chinese VC dummy to control for systematic differences between Chinese VCs and foreign VCs in their investment exits.

Estimation results show that if the VC investment is made at an early/seed stage, then it is more likely that this VC investment will have a successful exit, and the time to exit will be shorter. Chinese VCs seem to be more likely to have successful exits, and the time to exits would be shorter. When the median market-to-book ratio in the high-tech industry in the year is higher, the likelihood of successful exits in the year is higher, which shows that VCs tend to time the market when they consider their exits.

Table 4.3 reports the effects of VC reputation on the asset productivity of VC-backed IPOs. VC reputation is positively and significantly correlated with the asset productivity of VC-backed portfolio companies at their IPOs.

In summary, our estimation results support our hypothesis that better reputation of VCs is associated with more successful investment exits, shorter time to exits, and higher asset productivity of VC-backed portfolio companies at the IPOs in China.

Table 4.3 Tobit analysis of asset productivity (sales to assets) of VC-backed IPOs

	Log(1 + sales-to-book-assets)	
	(1)	(2)
IPO Capitalization share (Lead VC reputation)	0.038***	0.038***
	[0.00]	[0.00]
Lead VC connectedness		0.001
		[0.53]
VC syndicate size	-0.012**	-0.012**
	[0.03]	[0.03]
Total VC funding across all rounds	-0.0002	-0.0002
	[0.23]	[0.20]
Median market-to-book ratio in the high-tech industry in the year	0.013**	0.013**
	[0.03]	[0.02]
Log(aggregate fund inflows in the VC industry in the previous quarter)	-0.013	-0.017
	[0.32]	[0.25]
Log(number of IPOs in the previous quarter)	0.000	0.000
	[0.98]	[0.93]
Log(number of M&A deals in the previous quarter)	-0.0005	-0.0004
	[0.69]	[0.78]
Indicator = 1 if lead VC investment is at an early/seed stage	-0.033	-0.032
	[0.24]	[0.25]
Log(lead VC's age)	-0.045	-0.048
	[0.13]	[0.11]
Indicator = 1 if lead underwriter is in the top quartile by rank	-0.029	-0.035
	[0.68]	[0.62]
Median sales–to-book assets ratio in IPO firm's industry in the year of exit	0.021***	0.021***
	[0.00]	[0.00]
Observations	73	73

The sample in the regression consists of VC investments in China between 1997 and 2007, in companies that received their first round of VC funding beginning in 1997, and for which relevant data are available. The Tobit model is estimated with log of 1 plus sales-to-book-assets of the VC-backed portfolio company at the IPO being the dependent variable. The portfolio company's sales and book assets are the last reported annual revenues and total book assets of the company before the IPO. For definitions of control variables, please see Section 4.3.3 in the chapter. Robust p-values are in brackets. Significance at the 1 percent, 5 percent, and 10 percent levels is denoted by ***,**, and *, respectively.

4.5 VC age and VC investments in China: The grandstanding hypothesis

4.5.1 Literature review

Section 4.4 shows that the reputation of VCs plays an important role in determining their investment outcomes in China. But how do VCs build up their reputation? One way to do it in the United States, as Gompers (1996) indicates, is for young VC firms to take companies public faster and earlier than older VC firms. They can also signal the high quality of their investments by greater underpricing on the first day (that is, greater first-day return). This way, young VC firms are able to establish a good reputation by providing a track record of successful exits. Gompers (1996) calls this hypothesis the "grandstanding" hypothesis.

His empirical analysis of VC-backed IPOs in the United States supports the grandstanding hypothesis. Specifically, he finds that for companies backed by young VCs in the United States, the VCs serve on the boards of the portfolio companies for shorter periods of time. The VC-backed firms are indeed younger and more underpriced at their IPOs than those of older VCs. However, by rushing a portfolio firm to IPO, the VC incurs costs of signaling. Specifically, the shorter the duration of the VC's service on the board of the portfolio company before its IPO, the more premature the IPO is. As a result, the VC would receive a smaller equity stake because of this premature IPO. Do young VCs in China also "grandstand" to establish their reputation? We would like to answer this question in this section.

4.5.2 Data and methodology

We collect most data from the CVSource data set developed by the ChinaVenture Group. We collect the first-day return and standard deviation of stock return data from China Stock Market and Accounting Research (CSMAR) data set developed by Shenzhen GTA Co. Ltd. Wenxiu Sun at Xi'an Jiaotong University in China conducted the raw data collection and initial data analysis.

Our research methodology is similar to that of Gompers (1996). Specifically, we estimate the following industry-fixed effects models:

$$Y_{i,j} = \beta' X_{i,j} + \alpha_j + \varepsilon_{i,j}$$

where i indexes the firm, j indexes the industry, $Y_{i,j}$ refers to the duration of the VC's service on the board of the portfolio company before its IPO, the portfolio firm's age at IPO, IPO underpricing (the first day's closing price minus the opening price divided by the opening price), and the percentage of equity held by all venture firms prior to IPO, respectively, and X is a vector of independent variables. We examine 342 VC-backed IPOs in China between November 29, 1996, and November 15, 2011.

The median age of VCs in our sample is five years, so we define "young" VCs as those VCs younger than five years old, which is the key independent variable. The control variables include the number of IPOs in the previous four months (to measure IPO timing), the log of IPO offering size, underwriter rank, equity stake of all venture firms prior to IPO, VC under management, the standard deviation of stock returns from day 2 to day 20 after the IPO.

4.5.3 Estimation results

Table 4.4 shows that young VC firms do indeed serve on the boards of portfolio firms for significantly shorter periods of time. It also shows that for the portfolio companies backed by young VC firms, the time

Table 4.4 Young VC, duration of VC's board service, and time between initial VC funding and IPO

	Duration of VC's Board Service (months)		Time Between Initial VC Funding and IPO (months)	
	(1)	(2)	(3)	(4)
Young VC dummy	–5.715**	–5.305**	–16.644***	–17.697***
	[0.016]	[0.027]	[0.000]	[0.000]
Number of IPOs in the 4 months prior to IPO	–0.172***	–0.172***	0.009	–0.011
	[0.000]	[0.000]	[0.813]	[0.773]
Log(VC investment amount)	–2.157*	–1.990*	0.582	1.934
	[0.077]	[0.097]	[0.784]	[0.361]
Underwriter ranking		0.022		0.057**
		[0.357]		[0.013]
Amount lead VC manages		0.005		–0.041**
		[0.568]		[0.021]
VCs' equity holdings in the firm before IPO				0.430***
				[0.000]
Industry dummies	Yes	Yes	Yes	Yes
Constant	Yes	Yes	Yes	Yes
Observations	342	342	342	342
Adjusted R-squared	0.290	0.291	0.116	0.167

The sample is 342 VC-backed IPOs between November 29, 1996, and November 15, 2011, in China. The dependent variables are (1) the length of time that the lead VC has been on the IPO firm's board of directors (in months) at IPO and (2) the time between the date when the portfolio firm received the first VC funding and its IPO. The key independent variable is "Young VC dummy", which equals 1 if the age of VC is less than five years. For the definitions of control variables, please see Section 4.5.2. Robust p-values are in brackets, and ***,**, and * denote significance at 1 percent, 5 percent, and 10 percent levels, respectively.

between VC funding and IPO is significantly shorter. Both results support the grandstanding hypothesis.

Table 4.5 shows that there is no statistically significant difference between the underpricing of IPOs backed by young VCs and old VCs in China, which does not lend direct support to the grandstanding hypothesis.

Table 4.6 shows that VC age is positively and significantly correlated with the percentage of equity held by all venture firms prior to IPO. In other words, young VC firms tend to hold less equity in the IPO firm. Especially interesting is that the shorter the duration of the VC's service on the board of the portfolio company before its IPO, the smaller the percentage of equity held by all VC firms. This

Table 4.5 Young VCs and IPO underpricing

	IPO Underpricing (First-day return)	
	(1)	**(2)**
Young VC dummy	–0.113	–0.053
	[0.395]	[0.682]
Number of IPOs in the 4 months prior to IPO	–0.006***	–0.004***
	[0.000]	[0.000]
Log(VC investment amount)	–0.334***	–0.323***
	[0.000]	[0.000]
Standard deviation of stock returns from day 2 to day 20 after the IPO	6.026	5.854
	[0.240]	[0.234]
Log(Company Age)		–0.048
		[0.305]
Log(Duration of VC's board service)		0.332***
		[0.000]
Underwriter ranking		–0.001
		[0.438]
Amount lead VC manages		–0.001
		[0.112]
Industry dummies	Yes	Yes
Constant	Yes	Yes
Observations	342	342
Adjusted R-squared	0.360	0.404

The sample is 342 VC-backed IPOs between November 29, 1996, and November 15, 2011, in China. The dependent variable is IPO underpricing (that is, first-day return). The key independent variable is "Young VC dummy", which equals 1 if the age of VC is less than five years. For the definitions of control variables, please see Section 4.5.2. Robust p-values are in brackets, and ***,**, and * denote significance at 1 percent, 5 percent, and 10 percent levels, respectively.

Table 4.6 VC age and VCs' equity holdings in portfolio companies before their IPOs

	Percentage of Equity Held by VC in the Portfolio Company Prior to IPO	
	(1)	(2)
Log(VC age)	2.410***	1.883**
	[0.004]	[0.026]
Number of IPOs in the 4 months prior to IPO	0.042**	0.053***
	[0.018]	[0.006]
Log(VC investment amount)	–1.045	–1.058
	[0.292]	[0.314]
Log(Company age)		1.304*
		[0.087]
Log(Duration of VC's board service)		2.429*
		[0.075]
Underwriter ranking		–0.016
		[0.187]
Amount lead VC manages		0.010
		[0.433]
Industry dummies	Yes	Yes
Constant	Yes	Yes
Observations	337	337
Adjusted R-squared	0.008	0.019

The sample is 337 VC-backed IPOs between November 29, 1996, and November 15, 2011, in China. The dependent variable is the percentage of VC's equity holdings in portfolio companies before their IPOs. The key independent variable is "Young VC dummy", which equals 1 if the age of VC is less than five years. For the definitions of control variables, please see Section 4.5.2. Robust p-values are in brackets, and ***,**, and * denote significance at 1 percent, 5 percent, and 10 percent levels, respectively.

is consistent with the grandstanding hypothesis because for more premature IPOs, VC firms are expected to receive smaller equity stakes.

To summarize, we have found mixed results regarding the grandstanding hypothesis in China. On the one hand, a young VC would serve on the board of the portfolio company for a shorter period of time before IPO, and it would take less time for a VC to package the portfolio company for an IPO. Thus, a young VC would rush the portfolio company to an early IPO to signal a successful exit and establish a good reputation. Also, because of the premature IPO, the VC would receive a smaller equity stake at the IPO. These results are consistent with the grandstanding hypothesis. On the other hand,

IPOs backed by young VCs are less underpriced, which does not lend direct support to the grandstanding hypothesis. However, as is well known, the extent of underpricing is determined by many factors. A promising future research direction is to investigate various determinants of the underpricing of VC-backed IPOs in China. In particular, our result that IPOs backed by young VCs are less underpriced is new in the literature. This result differs from results from studies on grandstanding in other countries, such as Wang, Wang, and Lu (2003), who find that in Singapore, IPOs backed by younger VC firms are more underpriced.

4.6 VC syndication in China: the value-added hypothesis versus the improved selection hypothesis'

4.6.1 Literature review

VC syndication occurs when VCs jointly invest in a project in the same financing round. It has become very common since the 1980s. According to Tian (2012), about 70 percent of VC investments worldwide between 1980 and 2005 were syndicated investments, and roughly 88 percent of VC-backed IPOs were backed by syndicated VC investments.

The main benefit of syndication is that multiple VCs can pool together their different skills, information, industry expertise, and networks. Sah and Stiglitz (1986) show that group decision making is superior to individual decision making. As a result, we may expect better investment outcomes (such as more successful exits) with syndicated VC investments. This is the "value-added hypothesis."

The main cost of syndication is that the lead VC must share profits with other VCs if the syndicated VC investment turns out to be successful. This cost prompts Brander, Amit, and Antweiler (2002) to develop the "improved venture selection" hypothesis. Specifically, they argue that a VC would only seek syndication if it expects the return on the investment to be in the intermediate range. The logic is that if it expects the return to be definitely above its hurdle rate, then it would not seek syndication for fear of sharing profits with other VCs. If it expected the return to be much lower than its hurdle rate, then it would not seek syndication because it would definitely reject the project. If the expected return is in the intermediate range, and the lead VC has doubt over an investment, it would probably seek a second opinion from another VC. The improved venture selection hypothesis thus predicts that syndicated

VC investments would have worse investment outcomes (such as fewer successful exits) than standalone investments.

Brander, Amit, and Antweiler (2002) find that in Canada, syndicated VC investments have higher returns, which supports the value-added hypothesis. Das, Jo, and Kim (2011) find that in the United States, syndicated VC investments have a higher likelihood of successful exits, and shorter time to exit. These results from the United States also support the value-added hypothesis. However, Fleming (2004) finds that in Australia, syndicated VC investments have lower returns, which supports the improved selection hypothesis.

It appears that all prior studies on VC syndication use data from developed countries. Studies on VC syndication in emerging markets are rare, and to the best of our knowledge, ours is the first study on VC syndication in the world's largest emerging market, China. Specifically, our research question is: does VC syndication lead to more or fewer successful investment exits in China?

4.6.2 Data and methodology

We collected data on 7606 VC investments in China between 1989 and 2011. The data collection and initial data analysis were conducted by Xiaoyu Wang and Xiao Lu at Xi'an Jiaotong University in China. Among these 7606 VC investments, only 1818 were syndicated. The proportion of syndicated VC investments (24 percent) was much lower than the proportion of syndicated VC investments (79 percent) in the United States, as reported by Das, Jo, and Kim (2011).

Similarly to Section 4.1 of this chapter, we define a VC investment exit as a successful one if the portfolio company goes public through an IPO or is acquired by another company through an M&A. For the 1818 syndicated VC investments, 22 percent of the portfolio companies went public, while for the 5788 standalone VC investments, only 11 percent of the portfolio companies went public. For the syndicated VC investments, 6.4 percent of the portfolio companies were acquired by another company. For the standalone VC investments, only 4.4 percent of the portfolio companies were acquired by another company. Overall, the univariate comparisons show that in our sample, syndicated VC investments have a successful exit rate of 28.4 percent, while standalone VC investments have a successful exit rate of 15.4 percent. In other words, syndicated VC investments almost double the successful exit rate in China.

The univariate comparisons are suggestive but not conclusive, because many other factors that may affect VC investment exits have been omitted. To control for these factors, we turn to multivariate regressions. Specifically, we estimate the following Logit regressions:

$$\begin{aligned} Exit = \beta^{*}\,\text{sync} + \text{controls} + \text{VC stage dummies} \\ + \text{industry dummies} + \text{location dummies} + \text{year dummies} + \varepsilon \end{aligned}$$

where *Exit* refers to the IPO dummy or the M&A dummy, or the IPO/M&A dummy. The key independent variable is "sync", a dummy variable that equals 1 if the VC investment is syndicated. The control variables include the log of the amount of VC investments, the number of successful investment exits made by the VC, the number of investments made by the VC, and the average amount of each investment made by the VC. VC stage dummies include dummies for stages such as early, development, expansion, and later stages. Industry dummies include dummies for IT, biotech, finance, media, energy, and so on. Location dummies include dummies for Beijing, Shanghai, Hong Kong, Taiwan, and so on.

If the coefficient of "sync" is positive and significant, then our results support the "value-added hypothesis." If the coefficient of "sync" is negative and significant, then our results support the improved selection hypothesis.

4.6.3 Estimation results

Table 4.7 shows that syndicated VC investments are associated with a significantly higher probability of successful exits, that is, IPOs, M&As, and IPOs/M&As. These results support the value-added hypothesis. It is also interesting to notice that successful exits seem to be persistent because the coefficient on the variable "number of successful exits for VC in history" is positive and significant.

4.7 The effects of VC capital inflows on VC valuation

4.7.1 Literature review

Gompers and Lerner (2000) show that the surges of inflows of capital into VC funds increase the valuation of these funds' new investments in the United States. They explain this by the "money-chasing deals hypothesis" – too many VC funds competing for a limited number of attractive projects to invest in. It is particularly interesting to examine

Table 4.7 Logit regressions of investment exits on VC syndication

	(1)	(2)	(3)	(4)	(5)	(6)
	IPO/M&A	IPO	M&A	IPO/M&A	IPO	M&A
Syndicated VC	0.779*** [0.000]	0.801*** [0.000]	0.430*** [0.000]	0.664*** [0.000]	0.707*** [0.000]	0.191** [0.038]
Log (amount of investment)				–0.134*** [0.000]	–0.190*** [0.000]	0.067* [0.066]
Number of successful exits for VC in history				0.052*** [0.000]	0.057*** [0.000]	0.015** [0.023]
Number of investments for VC in history				–0.011*** [0.000]	–0.012*** [0.000]	–0.004*** [0.002]
Average amount of each investment for VC in history				0.001*** [0.000]	0.001*** [0.000]	0.000 [0.269]
Location dummies	Yes	Yes	Yes	Yes	Yes	Yes
VC stage dummies	Yes	Yes	Yes	Yes	Yes	Yes
Industry dummies	Yes	Yes	Yes	Yes	Yes	Yes
Year dummies	Yes	Yes	Yes	Yes	Yes	Yes
Constant	Yes	Yes	Yes	Yes	Yes	Yes
Observations	7606	7606	7580	4647	4647	4631
Pseudo R-squared	0.192	0.220	0.130	0.223	0.245	0.144

The sample is 7606 VC investments in China between 1989 and 2011. The dependent variables are dummy variables for (1) IPO/M&A, (2) IPO, and (3) M&A. The key independent variable is the dummy variable "Syndicated VC", which equals 1 if more than one VC invests in the same project in the same round. For the definitions of control variables, please see Section 4.6.2. Robust p-values are in brackets, and ***,**, and * denote significance at 1 percent, 5 percent, and 10 percent levels, respectively.

this hypothesis in China. This is because in China, the formal financial sector, that is, banks and stocks markets, is underdeveloped, and funds from the formal financial sector are mainly channeled to the state-owned enterprises (Allen, Qian, and Qian, 2005; Ayyagari, Demirguc-

Kunt, and Maksimovic, 2010). As a result, many promising startup firms in China cannot get access to necessary funding. Would the excess supply of "deals" in China invalidate the money chasing deals hypothesis? In other words, would the rapid growth of VC funds in China boost the valuation of their VC investments? This is the research question in this section.

4.7.2 Data and methodology

We collect data from the CVSource data set. The sample is 1075 VC investments with available valuation data that occurred between January 1994 and December 2008. Yuhang Wei conducted the raw data collection and initial data analysis. We estimate the following regression:

$$\begin{aligned}\log(\text{Pre-money Valuation}) = \beta_0 + \beta_1 \log(\text{VC inflow}) + \log(\text{industry index}) \\ + \text{VC stage dummies} + \text{industry dummies} \\ + \text{location dummies} + \varepsilon.\end{aligned}$$

We compute "Valuation" (Pre-money Valuation) as follows:

$$\begin{aligned}\text{Pre-money valuation} = (1 - \text{percentage of equity held by VC}) \\ \times \text{post-money valuation}\end{aligned}$$

where "post-money valuation" is the product of the price and the number of shares outstanding after the financing round. "VC inflow" is the amount of VC funds inflow in the four quarters prior to the financing. The industry index is the public stock market valuations of publicly traded firms in the same industry as the firm at the beginning of the month of the financing. It is either value-weighted or equal-weighted. VC stage dummies include the early-stage dummy, development stage dummy, and later stage dummy.

Upon closer inspection, we realize that there may be an endogeneity issue in the above regression. Specifically, even though capital inflows into VC funds may affect VC investment valuation, the causality may go the other way; that is, VC funds may attract more capital because their valuation rises. To tackle this endogeneity, we exploit an exogenous policy shift. On November 15, 2005, the State Development and Reform Committee and ten other ministries promulgated *Interim Measures for the Administration of Startup Investment Enterprises*. This exogenous policy shift provided various supportive measures to encourage

Table 4.8 VC inflow and pre-money valuations of financing rounds

	Log(pre-money valuation)			
	OLS		2SLS	
	(1)	(2)	(3)	(4)
Log(inflow of VC)	0.116**	0.111*	0.377***	0.372***
	[0.045]	[0.054]	[0.000]	[0.000]
Log(equal-weighted industry index)	−0.073		−0.134*	
	[0.369]		[0.089]	
Log(value-weighted industry index)		0.018		−0.072
		[0.793]		[0.322]
VC stage dummies	Yes	Yes	Yes	Yes
Industry dummies	Yes	Yes	Yes	Yes
Location dummies	Yes	Yes	Yes	Yes
Adjusted R-squared	0.289	0.288	0.247	0.247
Observations	1075	1075	1075	1075

The sample is 1075 VC investments with available valuation data that occurred between January 1994 and December 2008 in China. The dependent variable is log(pre-money valuation), where pre-money valuation is defined as the product of the price paid per share in the financing round and the number of shares outstanding before the financing round. The key independent variable is the logarithm of the inflow into VC funds in the four quarters prior to the financing. For the definitions of control variables, please see Section 4.7.2. The instrumental variable used in the first stage regression of the 2SLS estimation is the exogenous policy shift in 2005 that increased the inflow into VC. Robust p-values are in brackets, and ***,**, and * denote significance at 1 percent, 5 percent, and 10 percent levels, respectively.

VC investments. As a result, capital inflows into VC funds in China significantly rose. A t-test shows that the average annual capital inflow into VC funds between 2005 and 2008 is significantly higher than that between 1994 and 2004. On the other hand, this policy shift was not expected to directly affect VC investment valuation. Therefore, we use this policy shift as an instrumental variable.

4.7.3 Estimation results

Table 4.8 shows that the VC inflow is positively and significantly correlated with the pre-money valuation of portfolio companies, even after controlling for endogeneity by using the instrumental variable (the exogenous policy shift in 2005). In fact, after we control for endogeneity, the results are even stronger, both economically and statistically. This result shows that even in China, where startups in the private sector have very limited access to the formal financial sector, the money chasing deals phenomenon is still relevant.

4.8 Conclusions

VC investments have grown rapidly in China during 1985–2012. However, research on this topic is quite scarce. In this chapter, we analyze newly available data to provide insights into the effects of VC reputation and syndication on VC investment outcomes in China. We also test the validity of the money chasing deals hypothesis in China, that is, whether VC fund inflows affect the valuation of these funds' new investments.

Our analysis of the latest data on China's VC investments shows that VC reputation and syndication do matter in China. Specifically, we find that investments made by more reputable VCs were significantly more likely to exit successfully, and the portfolio company's asset productivity (sales to assets) was also significantly higher. Young VCs rushed portfolio companies to early IPOs to signal their successful exits and gain a good reputation, which was consistent with the grandstanding hypothesis. But IPOs backed by young VCs were less underpriced, which was not consistent with the grandstanding hypothesis. In terms of VC syndication, we find that syndicated VC investments were associated with a significantly higher probability of successful exits, that is, IPOs, M&As, and IPOs/M&As. These results are consistent with the value-added hypothesis. Lastly, we confirm that in China, when the VC fund inflows surged, the valuation of the funds' new investment significantly rises, even after controlling for endogeneity. This result supports the money chasing deals hypothesis. This result is interesting because in China, startups have very limited access to funding. As a result, the supply of potentially promising projects seems to exceed the supply of VC funding. The money chasing deals hypothesis has found support even in China's market environment, which confirms the generality of the money chasing deals hypothesis.

References

Ahlstrom, D., Bruton, G. D., and Yeh, K. S. 2007. Venture capital in China: past, present and future. *Asia Pacific Journal of Management,* 24: 247–268.

Aizenman, J., and Kendall, J. 2008. The internationalization of venture capital and private equity. NBER working paper. Forthcoming, *Journal of Economic Studies*.

Allen, F., Qian, J., and Qian, M. 2005. Law, finance, and economic growth in China. *Journal of Financial Economics* 77: 57–116.

Armour, J., and Cumming, D. 2006. The legislative road to Silicon Valley. *Oxford Economic Papers* 58: 596–635.

Ayyagari, M., Demirguc-Kunt, A., and Maksmovic, V. 2010 Formal versus informal finance: evidence from China. *Review of Financial Studies*, 23: 3048–3097.

Balvers, R., McDonald, B., and Millier, R. 1988. Underpricing of new issues and the choice of auditor as a signal of investment banker reputation. *Accounting Review*, 63: 605–622.

Batjargal, B. 2007. Network triads: transitivity, referral and venture capital decisions in China and Russia. *Journal of International Business Studies*, 38: 998–1012.

Batjargal, B., and Liu, M. 2004. Entrepreneurs' access to private equity in China: the role of social capital. *Organization Science*, 15: 159–172.

Berkman, H., Cole, R., and Fu, J. 2011. Political connections and minority-shareholder protection: evidence from securities-market regulation in China. *Journal of Financial and Quantitative Analysis*, 45: 1391–1417.

Bottazzi, L., Da Rin, M., and Hellmann, T. 2008. Who are the active investors? Evidence from venture capital. *Journal of Financial Economics*, 89: 488–512.

Brander, J. A., Amit, R., Antweiler, W. 2002. Venture-capital syndication: improved venture selection vs. the value-added hypothesis. *Journal of Economics & Management Strategy*, 11: 423–452.

Bruton, G. D., and Ahlstrom, D. 2003. An institutional view of China's venture capital industry. Explaining the differences between China and the west. *Journal of Business Venturing*, 18: 233–259.

Carter, R., and Manaster, S. 1990. Initial public offerings and underwriter reputation. *Journal of Finance*, 45: 1045–1068.

Carter, R., Dark, F., and Singh, A. 1998. Underwriter reputation, initial returns, and the long-run performance of IPO stocks. *Journal of Finance*, 53: 285–311.

Chemmanur, T., and Fulghieri, P. 1994. Investment bank reputation, information production, and financial intermediation. *Journal of Finance*, 49: 57–79.

Chemmanur, T., Krishnan, K., and Nandy, D. 2011. How does venture capital financing improve efficiency in private firms? A look beneath the surface. *Review of Financial Studies*, 24: 4037–4090.

Cochrane, J. H. 2005. The risk and return of venture capital. *Journal of Financial Economics*, 75: 3–52.

Da Rin, M., Di Giacomo, M., and Sembenelli, A. 2011. Entrepreneurship, firm entry, and the taxation of corporate income: evidence from Europe. *Journal of Public Economics*, 95: 1048–1066.

Das, S. R., Jo, H., and Kim, Y. 2011. Polishing diamonds in the rough: the sources of syndicated venture performance. *Journal of Financial Intermediation*, 20: 199–230.

Fleming, G. 2004. Venture capital returns in Australia. *Venture Capital*, 6: 23–45.

Gompers, P. A. 1996. Grandstanding in the venture capital industry. *Journal of Financial Economics*, 42: 133–156.

Gompers, P., and Lerner, J. 2000. Money chasing deals? The impact of fund inflows on private equity valuations. *Journal of Financial Economics*, 55: 281–325.

Hasan, I., Wachtel, P., and Zhou, M. 2009. Institutional development, financial deepening and economic growth: evidence from China. *Journal of Banking and Finance*, 33: 157–170.

Kenney, M., Han, K., and Tanaka, S. 2004. Venture capital industries in East Asia. In: Yusuf, S., Altaf, M., and Nabeshima, K. (eds) *Global Change and East Asian Policy Initiatives*. Oxford University Press, Oxford, pp. 391–427.

Kenney, M., Han, K., and Tanaka, S. 2007. Venture capital in Asia. In: Rowen, H., Hancock, M. G., and Miller, W. F. (eds) *Making IT: The Rise of Asia in High Tech*. Stanford University Press, Stanford, pp. 290–32.

Klapper, L., Laeven, L., and Rajan, R. 2006. Entry regulation as a barrier to entrepreneurship. *Journal of Financial Economics*, 82: 591–629.

Kortum, S., and Lerner, J. 2000. Assessing the contribution of venture capital to innovation. *Rand Journal of Economics*, 31: 674–692.

Lane, W., Looney, S., and Wansley, J. 1986. An application of the Cox proportional hazards model to bank failure. *Journal of Banking and Finance*, 10: 511–531.

Lerner, J. 2009. *Boulevard of Broken Dreams*, Princeton University Press, Princeton, NJ.

Li, Y., and Zahra, S. 2012. Formal institutions, culture, and venture capital activity: a cross-country analysis. *Journal of Business Venturing*, 27: 95–111.

Megginson, W., and Weiss, K. 1991. Venture capitalist certification in initial public offerings. *Journal of Finance*, 46: 879–904.

Ministry of Science and Technology of China. 2003. China VC Investment Development Report (2003).

Ministry of Science and Technology of China. 2011. China VC Investment Development Report (2011).

Nahata, R. 2008. Venture capital reputation and investment performance. *Journal of Financial Economics*, 90: 127–151.

Oster, S. 2001. Nothingventured. AsiaWeek.com, July 27–August 3.

Qian, P., and Zhang, W. 2007. Returns on Chinese venture capital investment and their determinants. *Economic Research Journal*, 52: 78–90.

Sah, R., and Stiglitz, J., 1986. The architecture of economic systems: hierarchies and polyarchies. *American Economic Review*, 76: 716–727.

Samila, S., and Sorenson, O. 2011. Venture capital, entrepreneurship and economic growth. *Review of Economics and Statistics*, 93: 338–349.

Sorensen, M. 2007. How smart is smart money? A two-sided matching model of venture capital. *Journal of Finance*, 62: 2725–2762.

Tian, X. 2012. The role of venture capital syndication in value creation for entrepreneurial firms. *Review of Finance*, 16: 245–283.

Titman, S., and Trueman, B. 1986. Information quality and the valuation of new issues. *Journal of Accounting and Economics*, 8: 159–172.

Wang, C. K., Wang, K., and Lu, Q. 2003. Effects of venture capitalists' participation in listed companies. *Journal of Banking and Finance*, 27: 2015–2034.

Wang, L., and Wang, S. 2011. Cross-border venture capital performance: evidence from China. *Pacific-basin Finance Journal*, 19: 71–97.

Zero2IPO.com. 2012. China venture capital investment research report.

Zhang, X., and Liao, L. 2011. VCs' background, IPO underpricing and post-IPO performance. *Economic Research Journal*, 56: 118–132.

5

Growth and Challenges in the Development of Institutional Investors in China

Liming Wang, Ningyue Liu, and Shuo Wang

5.1 Introduction

China's rapid and sustainable growth since its economic reform in 1978, with an average gross domestic product (GDP) growth rate of 9.97 percent (China Stock Market and Accounting Research (CSMAR), 2012), has propelled it to become the second largest economy in the world. The total circulating capitalization of the stock market reached 16.5 trillion Chinese *yuan* (RMB) in 2011, a ten-fold increase in ten years (China Securities Regulation Commission (CSRC), 2012a). This provides enterprises with abundant capital for their growth, and has become one of the key channels for investment. The reform and opening-up of capital markets continuously stimulates the growth of institutional investors, and in turn, the institutional investors have brought in considerable capital through various investment strategies. Despite the heavy restriction on foreign and domestic institutional investors, they have already become an important player in China's capital markets.

This chapter attempts to contribute to the current discussion on institutional investors in China's capital markets. The chapter is organized as follows: a comprehensive introduction to institutional investors in China is presented in the next section. It starts with an overview focusing on the most important ones (Qualified Foreign Institutional Investors [QFIIs] and domestic funds) and at the same time covering the others. Specifically, changes in policies and regulations related to these institutional investors will be outlined. In addition, the recent growth of these institutional investors and the challenges they are facing now will be addressed. This is followed by an empirical analysis of what firm attributes impact on the security holdings of foreign and domestic funds. By indicating the differences and similarities between these funds, the findings of the chapter will be useful to policy makers in nurturing and developing institutional investors, and in balancing the stability of markets and the opening-up process in China. Finally, we compare and contrast our main findings in China to other countries and provide some concluding remarks.

5.2 Institutional investors

In developed countries, despite the late-2000s crisis, institutional investors continued expanding. From 2003 to 2010, investment funds in 28 Organisation for Economic Co-operation and Development (OECD) member countries[1] (out of 34) achieved on average a compound annual growth of 8.1 percent, and insurance corporations and pension funds have grown at an even faster speed of 11.3 percent (OECD.Stat, 2012).

Before the discussion on institutional investors in China, it is necessary to clarify the definition of institutional investors in this chapter. In a broader sense, investment made by all units qualified as an *institution* can be counted as institutional investors. This includes all households and legal or social entities. However, leaving out non-financial corporations or non-profit institutions, governments, and all households, we include financial corporations, namely banks, money market funds (MMF), securities investment funds, pension funds, investment banks, insurance companies and trust companies in our definition of institutional investors. In China, commercial banks are forbidden by law to directly invest in enterprises, or to participate in trust investment or securities business. MMF in China are categorized into securities investment funds, and the proportion with regard to net assets varies from 2.39 percent to 39.62 percent of all investment funds (Su, 2011). The role of investment banks in China is partly taken by so-called securities companies, which include consulting, brokerage business, securities business with its own accounts, securities underwriting, and asset management. Therefore, we can narrow our definition for our research purposes to securities investment funds, social security funds[2], securities companies, insurance companies, and trust companies. QFII is also worth researching, as it includes the most influential foreign institutional investors in China's capital markets.

In 2012, the total capital of QFII accounts reached 265 billion RMB (CSRC, 2012b). At the end of 2011, assets managed by investment funds reached 2191 billion RMB (Galaxy Securities, 2012), insurance companies stood at 121 billion RMB (excluding the shares of insurance companies and their subsidiaries), social security funds were 42 billion RMB, trust companies were 40 billion RMB, and securities companies stood at 37 billion RMB (Wind Database, 2012). Despite our intention to comprehensively address all these important players, most of our attention will be focused on the most influential investors, both domestic and foreign: securities investment funds and QFII. We discuss them in detail in Sections 2.2 and 2.3, but first review the general development of institutional investors.

In the 1990s the newly established stock market was dominated by individual investors, while the growth of institutional investors was also witnessed. In March 1998, the first closed-end fund was established in China, signifying the introduction of professional institutional investors. Since then, institutional investors have emerged quickly, actively influencing the development of Chinese capital markets. In September 2001, the first open-end fund was established, and ever since then the market has witnessed more and more funds with diversified products and investment styles. In 2002, the QFII scheme was initiated, allowing foreign investors to directly invest in China's stock market. In 2004, *Some Opinions of the State Council on Promoting the Reform, Opening up and Steady Growth of Capital Market* (GuoFa [2004] No. 3) indicated that, 'we should cultivate a group of faithful, law-abiding and professional institutional investors, and see to it that institutional investors, mainly fund management companies and insurance companies, become major forces in capital markets' (State Council, 2004). In December 2006 at the 10th China Securities Investment Fund Forum, the Chair of the CSRC, Shang Fulin, pronounced that 'the development of our capital markets is at a critical stage, and for the reform, opening and steady growth of our capital markets it is important to further enlarge the scale of institutional investors, to continue to improve the structure of institutional investors, and to gradually perfect the function of institutional investors' (Shang Fulin, 2011). After their rise and fall from the end of 2006 till the end of 2008, institutional investors have become more diversified, and much work has been done to prevent violent fluctuation. Thus in 2012, when talking about future tasks, the newly appointed Chair of the CSRC, Guo Shuqing, stated (CSRC, 2012c): '[The commission will] urge investment funds to transform into modern asset management institutions, encourage institutional investors including social security funds, enterprise annuities, and insurance companies to increase the proportion of their investment in the capital markets, actively expedite the nationwide inclusion of long-term capital, such as pension funds

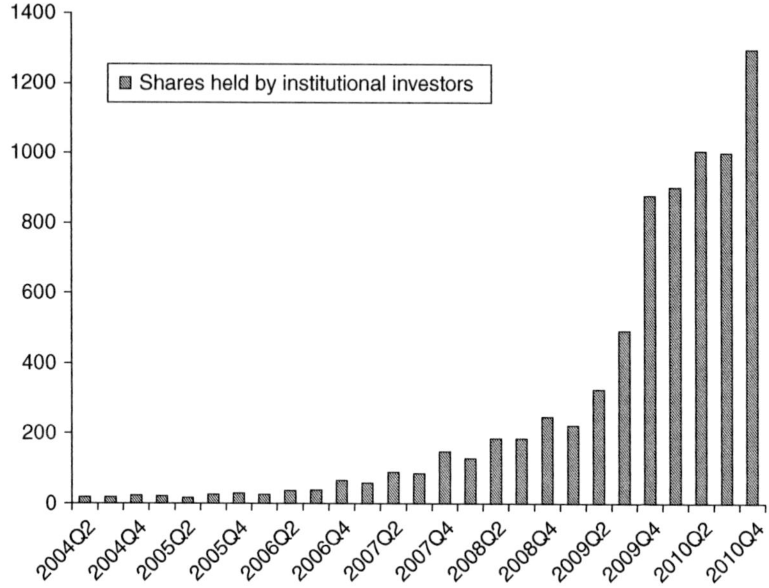

Figure 5.1 Growth of shares held by institutional investors

Note: Data from the Wind Database. Unit is one billion shares.

and housing funds, in capital markets. [It will] quicken the pace of attracting QFIIs, and increase their investment quota.'

Figure 5.1 illustrates the growth in shares held by QFIIs, securities investment funds, securities companies, social security funds, insurance companies and trust companies, from the second quarter of 2004 ('2004Q2') to 2010Q4. The holdings of institutional investors have grown at a tremendous speed, especially in 2007 and 2009, with 2010 showing further growth and ending in its fourth quarter at a peak of 1300 billion shares. However, there is not enough evidence for a correlation between deregulation and the growth of institutional investors during this period. In 2006, the regulation of QFII was officially enacted (though the approved quota did not abruptly change), and investment funds began to pay dividends to shareholders (however it wasn't until 2010Q2 that the number of shares held by these funds finally exceeded that of 2005Q4). The reform on non-tradable shares completed in 2007 prior to the main growth of institutional investors. Considering that the reforms such as the entry of social security funds in 2003 and insurance

Table 5.1 Development of institutional investors in recent years (in billion RMB)

Year	Market Circulating Capitalization	Among Which Held By Institutional Investors (%)	Market Total Capitalization	Market Index (000001.SS)
2006	2,470	42.5 (29.6)	8,990	2,675
2007	9,230	48.7 (40.7)	32,734	5,261
2008	4,508	54.6 (45.3)	12,193	1,820
2009	15,094	68.7 (59.1)	24,453	3,277
2010	19,269	70.9 (64.0)	26,614	2,808

Note: Data on institutional investors from China InfoBank Database (2012), percentages in brackets were calculated using Wind Database (2012), data of market indices and market capitalization from CSMAR Database (2012), 000001.SS is Shanghai Stock Exchange Composite Index.

companies in 2004 were even earlier, deregulation cannot explain the growth very well.

But what is striking is how well institutional investors performed during the years of crisis. Table 5.1 shows the recent growth of institutional investors in China's capital markets. During the dramatic downturn from late 2007 to late 2008, when the market index fell from 5261 to 1820, and during the process of the reform of non-tradable shares[3] (when the proportion of circulating [tradable] capitalization as a proportion of total capitalization rose from 27 percent in 2006 to 72 percent in 2010), institutional investors have managed to take over the market – from 42.5 percent in 2006, steadily through the crisis, to 70.9 percent at the end of 2010. It is important, however, to notice that in these statistics, a wider number of institutional investors are included than in our narrower definition. Guo Shuqing, Chair of the CSRC, stated in 2011 that 15.6 percent of the circulating capitalization of A-shares is held by 'professional institutional investors', while enterprise legal persons (enterprises recognized by law as having legal personality) hold 57.9 percent and natural persons (human beings) hold 26.5 percent ('Dialogue', 2012). Unfortunately, we could not find any further explanation for 'professional institutional investors', but considering the expansion of investment, and the relaxation of market regulations, institutional investors are certainly substituting for individual investors, and have become the main players in capital markets in China.

5.2.1 QFII in China

Despite the substantial impact of incoming Foreign Direct Investment (FDI) on China's economy, the opening-up for direct investment in the domestic securities market was very slow. The first domestic securities investment was made in 1992, when the first listed company in the B-share market[4] (Shanghai Vacuum Electron Devices Company, SVEC) opened to buying. The amount of foreign currency SVEC raised was equivalent to 420 million RMB at that time (Xu, 2012). However, with more and more Chinese companies listed abroad, the B-share market gradually lost its reason for existence. Since 2000, there has been no new initial public offering (IPO) in the B-shares market (Gao, 2011).

Joining the World Trade Organization (WTO) in 2001 entailed a series of reforms and opening-up for the Chinese government. The government adopted a whole set of policies to promote economic liberalization and to ameliorate the investment environment, including QFII. In May 2002, the Chair of the CSRC, Zhou Xiaochuan, formally addressed the planning of the QFII scheme at the 27th annual meeting of the International Organization of Securities Commissions (Zhou Xiaochuan, 2002). In August, the Forum on the Introduction of QFIIs took place in Shenzhen Stock Exchange.[5] At the forum, the State Administration of Foreign Exchange (SAFE) expressed its interest in the scheme and was willing to cooperate with the CSRC. The main concern was the impact of foreign investment on the Chinese securities and foreign exchange markets, but the majority of participants were optimistic about the size of China's securities markets and foreign exchange reserves. As addressed by the Chair of the CSRC, Zhou Xiaochuan (Zhou Xiaochuan's Speech, 2002), since the establishment of the two stock exchanges in China in 1990, by April 2002, 1175 companies had been listed, raising 810 billion RMB from over 670 million accounts, while securities investment funds reached a scale of 93 billion RMB, and foreign exchange reserves reached 212 billion RMB by the end of 2001 (CSMAR Database, 2012). This provided an adequate foundation for the introduction of foreign direct investments to China's main securities market.

Therefore, soon after the forum, two main regulations, the *Interim Measures* (CSRC Decree No. 12) and the *Interim Provisions* (SAFE Announcement No. 2 [2002]), were announced and entered into effect on 1 December 2002.[6] These allow qualified foreign institutional investors, subject to regulations and restrictions (shown in Table 5.2), to import a certain amount of foreign exchange funds converted into RMB (through special accounts under strict supervision), and to invest in the

Table 5.2 Qualification and restriction of QFII in 2002

	Years of Operation	Securities Assets under Management for Last Year	Paid-in Capital
Qualification			
Fund Management Companies	>5	>10 bn USD	
Insurance Companies	>30	>10 bn USD	>1 bn USD
Securities Companies	>30	>10 bn USD	>1 bn USD
Commercial Banks	N/A	>10 bn USD	Total assets world top 100
	Types	**Criteria**	
Restriction			
Share Percentage	Each QFII All QFIIs	In Each Listed Company <10% In Each Listed Company <20%	
Investment Quota	Each QFII	>50 million and <800 million USD	
Account	Each QFII	1	
Brokerage Company	Each QFII	1	
Investment Locked-in Time	Each QFII	1 Year	

Note: According to the *Interim Measures* (CSRC Decree No. 12) and the *Interim Provisions* (SAFE Announcement No. 2 [2002]). USD stands for US dollars.

securities market of mainland China, while capital gains and dividends can be converted into foreign exchange and remitted after approval.

Four years later, the *Interim Measures* was replaced by the revised *Measures* (CSRC Decree No. 36) promulgated jointly by the CSRC, SAFE and People's Bank of China (PBC) in 2006. The revised *Measures* lowered the requirement on years of operation and asset scale, allowed QFIIs to open direct accounts and to authorize at most three brokerage companies in each stock exchange, and shortened the investment locked-in time. The new *Measures* was complemented by a *Circular* (ZhengJian JiJin Zi [2006] No. 176) issued by the CSRC on the details of implementation.

In 2009, the SAFE announced its new *Provisions* (SAFE Announcement No. 1 [2009]) to deal with the growing foreign investment inflows. The quota for each QFII was increased from 50–800 million to 20–1000 million USD, locked-in time was further decreased, and the application process was simplified.

In 2011, the CSRC issued a *Guideline* (CSRC Announcement [2011] No. 12) for stock index futures investment for QFIIs, but only allowed QFIIs to use the futures for hedging purposes. As of April 2012, not a single QFII has participated in the futures market. In May 2012, the CSRC loosened the restriction on QFIIs' portfolios, cancelling the requirement of 'stock proportion no less than 50 percent' issued in 2010, but held on to the stipulation for cash 'no more than 20 percent' (CSRC, 2012).

The original total quota was set at just four billion USD in 2002 (Deng, 2007). In April 2005, when this limit was achieved, the total quota was more than doubled to ten billion USD (QFII quota, 2007). Even so, the investment quota approved for QFIIs roared from four billion USD in 2005, to ten billion at the beginning of 2007, reaching the top ceiling (ten billion, in Figure 5.2 we can see a flat period in 2007). To meet the pressing demand of investors and as a result of the second meeting of China-US Strategic Economic Dialogue, in 2007, the quota ceiling of QFII was raised again from ten billion to 30 billion USD. In April 2012, SAFE announced a further increase in the quota by 50 billion USD, making it 80 billion dollars in total. Although there was ample space before reaching the original quota ceiling, it (as argued) was aiming 'to introduce long-term investment into China's enhanced capital markets' (CSRC, 2012b).

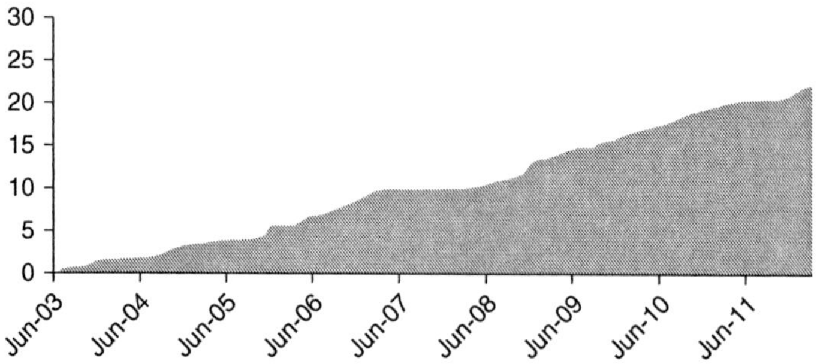

Figure 5.2 Cumulative total of QFII quota approved (in billion USD)

Note: Data from SAFE (2012).

By 9 March 2012, CSRC and SAFE had approved a total of 131 QFIIs. The first approvals were given to UBS AG, Nomura Securities, and Citigroup Global Markets Limited in June 2003, closely followed by Morgan Stanley & Co International Ltd, and Goldman Sachs & Co. There are now 158 foreign institutions from 23 countries qualified under the scheme, including 82 asset management companies, 11 insurance companies, 23 commercial banks, 13 securities companies, and 29 sovereign, pension, or endowment funds. With an accumulative investment of about 24 billion USD, the total capital scale of QFII accounts (including capital gains and dividends) has reached 42 billion USD (265 billion RMB), in which equities, bonds and bank savings account for 74.5 percent, 13.7 percent and 9.6 percent, respectively. The market capitalization of QFII holdings, however, still only accounts for about 1 percent of the circulating capitalization of the A-share market (CSRC, 2012b).

What is worth mentioning is a similar scheme known as RQFII set up in December 2011. RQFII stands for RMB Qualified Foreign Institutional Investors, where Hong Kong subsidiaries of fund management and securities companies meeting certain conditions can use RMB funds raised in Hong Kong in domestic securities investments within approved investment quotas. Theoretically, this provides another avenue for foreign fund management or securities companies to participate in China's financial market: a subsidiary can be established in Hong Kong to raise RMB funds, and use these to operate in the mainland's capital markets. However, this does not apply to foreign institutional investors who want to directly invest foreign capital into China.

From 30 December 2011 to 2 January 2012, nine fund management companies and twelve securities companies were approved under the RQFII scheme, hitting the total quota limit of 20 billion RMB (3.2 billion USD). These investments were subject to regulations including that a minimum of 80 percent of total investments were to be comprised of fixed income assets and a maximum of 20 percent in equities. It was reported that a preference would be given to existing subsidiaries of mainland companies ('Experts', 2011), and judging from the list of companies that were approved, this seems to be the case.

At the same time as the QFII quota was increased in April 2012, the total limit for RQFII funds was increased by 50 billion RMB to 70 billion RMB (11 billion USD). So far there have been several applications for RQFII quotas, but they will no longer be mainly invested in fixed income funds but instead listed in Hong Kong as exchange-traded funds investing in major A-shares ('Several Fund Management Companies', 2012).

5.2.2 Funds in China

The development of securities investment funds in China can be roughly categorized into four phases. The first phase was the early period from 1992 to 1997, prior to the enactment of the *Interim Measures on the Management of Securities Investment Funds*. In June 1992, the first corporate type closed-end investment fund—Zibo Town and Township Investment Funds Corp—was established with permission from the PBC, and listed on the Shanghai Stock Exchange (SHSE) in August 1993. The introduction of Zibo Funds initiated a short upsurge of investment funds, but due to the lack of regulations at this stage, by late 1993 the development of investment funds had stagnated.

The second phase witnessed the development of closed-end funds, due to the impact of the *Interim Measures* up to August 2001. In November 1997, the State Council Securities Committee (a former component of the CSRC) promulgated the *Interim Measures on the Management of Securities Investment Funds*, laying the foundation for the normalized development of China's investment funds. In March 1998, two closed-end investment funds of two billion RMB were approved by the CSRC, signifying the preface to the development of China's securities investment funds.

The third phase began with the development of open-end funds from September 2001, when the first open-end securities investment fund—Hua'an Innovation—was founded. In October 2003, the enactment of the *Law of the People's Republic of China on Securities Investment Fund* further strengthened regulations of investment funds, leading to a steady growth in securities investment funds.

The last phase commenced in 2006, marked by an extreme growth of open-end funds and a long gloomy recession. Within two years, the market index rose from over 1000 in January 2006 to 6000 in October 2007, bringing a boom in open-end securities investment funds. At this time, deregulation was complete and a variety of funds prospered in the markets. The growth of these funds was mainly market driven. However, since the bubble burst, assets managed by investment funds have lingered around 2000 billion RMB, while at the same time the number of funds has doubled (see Figure 5.3). Among these shrinking investment funds, assets managed by 'stock-oriented investment funds' of circulating capitalization of both stock markets has dropped from 32.84 percent in December 2007 to 9.70 percent in December 2011 (Galaxy Securities, 2012).

From the introduction of the first two closed-end funds in 1998, it took only five years for the number of funds to reach 95 in 2003. In December 2008, the total number of funds was 439, nearly five times the number five years before. By the end of 2011, the number

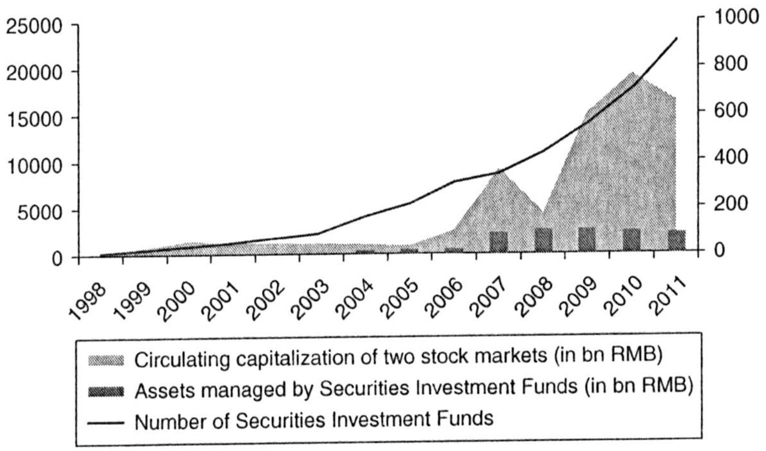

Figure 5.3 Growth of securities investment funds in China

Note: Left axis for circulating capitalization and assets managed by funds, right axis for number of securities investment funds, data from Galaxy Securities (2012), China InfoBank Database (2012), and CSRC (2012d).

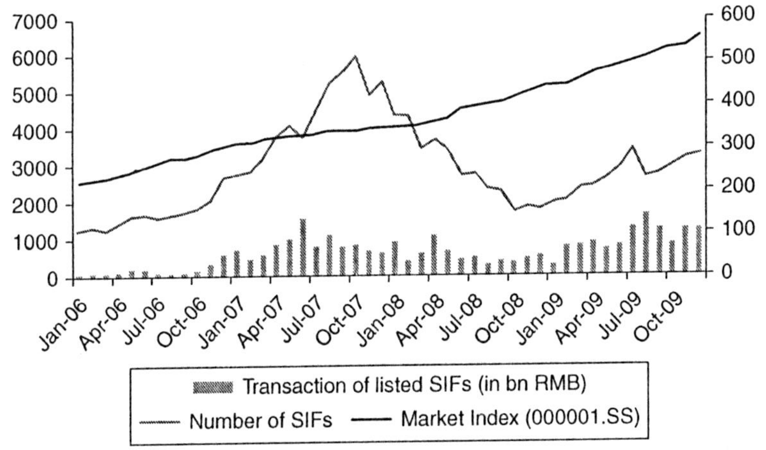

Figure 5.4 Market fluctuation from 2007 to late 2009

Note: Left axis for market index, and right axis for transaction and number of securities investment funds; Data from CSRC (2012d) and CSMAR Database (2012).

had doubled again. Compared to the continuous growth in the total number of funds, the volume of transactions has been much more volatile (see Figure 5.4), especially corresponding to the fluctuation of the stock market during 2007, when transactions dropped from a peak of

133 billion RMB (June 2007) to 28 billion RMB (August 2008). Despite fluctuations from time to time, if we make a regression with the transactional data, the growth is still remarkable: 15-fold between January 2006 and December 2009.

With the support of relevant policies, after ten years of rapid development, securities investment funds have become the largest and most important institutional investors in China's securities market. In 2009, the value of assets managed by securities investment funds exceeded two trillion RMB, with a compound annual growth rate exceeding 30 percent. In 2008, the holdings of securities investment funds accounted for 28.83 percent of the total circulating capitalization of the market, compared to 1.81 percent in 1998 ('Non-conventional Development', 2009).

5.2.3 Other institutional investors in China

As stated at the beginning of this section, apart from QFII and securities investment funds, there are other institutional investors in China including securities companies, social security funds, insurance companies, and trust companies.

Since 1996, many securities and trust investment companies have emerged and become important players in the securities market. In 1999, funds of insurance companies were allowed to indirectly enter the securities market by buying securities investment funds, but the investment should not exceed 5 percent of the insurance company's total assets (Zhu and Yan, 2001). In 2000, the CSRC adopted the policy of 'nurturing and developing institutional investors non-conventionally and innovatively' as one of the major strategies in developing China's securities market (Chen, 2001, p. 52). In 2001, the *Trust Law of the People's Republic of China* and the *Interim Measures on the Administration of the Investment of National Social Security Fund* were enacted, and this consolidated various forms of trust investments, affording the newly established national social security fund to partake in the stock market (with investment of funds and securities not to exceed 40 percent of total investments). In 2002, the *Insurance Law of the People's Republic of China* was amended, consolidating the insurance industry, and prohibiting insurance companies from establishing securities institutions. In 2003, the national social security fund was allowed to partake in stock markets via entrusting with six fund management companies. In 2004, the *Interim Measures for the Administration of Stock Investments of Insurance Institutional Investors* was enacted jointly by the China Insurance Regulatory Commission and the CSRC, allowing insurance companies to invest directly in the stock market with strict conditions regarding qualification and limitations

(5 percent of total capital). In 2009, due to speculative use of multiple accounts held by trust companies in initial public offerings, they were banned from opening new securities accounts (Luo, 2011). As of April 2012, this ban has not yet been lifted.

Guided by the laws and regulations that were gradually improved, securities companies, social security funds, insurance companies and trust companies have achieved remarkable growth in recent years. Securities companies have grown from three billion RMB in the late 1980s, to a cohort of 107 companies owning assets of more than two trillion RMB in 2009, and investments of 37 billion RMB in the stock market. In 2009, 230 insurance companies in China controlled assets of 3.38 trillion RMB, and the cap for investment in the stock market was raised to 20 percent of total assets ('Non-conventional Development', 2009). The total holdings of insurance companies were worth 92 billion RMB at the end of 2009. In 2011, the national social security fund had a balance of 2.87 trillion RMB, of which pension funds accounted for 1.92 trillion RMB ('Pension Funds', 2012). The fund holds 42 billion RMB in the stock market, far below the limit of 40 percent of its total investment. Figure 5.5 shows that, from 2005 to 2010, all types of institutional investors increased their holdings in listed companies. During this

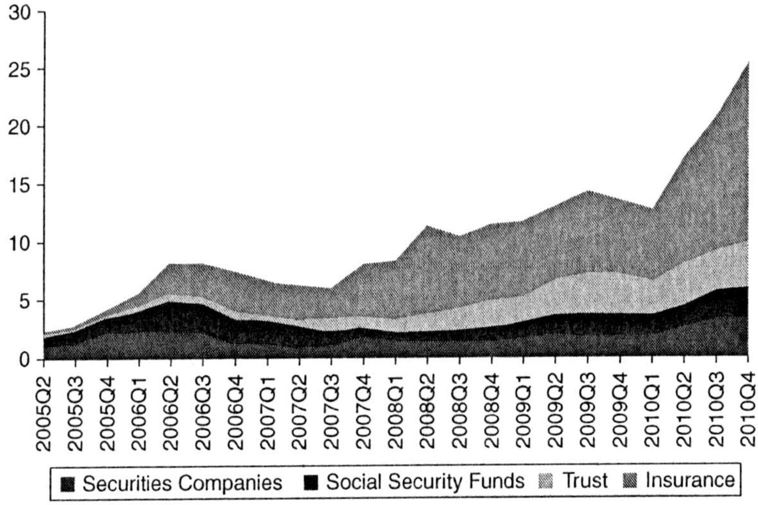

Figure 5.5 Number of circulating shares held by various institutional investors in both stock markets, in billions

Note: Wind Database, since 2010 insurance holdings excluding China Life Insurance Company that transformed 19 billion formerly non-tradable shares to tradable shares in January 2010.

period, holdings of securities companies and social security funds had a three-fold increase, trust companies had a 16-fold increase, and insurance companies showed more than a 150-fold increase. But compared to the growth of these companies, their investment in the stock market is still expanding at a slower pace.

5.2.4 Challenges

So far we have discussed six types of institutional investors: QFII, securities investment funds, securities companies, insurance companies, social security funds, and trust companies. In a developing country such as China, the entire capital market was brand new, regulations had to be formed and many lessons have been learned in the establishment and development of markets. In this sense, the success of China's capital markets is remarkable. However, the development of institutional investors is still obstructed by many factors in China.

An overarching challenge all institutional investors have to face is the underdevelopment of China's capital markets. The stock market is still a 'policy market', heavily influenced by information emanated from policy makers. It lacks adequate supervision of listed companies, which hardly pay any dividends. The derivatives market is also underdeveloped and prone to fluctuation. Therefore, markets are exposed to high uncertainty, as well as credit and fluctuation risks.

QFII in China is still highly regulated. As specified earlier, qualification is hard to achieve, and there are strict rules for brokerage companies and operation of their accounts. The restrictions were considered necessary for the smooth introduction of foreign capital, but at only 1 percent of total market capitalization, there is room for further deregulation. What is also interesting is that it is interlocked with China's foreign exchange mechanism. QFII is attractive not only because of the Chinese companies listed in it, but due to appreciation in the RMB currency. As free exchange is not possible, QFII has become an ideal way to circumvent regulations. Reforming of China's foreign exchange mechanism is another uncertainty for the QFII scheme.

Domestic securities investment funds were hugely successful in 2007. However, these funds are now shrinking and losing their analysts. There are both external and internal challenges. Externally, the stock market has been in recession since 2009, and most funds are experiencing loss, which discourages investment in these funds, and fund raising has become very difficult. But at the same time, more funds are entering the market, increasing competition among them. Internally, investment funds rapidly grew in reputation, but their management is underdeveloped. There is a shortage of experienced specialists, and as private equity funds are more generous in paying their analysts, those few with experience leave the funds. Corporate culture, hierarchical structures, reward systems, and decision making processes, are some other challenges facing funds.

Social security funds are held back by public debate on whether they should be involved in the stock market or not. Because China's stock market is more speculative in nature, it is hard to ensure the security of fund investments. But not entering the market seems a bad option as well. Due to inflation (5.6 percent and 3.3 percent, consumer price index of 2011 and 2010, respectively) and low interest rates for bonds and bank savings, pension funds had less than 2 percent gains in 2011 and 2010, actually resulting in a loss of 130 billion RMB in two years ('State Council', 2012). So far, the national social security fund is the only social security fund that is allowed to invest in the stock market. Many more regional funds are still blocked from it. While ten years have passed, and capital markets have advanced greatly with many new products (such as index futures) being developed, the national social security fund is still regulated by the *Interim Measures* of 2001.

For insurance companies, regulation and human resources are two major concerns. Securities companies face the challenge of expansion of commercial banks. Trust companies are still banned from opening securities accounts, but if allowed, they might benefit from the emerging private equity funds.

Although institutional investors are faced with many challenges in the market, constant reform and opening-up are also ongoing. The Chair of CSRC, Guo Shuqing, addressed these areas in his reform plans (CSRC, 2012c): the public offering system, transparency and supervision of listed companies, a delisting mechanism, product diversity, regulation codification, and insider trading, among others. But different investors have different traits, and to the policy maker, these traits are important for better management of markets. Therefore, it is beneficial to investigate the investment behavior of QFIIs and domestic funds, and examine their similarities and differences.

5.3 The preference of QFII and domestic funds

In the previous section, a comprehensive introduction to institutional investors in China is presented. In this section, we will provide empirical evidence on how institutional investors allocate assets across different firms in Chinese stock markets.

In spite of the exceptional growth of QFII in China, there is limited research on how QFIIs determine their allocations across different listed companies and the factors influencing their investment behavior. In this section, we will examine what firm attributes impact the security holdings of QFIIs and Securities Investment Funds, which are the largest domestic institutional investors in China.[7]

5.3.1 Literature review and research hypothesis

5.3.1.1 Literature review

Kang and Stulz (1997) adopt data for Japan from 1975 to 1991 and find that foreign investors hold disproportionately more shares of firms in manufacturing industries, large firms, and firms with good accounting performance, low unsystematic risk, and low leverage. Dahlquist and Robertsson (2001) analyze the determinants of foreign ownership in Swedish firms and find that foreigners have a preference for large firms, firms paying low dividends, and firms with large cash positions on their balance sheets. Foreign investors also tend to underweight firms with a dominant owner.[8] Covirg et al. (2006) investigate a range of stock preferences among domestic and foreign fund managers in 11 developed countries and conclude that foreign fund managers have less information about stocks in local markets than their domestic counterparts. They find that ownership by foreign funds is related to the size of foreign sales, index membership and stocks with foreign listings.

Fast growing emerging markets are attractive to foreign institutional investors, with portfolio investments by them being the most important source of capital for emerging markets, in particular during the 1990s (Frenkel and Menkhoff, 2004). Aggarwal et al. (2005) look at the portfolio holdings of 576 US mutual funds invested in emerging markets as at February 2002, and analyze both country- and firm-level disclosure and institutional policies that influence mutual funds' allocation choices. At the firm level, US funds have a preference for firms that adopt discretionary policies such as greater accounting transparency and the issuance of an American Depositary Receipt (ADR).

5.3.1.2 Research hypothesis

Most of the previous studies emphasize the impact of financial characteristics, for example, size, on the share holdings of institutional investors (Dahlquist and Robertsson, 2001). However, Leuz et al. (2009) believe that corporate governance, for example, ownership structure, is another group of factors that are considered when investment decisions are made. We examine whether this is also the case for foreign institutional investors in China. Given the potential long-term investment benefits, we expect to find that foreign investors (representing sophisticated investors) are more likely to consider the corporate governance characteristics of firms. Given the short history of the local markets, the trading experience and investment sophistication of Chinese investors are unlikely to be comparable with investors from developed markets (Ng and Wu, 2007). We expect that Chinese domestic institutional investors (representing relatively less sophisticated investors) might have a preference for financial characteristics, given the short-term capital gain. Specifically, domestic fund managers may put more emphasis on firm's financial characteristics, for example return on shareholders, which is measured by earning per share in this paper. For these reasons, we propose the following hypothesis.

Hypothesis: Corporate governance (financial characteristics) has a significant impact on the investment of foreign (domestic) institutional investors.

5.3.2 Data and methodology

5.3.2.1 Data

The shareholder data of foreign funds and domestic funds are all sourced from the Wind database while financial and corporate governance data are from CSMAR at GTA Research Service Center. The data is annual and covers the period 2003 to 2009. In order to investigate the behavior of foreign and domestic funds, our sample includes only those companies whose stocks are held by either foreign funds, domestic funds, or both. Foreign and domestic funds' portfolio holdings consist of 858 and 6793 firm-year observations respectively.

5.3.2.2 Methodology

We examine the impact of a comprehensive range of firm-level characteristics, including financial and corporate governance indicators, on the investment decisions of foreign and domestic funds. The firm-level characteristics are divided into two groups: financial indicators and corporate governance indicators. In each group, we chose a range of indicators to measure the firm-level characteristics according to previous literature and the characteristics of Chinese capital markets. Drawing on existing studies, we use capitalization to measure size, current ratio to measure short-term liabilities paying capability, long-term liabilities ratio to measure long-term liabilities paying capability, earnings

Table 5.3 Indicator definition

Classification	Indicator	Formula
Financial Indicators		
Size	Capitalization	ln (capitalization)
Short-term liabilities paying capability	Current ratio	current assets/current liabilities
Long-term liabilities paying capability	Long-term liabilities ratio	long-term liabilities/total liabilities
Financial risk	Degree of financial leverage	earnings before interest and taxes (EBIT)/ (EBIT–financial cost)
Return on shareholders	Earnings per share	net profit/total shares outstanding
Profit	Return on equity	net profit/average total equity
Cash flow	Free cash flow	net profit+ amortization/ depreciation–changes in working capital–capital expenditures
Growth	Growth rate of total assets	(ending total assets–beginning total assets)/beginning total assets
Operating capability	Turnover rate of receivables	operating income/average receivables
Corporate Governance Indicators		
Ownership structure	Percentage of state-owned shares	number of state-owned shares/number of total shares
Ownership concentration	Z index	number of shares held by the largest circulating shareholder/number of shares held by the second largest circulating shareholder
Management structure	Number of directors	number of directors
	Duality of chairman and CEO	a dummy variable equal to 1 if chairman and CEO is one person and 2 otherwise
	Percentage of independent directors	number of independent directors/ number of directors
Compensation of management	ln of sum of top three compensation of senior executives	ln of sum of top three compensation of senior executives

Note: In this table, we explain the financial indicators and corporate governance indicators employed in the chapter. We divide the comprehensive range of financial characteristics into nine subgroups, namely size, short-term liabilities paying capability, long-term liabilities paying capability, financial risk, return on shareholders, profit, cash flow, growth, and operating capability. We divide the comprehensive range of corporate governance characteristics into four subgroups, namely ownership structure, ownership concentration, management structure, and compensation of management. In the last column, we also introduce the way to calculate the indicator.

per share to measure return on shareholders, and return on equity to measure company profit. In addition to these five firm-level characteristics, our analysis also includes four additional characteristics, namely financial risk, cash flow, growth, and operating capability. In order to investigate a comprehensive range of firm-level characteristics, we also add cash flow and operating capability, which are important company characteristics not included in previous studies.

Previous studies suggest that institutions are good at investing in firms with better corporate governance structures. Leuz et al. (2009) study 4409 firms from 29 countries and find that foreigners invest less in firms with governance problems. For ease of comparison, we first chose the same attributes as Dahlquist and Robertsson (2001), that is, ownership concentration, and Bushee et al. (2009), that is, management structure. In addition to these two classifications, our analysis also includes two more measures, namely ownership structure and compensation of management. We use the percentage of state-owned shares in the ownership structure subgroup (Naughton, 2007). Finally, compensation of management is also an important characteristic of a company and is also included here. Indicator definitions are given in Table 5.3.

5.3.3 Empirical results

In this section, we focus on analyzing the firm-level drivers that influence foreign and domestic investors' allocation choices.[9] Both fixed effects models (FEM) and random effects models (REM) are used in this study to examine the relationships (Greene, 2002).[10] Consistently with previous studies in the literature, we track funds' portfolio holdings using the percentage relative spread (see Dahlquist and Robertsson [2001] and Kang and Stulz [1997]).[11] The percentage relative spread captures funds' deviations from investment allocations predicted by Chinese market portfolios.[12]

The third column of Table 5.4 reports the results for the model where the percentage relative spread of foreign funds is regressed on the financial indicators and the corporate governance indicators. We also control for industry and year effect by adding industry and yearly dummy variables into the model. In order to take account of the introduction of new regulations on QFIIs in 2006, a dummy variable is included in the final empirical model. The dummy variable, year 2006, is assigned a value of one if the year is after 2006 and zero otherwise. Table 5.4 reveals several findings on foreign institutional investors' preferences. Inconsistently

Table 5.4 Preferences of QFIIs and domestic funds

Classification	**Indicator**	**QFIIs**	**Domestic Funds**
Size	ln of capitalization	0.5155	0.0396***
		(1.11)	(3.57)
Short-term liabilities paying capability	current ratio	–0.2216	0.0077*
		(–0.92)	(1.73)
Long-term liabilities paying capability	long-term liabilities ratio	1.2435	–0.0212
		(0.99)	(–0.63)
Risk	degree of financial leverage	0.0250	–0.0039
		(0.11)	(–1.01)
Return on shareholders	earnings per share	–0.9645	0.0740***
		(–1.31)	(3.23)
Profit	ROE	4.6125*	–0.0248
		(1.85)	(–0.38)
Cash flow	free cash flow	–0.0194***	0.0002
		(–2.56)	(0.51)
Growth	growth rate of total assets	–1.0335*	–0.0058
		(–0.92)	(–0.48)
Operating capability	turnover rate of receivables	–0.0001	0.0001
		(–0.01)	(0.78)
Ownership structure	percentage of state-owned shares	2.1179**	–0.0769***
		(2.27)	(–2.80)
Ownership concentration	Z index	–0.0296***	–0.0024***
		(–3.27)	(–6.93)
Structure of management	number of directors	0.0124	0.0068**
		(0.10)	(2.04)
	duality of chairman and CEO	–0.0312	0.0065
		(–0.04)	(0.50)
	percentage of independent directors	–1.8448	0.1969**
		(–0.40)	(2.11)
Compensation of management	ln of sum of top three compensation of senior executives	0.8696*	–0.0043
		(1.91)	(–0.45)
Dummy variable	year 2006	–5.3861***	
		(–4.42)	
Industry		control	Control
Year		control	Control
Intercept		–17.2309	–0.9145***
		(–1.64)	(–3.33)
Model		Fixed	Fixed
Hausman		50.37	116.96

Continued

Table 5.4 Continued

Classification	Indicator	QFIIs	Domestic Funds
P-value of Hausman		0.0000	0.0000
Overall R^2 (%)		11.01%	5.32%
F test		4.18	7.81
P-value of F test		0.0000	0.0000
N		858	6,793

Note: In this table, a fixed effects model is used to explain factors impacting on the investments of foreign funds and domestic funds in China's Stock Market. The results of foreign and domestic funds are reported in the third and the last column respectively. The dependent variable is the percentage relative spread of foreign institutional investors in each company. The independent variables are financial and corporate governance firm-level characteristics. We also include the industrial and year dummy variables to control the industrial and year effect respectively. For each independent variable, the table reports the coefficient above and the t-statistic in parentheses below. The superscripts of coefficient denote the significance of the coefficient (***, **, * representing significance at 1%, 5%, and 10% levels respectively). We report the intercept, t-statistics of the intercept in parentheses below, the model type in this table, the Hausman test value, p-value of Hausman test and number of observations at the end of Table 5.4. The specification test devised by Hausman (1978) tests if the null hypothesis of the coefficients estimated by the efficient random effects estimator are the same as the ones estimated by the consistent fixed effects estimator. If they are insignificant, then it is safe to use random effects. If you get a significant p-value, however, you should use fixed effects.

with prior research in developed markets (see Aggarwal et al., 2005; Dahlquist and Robertsson, 2001; Kang and Stulz, 1997), we find that firm size as measured by the natural logarithm of capitalization is not one of the strongest determinants of foreign institutional investors' investment decisions in China. Furthermore, the insignificant relationship between foreign institutional investors' ownership and firms' profit is inconsistent with the finding in Kang and Stulz (1997) on Japanese data. There is no significant relationship between foreign institutional investors' ownership and firms' liabilities paying capability, no matter whether it is short-term or long-term. Finally, free cash flow indicates a negative relationship, statistically significant at the 1 percent level. This result indicates that foreign institutional investors prefer firms with less free cash flow, which is inconsistent with the findings of Dahlquist and Robertsson (2001).

Regarding corporate governance, the percentage of state-owned shares and the Z index are statistically significant with the ownership of foreign institutional investors. The results indicate that foreign institutional investors have a preference for firms with a larger percentage of state-owned shares. The influential role of government policy is a feature of the Chinese market. Naughton (2007) believes that Chinese market fluctuations are better explained as reactions to government policy changes rather than as a reaction to changes in underlying fundamentals of individual companies. This unique characteristic in Chinese markets drives foreign funds to invest more in firms with a larger percentage of state-owned shares because the higher the percentage of state-owned shares in a company the closer the relationship with the Chinese government. Consistently with Dahlquist and Robertsson (2001) and Huang and Zhu (2011), there is a negative relationship between foreign institutional ownership and firms' ownership concentration measured by the Z index, implying that foreigners avoid companies with a dominant owner.[13] Another notable significant finding is the year 2006 dummy variable. The statistically significant coefficient with a negative sign for the 2006 dummy variable indicates that the investment of QFIIs declined after 2006, although CSRC had new regulations to increase the investment quota of QFIIs in China. However, it is more likely that this dummy variable is taking account of the substantial volatility in Chinese stock markets post 2006. Following the global economic downturn, the Shanghai Stock Exchange Composite Index fell from a peak of 6092 points on 16 October 2007 to a trough of 1719 on 3 November 2008. In particular, Kaminsky et al. (2001) conclude that although international mutual funds are one of the main sources of capital flows to emerging economies, withdrawals from emerging markets during crisis are large. Our results provide further indications of the sensitivity of institutional investment to downturns in the market.

The last column of Table 5.4 presents factors impacting on domestic funds' investment behavior. Several notable observations emerge from Table 5.4. Firm size has significant explanatory power, indicating that domestic funds prefer large firms, which is consistent with the findings of Huang and Zhu (2011). Although not a critical indicator for foreign funds, earnings per share is a significant financial factor influencing domestic funds' investment behavior. For both foreign and domestic funds, ownership structure is a dominant factor influencing their investment behavior but for different reasons. Clearly the investment preferences of foreign and domestic funds differ substantially.

The conventional view is that government intervention has a negative impact on firm performance. However, Cao et al. (2011) highlight the potential of political promotion providing incentives for managers in Chinese state-owned enterprises (SOEs) to maximize firm value, which has a positive impact on corporate performance. Our findings in relation to the behavior of foreign investors are consistent with this literature on political connections. On the other hand, Firth et al. (2010) find that the government exerts political pressure on domestic mutual funds to accept a compensation package to complete the split share structure reforms swiftly. Specifically, the negative and significant relationship between mutual fund ownership and the final compensation ratio indicates that mutual funds help SOE firms complete the reform at lower cost that actually damages their own returns. Research also indicates that foreign institutional investors tend to gain superior bargaining power in China, while local funds yield to political pressure from governments (Huang and Zhu, 2011). Inferior bargaining power coupled with adverse political pressure from governments, compared to foreign institutional investors, has the implication that domestic funds in China invest less in firms with a high percentage of state-owned shares. Finally, foreign institutional investors require approval by stock market authorities, for example CSRC and SAFE, under the QFIIs scheme, which further underlines the political influence.

We conclude that the drivers of foreign funds in emerging markets are not consistent with those in developed markets, for example, size, liabilities paying capability and profit (see Dahlquist and Robertsson, 2001; Kang and Stulz, 1997). Foreign investors in China place more emphasis on corporate governance characteristics. In particular, they have a preference for firms with a high percentage of state-owned shares as these are perceived to indicate more political connections. Consistently with the finding in Leuz et al. (2009), corporate governance is indeed an important factor influencing the investment decisions of foreign institutional investors. In contrast, however, domestic funds place greater emphasis on financial characteristics, for example, size and return on shareholders as well as corporate governance structures. Therefore, our research hypothesis, that corporate governance (financial characteristics) has a significant impact on the investment of foreign (domestic) institutional investors, is supported. We conclude that the investment preferences of foreign and domestic funds differ substantially.

5.4 Comparison with other emerging markets

In this section, we will briefly compare the institutional investors in China with those in other emerging markets. First, the positions and growth of institutional investors in other emerging countries will be outlined. Second, we will discuss the findings regarding QFIIs compared with the experience of other emerging markets.

5.4.1 Comparison with institutional investors in other emerging markets

According to a 2010 survey (International Organization of Securities Commissions, 2012) on institutional investors in 25 emerging economies, securities investment funds, securities companies, social security funds and insurance companies are present in nearly all 25 jurisdictions surveyed, although the proportions of institutional investors to the total market capitalization vary largely from 17 percent (in China) to 91 percent (in Malaysia) in these jurisdictions. Moreover, the structure of institutional investors in these economies could largely differ from each other. For instance, in Korea, institutional investors (excluding banks) hold 13 percent of the aggregate value of listed stocks (Song, 2012), which is similar to mainland China (15.6 percent, 'professional institutional investors') as discussed before. But, in stark contrast to the foreign investment in mainland China's capital market (1 percent), the foreign investment in the Korean stock market constituted 30 percent of the total market capitalization (Song, 2012). This is partly due to a regulatory difference: Korea abandoned the ceiling of foreign ownership of listed stocks and bonds as early as 1998, while mainland China still maintains a 20 percent limit (see Table 5.2).

Consistently with our findings from China, institutional investors have enjoyed a booming period in other emerging economies over, roughly, 2008 to 2010: the average annual growth of the total assets managed by securities investment funds, securities companies, and insurance companies in 25 jurisdictions is 25.4 percent, 29.5 percent and 21 percent from 2008 to 2010, respectively (International Organization of Securities Commissions, 2012). Despite the similar growth, the actual level of development again differs. As we discussed in Section 5.2.4, the assets of contractual funds (pension and insurance funds) in China only account for around 11 percent of its GDP in 2011, while the percentage over ten years ago for Thailand, Brazil, Korea, and Chile was already 10.7 percent, 17.4 percent, 31.0 percent, and 77.5 percent, respectively (Fratzscher, Kim, and del Valle, 2001). It is apparent that institutional investors have shown rapid growth in all emerging markets, but varied largely in the structure and level of their investment from one to another.

5.4.2 Comparison with foreign institutional investors in other emerging markets

There are a number of emerging markets that have permitted investments by foreign institutional investors. These markets were conservative in the initial phases and gradually relaxed the restrictions on the investment of foreign institutional investors. For example, to bring in foreign investment and related expertise, Taiwan first opened its securities market to foreign investment in 1982 (Lin and Chen, 2006). In the next twenty-one years, reform on foreign investment regulation took place in three phases (Lu, 2003), extending investors' portfolio from indirect investment with beneficiary certificates of funds, to direct investment of QFIIs (in 1991), and to that of General Foreign Individual Investors (GFIIs). Similar to what happened in Taiwan, a continuous relaxation in the regulation of QFIIs has been witnessed in mainland China since its inception: raising quotas, expanding investment products, and reducing criteria of eligibility. Mainland China will permit direct investment of foreign individuals in the securities market when the regulators think appropriate.

Furthermore, the development of foreign institutional investors in emerging markets is viewed in a positive light internationally as it is a clear indicator of market development. India opened its doors to foreign institutional investors in September 1992 as part of its initiative to liberalize its capital markets. Gordan and Gupta (2003) suggest that the portfolio flows to India have been less volatile when compared with many other emerging markets. The cumulative net foreign institutional investors' investment in India was approximately 17.4 trillion US dollars in August 2003, which was 9 percent of the market capitalization of Bombay stock exchange. Lin and Shiu (2003) report that, although small, trading by QFIIs is steadily growing. The QFII ownership rapidly increased from 2 percent in 1994 to 10 percent in 2000. Vo (2010) provides the introduction to institutional investors in Ho Chi Minh City Stock Exchange, Vietnam. One of the most prominent features in Vietnam stock markets is the dramatic growth in the level of foreign institutional investors' ownership. The average of ownership of foreign investors increased from 10.16 percent in 2007 to 17.46 percent in 2008 in the Vietnam stock market. Similar to other emerging markets, the number of QFIIs in China has increased from 10 at the beginning of the scheme in 2003 to 157 by the end of September 2012. Moreover, the total investment quota of QFIIs has grown from 425 million US dollars in 2003 to 30.8 billion US dollars by the end of September 2012.[14]

Finally, a number of empirical studies have investigated the preference of foreign institutional investors. Vo (2010) employs the data from Vietnam stock markets and finds that foreign institutional investors avoid firms with dominant shareholders, which is consistent with our findings in this chapter. McKinsey and Company (2002) have highlighted the importance of governance to the investment decisions in the global market. This study also stresses that corporate governance considerations dominate any other issues when it comes to investment decisions in East Asia. Each of these markets has its unique features, with its own local laws, regulations, and market practices. These characteristics lead to different behaviors and preferences of foreign institutional investors in these markets. In this chapter, the size of firms was found inadequate as an explanation on the investment of foreign institutional investors. However, Lin and Shiu (2003) conclude that foreign companies prefer large firms, and firms with high export ratio in the Taiwan stock market.

5.5 Conclusion

In this chapter, we have outlined the development of institutional investors in China's capital markets, including how regulations have been gradually established and reformed, and how investors prospered in such a short period of time—in the sense of size and importance to the market—partly due to deregulation, and partly due to vigorous development of the market. Then we turned to the two most important actors: QFIIs and funds. We followed the development of the QFII scheme, witnessed its remarkable growth, and also referred to the most recent scheme that allows RMB funds to enter China via Hong Kong. The development of funds in China can be identified in four phases, in the last one of which they rapidly became popular, yet experienced a downturn and remained declining since then. Other institutional investors such as securities companies, social security funds, insurance companies, and trust companies were also discussed, in terms of relevant regulations and growth in their investments. But if we compare the growth with their size, their investment in the stock market is very limited. Next, we discussed the challenges that obstruct further growth, from market risks to rigorous regulations, from external market reliance to internal management issues, and from public debate to out-dated regulation. These challenges need to be addressed, and comprehensive reforms have been announced by the CSRC.

We then turned to examine the preferences of QFII and domestic funds. We find that corporate governance characteristics such as ownership structure and concentration play a significantly strong role in determining foreign funds holdings, whereas some basic financial indicators such as size and profit of firms do not have a substantial impact, which is inconsistent with findings in developed markets. Our results indicate that for foreign institutional investors, corporate governance has a significant impact on the investment decisions, and the ownership structure of Chinese listed firms is found to be especially attractive to them. Our empirical findings will be of value to policy makers in China in particular, in gauging the important drivers of foreign institutional investors. Finally, given the increasing significance of foreign financing and the fact that access to foreign capital is uneven across firms, it is important for firms to fully understand the factors that influence investors' behavior. In particular, stocks with high foreign ownership outperform stocks with low foreign ownership (Huang and Shiu, 2006).

The development of institutional investors in China has been through a long and winding path since the 1990s. We hope this chapter provides not only an overall review but also a rigorous empirical analysis on the development of institutional investors in China, and contributes to a better understanding of the behavior of QFIIs and funds, and future policy making in this respect.

Acknowledgement

We thank Taylor & Francis for granting us permission to reprint 1 table and 3 pages from 'Domestic and foreign institutional investors' behavior in China', *European Journal of Finance* (Forthcoming).

Notes

1. Excluding Switzerland, Norway, Ireland, Germany, Finland and New Zealand. Data for 2010 was incomplete for Estonia and Italy; the authors used the data of the previous year.
2. In China, the social security system is comprised of the national and local social security funds (including pension funds). As at March 2012, local social security funds are not allowed to invest in the stock market.
3. In China's capital markets, total capitalization contains negotiable shares and non-negotiable (restricted negotiable) shares. Those negotiable shares in the stock market are so-called circulating shares. Non-negotiable shares are comprised of state-owned shares, state-owned legal person's shares, domestic legal person's shares, foreign legal person's shares, staff shares, preference shares, and others (China Securities Depository and Clearing Corporation, 2006, p. 107).
4. The B-shares market was established in 1992 to help to channel foreign investment into the Chinese market. The par value of the stocks is in RMB, but investors use US or HK dollars to buy the B-shares.
5. China's two domestic stock exchanges, the Shanghai Stock Exchange and the Shenzhen Stock Exchange, were established in December 1990 and July 1991, respectively.

6. On 27 December 2002, Chair Zhou was transferred to the People's Bank of China, and the then President of the Agricultural Bank of China Shang Fulin succeeded in his post (until October 2011, when he moved to the China Banking Regulatory Commission). The current Chair of the CSRC in 2012 is Guo Shuqing.
7. In Section 5.3, we select Securities Investment Funds as the representative of Chinese domestic institutional investors due to the relatively large size and long history (hereinafter domestic funds).
8. Dahlquist and Robertsson (2001) find there is a negative relationship between foreign institutional ownership and ownership concentration, implying that foreigners avoid companies with a dominant owner.
9. Consistently with a number of studies examining developed markets (Dahlquist and Robertsson, 2001; Aggarwal et al., 2005), our approach focuses primarily on contemporaneous relationships. Given the emerging nature of the market, the low level of foreign ownership and the limited channels of corporate participation, we would expect there to be no potential for endogeneity in our study.
10. Hausman (1978) designed a test to indicate the appropriateness of the FEM versus the REM and decide which is a better one. The null hypothesis states REM as the correct form while the alternative is FEM.
11. The percentage relative spread measures the over- and under-investment of funds by calculating the difference between the firms' allocated weight and the Chinese market weight for each firm.
12. Dahlquist and Robertsson (2001) compare the portfolio of foreign investors with the Swedish market portfolio. Kang and Stulz (1997) also adopt Japanese market portfolio as a benchmark to analyze the investment of foreign investors.
13. The opposite signs for ownership of state-owned shares and the Z index are not in conflict. The Z index equals the number of shares held by the largest circulating shareholder divided by the number of shares held by the second largest circulating shareholder. It stresses the control power of the largest shareholders. Even for the firm with a high percentage of state-owned shares as the largest shareholder, Z index will still be small as long as the number of shares held by the second largest shareholder is also large.
14. The source is the Investment Quota Approval Form of QFIIs issued by SAFE, 29 September 2012.

References

Aggarwal, R., Klapper, L., and Wysocki, P. 2005. Portfolio preferences of foreign institutional investors. *Journal of Banking and Finance*, XXIX: 2919–2946.

Bushee, B., Carter, M. E., and Gerakos, J. 2009. Institutional investor preferences for corporate governance mechanisms, *SSRN Working Paper Series*.

Cao, J., Lemmon, M., Pan, X., Qian, M., and Tian, G. 2011. Political promotion, CEO incentives, and the relationship between pay and performance, *SSRN Working Paper Series*.

Chen, Z. 2001. What is Hua'an innovative open-end fund? *China Economic Information*, XII: 52–4.

Covirg, V., Lau, S. T., and Ng, L. 2006. Do domestic and foreign fund managers have similar preferences for stock characteristics? A cross country analysis, *Journal of International Business Studies*, XXXVII: 407–429.

China InfoBank Database. 2012. http://www.infobank.cn/, date accessed 25 May 2012.

CSMAR Database. 2012. GTA Data, http://www.gtarsc.com, date accessed 25 May 2012.

'The CSRC Loosens the Restriction to QFII on Stock Investment Proportion' (2012) *Xinhua News*, http://news.xinhuanet.com/fortune/2012-05/15/c_123130305.htm, 15 May 2012, date accessed 25 May 2012.

CSRC. 2012a. *Statistics of January 2012*, http://www.csrc.gov.cn/pub/zjhpublic/G00306204/zqscyb/201203/t20120316_207256.htm, 16 March 2012, date accessed 25 May 2012.

CSRC. 2012b. *QFII Investment Quota to Be Increased by 50 Billion RMB*, http://www.csrc.gov.cn/pub/newsite/bgt/xwdd/201204/t20120403_208155.htm, 3 April 2012, date accessed 25 May 2012.

CSRC. 2012c. *2012 National Work Conference on Securities and Futures Regulators Convened, GuoShuqing Attended*, http://www.gov.cn/gzdt/2012-01/09/content_2040534.htm, 9 January 2012, date accessed 25 May 2012.

CSRC. 2012d. *Securities Market Monthly Report*, http://www.csrc.gov.cn/pub/newsite/sjtj/zqscyb/, date accessed 27 May 2012.

Dahlquist, M., and Robertsson, G. 2001. Direct foreign ownership, institutional investors, and firm characteristics. *Journal of Financial Economics*, LIX: 413–440.

Deng, L. 2007. Analysis on the potential impact of QFII scheme to the governance of China's listed companies. *Zhejiang Finance*, II: 41–2.

'Dialogue between People's Daily and GuoShuqing: Nine Questions about the Capital Market' (2012) *People's Daily*, http://finance.people.com.cn/stock/GB/17260486.html, 1 March 2012, date accessed 25 May 2012.

'Experts: RQFII Helps China-funded Securities Companies to Attract Customers' (2011), *Wenweipo*, http://trans.wenweipo.com/gb/paper.wenweipo.com/2011/12/15/FI1112150005.htm, 15 December 2011, date accessed 25 May 2012.

Firth, M., Lin, C., and Zou, H. 2010. Friend or foe? The role of state and mutual fund ownership in the split share structure reform in China. *Journal of Financial and Quantitative Analysis*, XLV: 685–706.

Frenkel, M., and Menkhoff, L. 2004. Are foreign institutional investors good for emerging markets?, *The World Economy*, XXVII: 1275–1293.

Fratzscher, O., Kim, Y., and del Valle, C. 2001. *Institutional Investors: Catalysts for China's Capital Markets*, http://siteresources.worldbank.org/extbanking/resources/china-instinv.pdf, date accessed 28 October 2012.

Galaxy Securities. 2012. *Industrial Report on Chinese Securities Investment Funds 2011*, China Galaxy Securities Company,http://download.cnfol.com/stock/2012/01/01.13/4.pdf, 6 January 2012, date accessed 25 May 2012.

Gao, C. 2011. Concerns over international board, *China Daily*, 9 May 2011.

Gordan, J., and Gupta, P. 2003. Portfolio flows into India: do domestic fundamentals matter?, *IMF Working Paper No. 03/20*.

Greene, W. H. 2002. *Econometric analysis*, 5th edn, Prentice Hall.

Hausman, J. A. 1978. Specification tests in econometrics. *Econometrica*, XLVI: 1251–1271.

Huang, R. D., and Shiu, C. 2006. Local effects of foreign ownership in an emerging financial market: evidence from qualified foreign institutional investors in Taiwan. *Financial Management*, XXXVIII: 567–602.

Huang, W., and Zhu, T. 2011. Foreign investment vs. state ownership: is there a political pressure? The illustrative case of qualified foreign institutional investors in China, *SSRN Working Paper Series*.

International Organization of Securities Commissions. 2012. *Development and Regulation of Institutional Investors in Emerging Markets*(FR04/12), June 2012.

Kaminsky, G. L., Lyons, R. K., and Schmukler, S. L. 2001. Mutual fund investment in emerging markets: an overview. *The World Bank Economic Review*, XV: 315–340.

Kang, J., and Stulz, R. M. 1997. Why is there a home bias? An analysis of foreign portfolio equity ownership in Japan. *Journal of Financial Economics*, XLVI: 3–28.

Leuz, C., Lins, K. V., and Warnock, F. E. 2009. Do foreigners invest less in poorly governed firms? *Review of Financial Studies*, XXII: 3245–3285.

Lin, A., and Chen, C. 2006. The impact of qualified foreign institutional investors on Taiwan's stock market. *Journal of Chinese Management Review*, IX: 1–27.

Lin, C. H. and Shiu, C.-Y. 2003. Foreign ownership in the Taiwan stock market: an empirical analysis. *Journal of Multinational Financial Management*, XIII: 19–41.

Lu, K. 2003. 'An overview of the Taiwanese qualified foreign institutional investor system. *China's Capital Account Liberalisation: International Perspectives* (BIS Papers No. 15), 141–51.

Luo, S. 2011. Analysis on the emergence and development of China's sunshine private equity. *China Market,* IX: 58–60.

McKinsey and Company. 2002. *Global Investor Opinion Survey on Corporate Governance*. McKinsey & Company, London, England.

Naughton, B. 2007. *The Chinese Economy Transitions and Growth*, The MIT Press, Cambridge, MA.

Ng, L. and Wu, F. 2007. The trading behavior of institutions and individuals in Chinese equity markets, *Journal of Banking and Finance*, XXXI: 2695–2710.

'Non-conventional Development: Institutional Investors Have Become the Dominant Force in the Securities Market'. 2009. *Shanghai Securities News,* http: //www.cnstock.com/paper_new/html/2009–09/25/content_71483209.htm, 25 September 2009, date accessed 25 May 2012.

OECD.Stat. 2012. Institutional Investors' Assets, date accessed 25 May 2012.

People's Bank of China. 2001. The Content and Time Frame of the Opening-up of China's Financial Industry after Joining WTO', http://www.pbc.gov.cn/publish/tiaofasi/273/1385/13854/13854_.html,01 December 2001, date accessed 25 May 2012.

'Pension Funds Entering the Stock Market Will Change the Structure of A-share Market in Long-term'. 2012. *Shanghai Securities News*, http://finance.people.com.cn/stock/GB/17703871.html, 20 April 2012, date accessed 25 May 2012.

'QFII Quota Expanded to 30 Billion US Dollars, the Market Embracing "Warm Wind" of Capital'. 2007. *Shanghai Securities News*, http://news.xinhuanet.com/fortune/2007–12/10/content_7224034.htm, 10 December 2007, date accessed 25 May 2012.

SAFE. 2012. *QFII Investment Quota Approval Situation Table*, http://www.safe.gov.cn/model_safe/glxx/glxx_detail.jsp?ID=120700000000000000, 9 March 2012, date accessed 25 May 2012.

China Securities Depository and Clearing Corporation. 2006. *China Securities and Settlement Statistical Yearbook*, http://www.chinaclear.cn/main/03/0305/1192763915494.pdf, date accessed 27 May 2012.

'Several Fund Management Companies Have Applied for Transborder ETF under RQFII Scheme'. 2012. *China Securities Journal*, http://finance.sina.com.cn/money/fund/20120413/013811813210.shtml, 13 April 2012, date accessed 25 May 2012.

'Shang Fulin: Firmly Develop and Strengthen the Cohort of Institutional Investors'. 2011. *Shanghai Securities News*, http://www.chinadaily.com.cn/dfpd/rs10nian/2011-09/23/content_13782174.htm, 23 September 2011, date accessed 25 May 2012.

Song, H.S. 2012. 'Enhancing institutional investors' role in the Korean stockmarket',http://www.kcmi.re.kr/eng/cmweekly/down1.asp?num=73&seq=1&filename=(2012-0410)weekly_Eng.pdf, date accessed 28 October 2012.

'State Council Approved 100 Billion Pension Funds of Guangdong Province to Be Operated by National Council for Social Security Fund'. 2012. *China Labour And Social Security News*, http://www.lm.gov.cn/SocialSecurity/content/2012-03/29/content_702285.htm, 29 March 2012, date accessed 25 May 2012.

State Council. 2004. *Some Opinions of the State Council on Promoting the Reform, Opening up and Steady Growth of Capital Market*, http://www.fdi.gov.cn/pub/FDI_EN/Laws/Securities/P020060620358568125911.pdf, 31 January 2004.

Su, C. 2011. 'Research on the development of money market fund in China. *South China Finance*, V: 67–70.

Vo, X. 2010. Foreign ownership in Vietnam stock markets – an empirical analysis, *MPRA, Working Paper.*

Wind Database. 2012. Wind Information, date accessed 25 May 2012.

Xu, H.W. 2012. '16 Years Ago China's Capital Market Embraced the First RMB Foreign Capital Stock, SVEC Sold out in Three Days after IPO' (in Chinese), *Youth Daily*, http://www.why.com.cn/epublish/other/node21750/userobject7ai161848.html, date accessed 25 May 2012.

'Zhou Xiaochuan: Opportunities and Obstacles of Emerging Markets'. 2002. *China Daily*, http://www.people.com.cn/GB/jinji/35/159/20020619/756585.html,19 June 2002, date accessed 25 May 2012.

'Zhou Xiaochuan's Speech on the Second International Conference on China's Securities Market'. 2002. *Xinhua News*, http://news.xinhuanet.com/zhengfu/2002-06/10/content_433346.htm, 10 June 2002, date accessed 25 May 2012.

Zhu, C., and Yan, J. 2001. A study on the linkage between China's insurance market and capital market (in Chinese). *Journal of Finance*, V: 103–10.

6
Impact of Foreign Bank Entry on the Performance of Chinese Banks

Yizhe Dong, Alessandra Guariglia, and Wenxuan Hou

6.1 Introduction

Since China joined the World Trade Organization (WTO) in 2001, the Chinese banking sector has entered a new era. In order to comply with its WTO commitments, the Chinese government has progressively removed regulatory obstacles and adopted numerous reforms to open up its banking sector to competition–both domestic and foreign. Regulation and supervision within the Chinese banking sector have also improved in order to meet international standards. Over the five-year period following entry into the WTO, the geographical coverage and business scope restrictions on foreign banks have gradually been removed. Since December 2006, all Chinese cities have allowed locally incorporated foreign banks to engage in both local and foreign currency business with all types of customers, and the Chinese banking sector has been fully opened up. The total assets of foreign banks reached 1.7 trillion RMB in 2010, with an average annual growth rate of 20.3 percent over the period from 2002 until 2010.

Previous empirical studies have found that the impact of foreign banks entering the local banking sector has been both positive in terms of improving the local banks' performance (Claessens et al., 2001), and negative in terms of destabilizing the local banking industry (Barajas et al., 2000). Foreign bank entry has brought technological advancements, better risk management, product innovation and international operations experience, which have helped local banks to improve their profitability and efficiency. On the other hand, foreign bank penetration can cause excessive competition for marginal customers, which could potentially lead to financial instability. There is a vast literature on the impact of foreign bank entry, including that by Claessens et al. (2001)

and Lensink and Hermes (2004) using cross-country analysis, Denizer (1999) on Turkey, Clarke et al. (1999) on Argentina, Hasan and Marton (2003) on Hungary, and Unite and Sullivan (2003) and Manlagñit (2011) on the Philippines. However, at present only limited research evidence exists in relation to the Chinese banking sector. This may be due to the limited availability of data, as the penetration of foreign banks only accelerated after 2003. It is important, therefore, to investigate the impact of foreign bank entry on the performance of Chinese banks as this will assist policy makers with their decisions and will also enable local bank management to prepare to meet the challenge created by foreign banks more effectively.

The main objective of this chapter is to provide new evidence to supplement the existing banking literature by investigating the impact of the presence of foreign banks on Chinese banks' profitability, efficiency and levels of risk. This study uses an unbalanced dataset that consists of 51 Chinese banks over the period from 2002 to 2010. The results provide strong evidence to suggest that foreign banks have an important role in facilitating the development of the local Chinese banking market. The increasing foreign banking presence has had the effect of boosting the profitability and improving the efficiency of the Chinese banking sector, while having no significant impact on the non-interest activities and risk levels incurred by the local market. This finding supports the open market policy and confirms the positive impact of foreign banks.

The remainder of this chapter is organized as follows: Section 2 provides background information about Chinese banking reforms and the presence of foreign banks. Section 3 briefly reviews some existing literature that has analyzed the impact of foreign bank entry. Section 4 discusses the model, variables and data employed in our empirical analysis. Section 5 discusses the empirical results. Section 6 presents our conclusions.

6.2 Chinese banking reform and foreign entry

6.2.1 Banking reform

Since the late 1970s, both before China joined the WTO and since then, the Chinese government has implemented a series of reforms and measures aimed at improving the efficiency of the Chinese banking system and encouraging Chinese banks to adhere to international standards. The four state-owned banks (the Big Four),[1] each of which initially had its own specific business focus, are now allowed to enter into a variety of commercial banking services, and the segmentation of these four banks has gradually diminished since 1985. In addition, the People's Bank of China (PBC) has relaxed the barriers to entry for new banks and, between 1985 and 1996, a number of new medium- and small-sized commercial banks entered the market. These banks are now known as joint-stock commercial banks (JSCBs) and operate nationwide with diversified ownership in direct competition with the Big Four. Two very significant laws—the Central Bank Law and the Commercial Bank Law—were enacted in 1995. This development further enhanced the legal status of the PBC and clarified the position of commercial banks whose primary purpose is to serve the market. Consequently, all Chinese banking legislation is now in accordance with the provisions of the Basel Committee on Banking Supervision (Chen et al., 2005).

In 2003, the Chinese government created the China Banking Regulatory Commission (CBRC) in order to increase the efficiency of the banking sector's regulatory and supervisory functions and leave the PBC free to focus on its responsibilities as a central bank. At the same time, the government initiated the 'pilot state-owned bank-overhaul programme', which aimed to accelerate the reform of the state-owned banks by injecting new capital, resolving problems related to under-performing loans and improving corporate governance. One particularly important strategy employed by the Chinese authorities for improving Chinese banks' corporate governance and management efficiency has involved encouraging Chinese banks to seek a listing on the stock exchange(s) through an initial public offering (IPO). By the end of 2011, 17 Chinese banks had launched IPOs on Chinese stock exchanges and/or the Hong Kong Stock Exchange. Moreover, realizing that Chinese banks would potentially face stiff competition when China's WTO commitments opened the Chinese banking sector to foreign banks, the CBRC promulgated new stringent capital adequacy rules based on the Basel I and (parts of the) Basel II Accords, to enhance risk management within the banking sector.

6.2.2 Foreign bank entry

In addition to the improvements to the internal banking sector, the reform process also involved the opening up of the market to foreign banks. Foreign banks were first allowed to open representative offices and branches in Special Economic Zones at the beginning of the 1980s. These geographical restrictions were then relaxed to include 23 cities in 1994. However, the banks' activities were strictly limited and their basic function was to provide foreign finance to support the operation of foreign enterprises within China. In 1999, the PBC further relaxed the geographical restrictions on foreign banks and allowed them to operate in all major Chinese cities. In addition, up to 2001, the PBC had granted approval to 32 foreign banks, allowing them to conduct RMB business in Shanghai, Shenzhen and their adjacent regions. Although the Chinese banking market became considerably more open in the 1990s, there were still many restrictions on foreign banks relating to consumers and business scope, and the development of foreign banks was substantially circumscribed by these restrictions.

A crucial milestone in the financial liberalization process was China's accession to the WTO in December 2001. In order to comply with its WTO commitments, the Chinese government progressively removed all geographical, business scope and customer restrictions in relation to foreign banking institutions, a process that was completed in 2006. The result is that the Chinese banking sector has now been completely opened up to foreign banks.[2] By the end of 2010, there were 37 locally incorporated foreign banks, 90 foreign bank branches, and 230 representative offices set up in China. Although most restrictions on foreign banks were removed after 2006, those wishing to open branches in China still have to overcome some obstacles, such as adopting local banking practices and adjusting to the local culture. As an important part of the banking reform process, the Chinese government has encouraged strategic investment by foreign banks in Chinese local banks. Under the regulations, the total ownership stake of all foreign investors in a local bank can be no more than 25 percent, while a single investor can own up to 20 percent. Strategic investment offers foreign banks the opportunity to expand into China without the risks and difficulties associated with establishing their own local affiliates. It also allows foreign financial institutions to form strategic partnerships and acquire an understanding of Chinese business culture and customers, which would not otherwise be possible. Since 1996, when foreign strategic investors were first permitted to invest in Chinese banks, foreign institutional investors have acquired a stake in 29 Chinese banks, with a total investment of 32.78 billion RMB by 2010. Therefore, the presence of foreign banks has been effectively boosted by the measures adopted after China's accession to the WTO.

6.3 Literature review

6.3.1 Impact of the presence of foreign banks

In general terms, the impacts of foreign banks on the domestic market come from competition and spillover effects, which suggests that the presence of foreign banks has forced rival banks to increase their efficiency. When banks (firms) possess competitive advantages, they are more likely to expand their business activities abroad in order to make extra profits. Therefore, it is normally assumed that multinational banks (firms) that are capable of expanding their business beyond their home country possess some competitive advantages (Hymer, 1960). Isik and Hassan (2002) show that foreign banks are more efficient than domestic banks due to their comparative advantages. Blomström and Kokko (1998) suggest that foreign participants not only serve to increase market competition, but also bring technological advancements and superior management skills, which in turn improve the core competitiveness of domestic banks (firms). Levine (1996) suggests that, due to the promotion and demonstration of more advanced banking services by foreign banks, domestic banks are inspired to improve the quality of their own services and become more efficient. Besides the direct impact on domestic banks, the presence of foreign banks also encourages the development of local accounting, auditing and other finance-related institutions. Pressure is exerted on the regulatory and supervisory systems of the local banking industry to become more rigorous in order to meet international standards. This is confirmed by Buch (1997), who investigated the impact of the presence of foreign banks on the Czech Republic, Estonia, Hungary and Poland. He suggests that opening the domestic market to foreign banks could prompt local regulatory bodies to make adjustments in order to comply with western standards and thus facilitate the reform of the banking system. Drakos (2003) also suggests that the presence of foreign banks contributes to a more efficient banking sector in a set of transitional countries.

Apart from these effects on their operations, foreign banks may also directly invest in domestic banks and become shareholders or strategic investors, which can result in significant impacts on local banks. Berger et al. (2009) suggest that (minority) foreign ownership could enhance the corporate governance and performance levels of Chinese domestic banks. Demirguc-Kunt and Huizinga (1999) suggest that, in developing countries, banks with foreign ownership are associated with higher profitability and interest margins. Grigorian and Manole (2002) also find that banks with foreign ownership are likely to be more efficient than their domestic counterparts. Fries and Taci (2005) show that, in 15 Eastern European transitional countries, private banks with substantial foreign ownership are more efficient than new domestic private banks and foreign private banks, while those private banks that have a majority domestic ownership are the least efficient. In addition, Bonin et al. (2005) find that, when they have a strategic foreign owner, banks are able to provide better services and have greater cost efficiency.

Although the presence of foreign banks may improve the efficiency and profitability of local banks, it may also have a negative impact on the domestic banking sector, for example by increasing risk levels and decreasing banking stability. Barajas et al. (2000) claim that, with the entry of foreign banks, the quality of loans and the profitability of domestic banks will deteriorate due to increased competition and/or high-quality customers switching from domestic to foreign banks. Unite and Sullivan (2003) also find that loan loss provisions increase with the presence of foreign banks. Claessens et al. (2001) suggest that the effects of foreign bank entry, in terms of increasing competition and lowering domestic banks' profits, may create a destabilizing effect on the financial system, especially when the regulatory and supervisory systems are not sufficiently mature. Grigorian and Manole (2002) explain this phenomenon by suggesting that foreign banks with high levels of capital are able to cherry-pick their customers. The best quality borrowers are selected by these foreign banks in order to improve the quality of their portfolios. The remaining borrowers, who are served by the domestic banks, are less favorable, which could increase the risks associated with offering them loans.

6.3.2 Evidence regarding foreign bank entry into China

Despite the vast literature on the impact of foreign bank entry, only a few studies have investigated the effects on the Chinese banking sector. This might be because the Chinese banking sector has only been opened to foreign banks or financial institutions, and only in a restricted way, during the past few decades. The penetration of foreign banks into China has accelerated in recent years, since China's entry into the WTO in 2001. Due to the limited data available, any analysis of the presence of foreign banks in China will be correspondingly limited. Nonetheless, some studies have been carried out. Shen et al. (2009) examine the impacts of foreign bank entry on the performance of 48 Chinese commercial banks, covering the period from 1997 to 2007. Their measures of a foreign banking presence are designed to assess both the country level and the bank level. The country level is measured by the ratio of the number of Chinese banks with foreign strategy investors (FSI) to the total number of Chinese banks. Meanwhile, their bank-level measure is the total number of FSIs owning a stake in the Chinese bank in question. Based on the country-level analysis, they find that the profitability of domestic banks, measured by return on assets, and the net interest income ratio and net interest margin all increase as the presence of foreign banks increases. This suggests that the positive influence on profitability may be due to banks taking FSI on board, as this could introduce new operational technology or facilitate co-operation. However, when they use the bank-level measure, the results show that the presence of foreign banks has a significant impact on both the profitability and the costs of the local banks. They argue that the difference in results for the two measures may be due to the fact that both profits and costs are increased and the effects are offset by each other. New operational practices introduced by foreign investors will require a larger capital investment, but they can also serve to increase revenues. Although the study is inspiring, the measures of foreign bank presence are not sufficiently comprehensive. The study only focuses on the influence of strategic foreign ownership and neglects the direct influence exerted by foreign banks in China. As the operation of foreign banks will cause direct competition, the impact of this on domestic banks might be different from the impact of foreign ownership, which represents an indirect means of entry and results in less direct competition.

Xu (2011) differs from Shen (2009) in constructing a foreign exposure index using the number of foreign bank branches located in the same city as the domestic bank to measure the domestic bank's degree of foreign exposure. The results show that the relationship between net interest margin and the presence of foreign banks is negative, while non-interest income and operational costs increase as a result of increased foreign bank penetration. Xu (2011) concludes that an increased foreign presence is associated with a more competitive and efficient domestic banking sector. Although the study uses a complex measure of foreign banking presence, the sample only covers the period from 1999 to 2006 and therefore it may not fully reflect the impact of foreign banks, because the restrictions on their entry to China and their operations in the country were only substantially removed after 2006. Therefore, this chapter endeavors to fill the gap and add new evidence to the literature by investigating the impact of the presence of foreign banks on the Chinese banking sector over the period from 2002 to 2010.

6.4 Empirical model, variables and data

6.4.1 The empirical model

The main aim of this chapter is to examine the impact of the presence of foreign banks on Chinese banking performance. Following Clasessens et al. (2001) and Unite and Sullivan (2003), our empirical model is constructed as follows:

$$P_{it} = \alpha + \beta_1 FBN_t + \beta_2 FBA_t + \gamma Z_{it} + \theta Macro_t + \varepsilon_{it}$$

where P_{it} represents various performance measures for bank i at time t; FBN_t and FBA_t are the indicators designed to measure the foreign presence; Z_{it} and $Macro_t$ are control variables, which capture the effects of bank-specific characteristics and macroeconomic factors on bank performance; ε_{it} is the error term and α, β, γ, and θ are estimated parameters.

6.4.2 Variables

We use five different bank performance indicators to capture different aspects of banks, which are as follows: net interest margin (NIM), return on assets (ROA), loan loss reserve ratio (LLR), non-interest income (NII), and efficiency ratio (ER). The foreign banking presence could influence the degree of competition within the local banking sector, which in turn could affect banks' profits in material terms (Blomstrom and Kokko, 1998; Xu, 2011). In order to capture this effect, we use NIM and ROA to measure the profitability of the banks. Levine (1996) suggests that the spillover effect from foreign investment not only increases competition but also improves the efficiency of the domestic banking system. Therefore, we include the ER, which is defined as the ratio of total costs to total income, as a proxy for bank efficiency. In addition, the infiltration of foreign banks is also likely to affect the risk levels among the local banking sector. Foreign banks with greater operational experience and higher quality customer service are able to cherry-pick higher profile customers (Grigorian and Manole, 2002). As higher quality customers are chosen and served by foreign banks, the remaining customers may be less favorable, and thus lending money to them may increase the risk levels incurred by domestic banks. Barajas et al. (2000) also argue that the quality of loans offered by local banks will be diminished as competition increases and/or as they lose higher quality customers to foreign banks. The loan loss reserve is designed to cover those loans on which borrowers are likely to default. When the loan loss reserve is increased, it indicates that the quality of loans has deteriorated and the risk levels incurred by a bank have increased, and vice versa. Thus, the LLR, which is defined as the ratio of the loan loss reserve to total earning assets, is used to measure the risk levels of the banks investigated in this study. The last performance indicator is the ratio of non-interest income to total assets, which captures a bank's non-interest-generating activities. Levine (1996) and Blomstrom and Kokko (1998) suggest that foreign direct investment is likely to bring new products, processes and technology to the domestic market and it is expected that non-interest-generating activities will increase as a result.

Following Lensink and Hermes (2004) and Manlagñit (2011), we use both the number of foreign banks (FBN) operating in China and the percentage of total foreign banking assets as a proportion of the total banking sector assets (FBA) to measure the presence of foreign banks. If foreign banks have an impact on the domestic banking industry, they should constitute a part of the market and should continuously increase their market share (Claessens et al., 2001). Thus, the share of total assets held by foreign banks in the Chinese banking sector is an appropriate measure of foreign bank penetration and also reflects whether foreign banks are actively competing with local banks. Moreover, the number of foreign banks operating in the Chinese banking sector provides an indicator of how many foreign rivals domestic banks have to compete with. The more foreign banks are operating, the greater will be the pressure on local banks to try to compete. Therefore, this measure is able to capture the impact of foreign banks in relation to increased competition.

In addition to the above variables, this study also incorporates several control variables that have the potential to influence a bank's performance. The first is the book value of equity over total assets (E/A), which is used to control for the risk of insolvency and the different risk preferences across banks. A further control variable is non-interest expenses (overhead expenses) over total assets (NIE/A), which is related to the efficiency levels of banks. The ratio of total loans to total assets (TL/A) is included in order to capture the size of interest-earning (core) activities. Funding is directly related to interest expenses and is also expected to influence the profitability of a bank. Other earning assets, including balances due from the central bank, inter-bank loans and other investments and securities, may suppress the net interest margin because they do not directly generate interest income (Xu, 2011). Thus, the variable of other earning assets over total assets (OEA/A) is also included in our model. The last control variable is market share (MS), which is used as a proxy for relative market power and is defined as the ratio of an individual bank's total assets to the total assets of all banks in a given year. The relative market power hypothesis asserts that banks with a large market share and well-differentiated products are able to exercise greater power within the market and earn supernormal profits (Berger, 1995; Shepherd, 1983).

Finally, we also include two macroeconomic control variables, GDP growth rate (GDP) and inflation rate (INF), in the model. The annual percentage growth rate of GDP is used to control for the general economic environment, which may have an influence on banks' profits and operations. When the general economic environment is favorable, banks' profits are usually boosted, and vice versa. The inflation rate is measured by the annual percentage change in the consumer price index and is expected to have a direct relationship with the nominal interest rate, which will influence the net interest margin and profits.

6.4.3 Data

Our sample is an unbalanced panel that includes 51 Chinese commercial banks over the period 2002–2010, and totals 300 observations. The sample comprises the 5 state-owned commercial banks (SOCBs), 12 national joint-stock commercial banks (JSCBs), 25 city commercial banks (CCBs) and 9 foreign banks. At the end of 2010, these 51 banks accounted for 82 percent of the total assets held by commercial banks in China. The data are mainly drawn from Bankscope, the Almanac of China's Finance and Banking Industry (ACFB, 2003–11) and CBRC annual reports (2004–10). The data on the macroeconomic control variables, the GDP growth rate and the inflation rate are extracted from the World Bank's Development Indicator database. Table 6.1 presents a summary of the definitions of the variables and the data sources, while Table 6.2 displays descriptive statistics of the variables for the period from 2002 to 2010.

6.5 Empirical results and discussion

The main aim of this study is to investigate the impact of the presence of foreign banks on the performance of the domestic banking sector in China. Five performance indicators are examined: net interest margin (NIM), return on assets (ROA), efficiency ratio (ER), non-interest income ratio (NII), and loan loss reserve ratio (LLR). Table 6.3 presents the regression results and identifies the relationships between the banking performance and the presence of foreign banks.

Table 6.1 Variable definitions and data sources

Variables	Definitions	Data sources
Dependent variables		
Net interest margin (NIM)	Net interest income over total earning assets	Bankscope
Return on assets (ROA)	Profit before tax over total assets	Bankscope
Loan loss reserve ratio (LLR)	Loan loss reserve over total earning assets	Bankscope
Efficiency ratio (ER)	Total costs over total income	Bankscope
Non-interest income (NII)	Non-interest income over total assets	Bankscope
Independent variables		
Foreign bank presence		
FBA	Total foreign bank assets over total banking sector assets	CBRC and ACFB
FBN	No. of foreign-funded banks (including locally incorporated foreign banks, foreign bank branches and representative offices)	CBRC and ACFB
Control variables		
Equity (E/A)	Book value of equity over total assets	Bankscope
Non-interest expenses (NIE/A)	Non-interest expenses over total assets	Bankscope
Loans ratio (TF/A)	Total loans over total assets	Bankscope
Other earning assets (OEA/A)	Other earning assets over total assets	Bankscope
Market share (MS)	A bank's total assets over total banking assets	Bankscope
GDP growth rate (GDP)	Annual percentage growth rate of GDP	World Bank
Inflation rate (INF)	Annual inflation rate	World Bank

6.5.1 Profitability analysis

Our empirical analysis shows that the presence of foreign banks has a positive and statistically significant effect on banks' net interest margin (NIM) and return on assets (ROA), which suggests that an increased foreign banking presence enhances the profitability of domestic banks. This positive impact could be attributed to the high-quality management skills and/or modern banking practices transferred from foreign banks to domestic banks, which in turn increase the profitability of the Chinese banking sector. This finding is consistent with that of Shen et al. (2009),

Table 6.2 Descriptive statistics of the variables

	Mean	Std. Dev.	Min.	Max.
NIM (%)	2.47	0.57	0.54	4.04
ROA (%)	1.05	0.52	−1.53	2.43
LLR (%)	1.39	1.49	14.4	0.07
ER (%)	44.3	15.9	14.55	135.5
NII (%)	0.44	0.16	0.05	1.7
FBA (%)	1.86	0.31	1.3	2.38
FBN	245	74.34	146	360
E/A (%)	5.33	3.48	−13.71	31.35
NIE/A (%)	1.06	0.33	0.098	0.33
TL/A (%)	58.38	10.91	30.45	78.5
OEA/A	23.64	15.12	3.4	46.5
MS (%)	1.9	3.931	0.08	17.37
GDP (%)	10.71	1.62	9.1	14.2
INF (%)	2.35	2.1	−0.8	5.9

Table 6.3 Empirical results

	NIM	ROA	ER	NII	LLR
FBN	0.001**	0.002***	−0.0002***	0.0002	−6.69
	(2.10)	(5.29)	(−2.89)	(0.92)	(−0.48)
FBA	0.893***	0.671***	−0.255***	0.141	−0.0003
	(3.61)	(3.21)	(−5.28)	(1.08)	(−0.04)
E/A	−0.002	−0.028***	0.012***	−0.012*	−0.002***
	(−0.21)	(−3.13)	(5.97)	(−1.85)	(−9.06)
TL/A	0.822	−0.928**	0.120	−0.704**	−0.002
	(1.64)	(−2.38)	(1.42)	(−2.47)	(−0.24)
NIE/A	0.586***	−0.051	0.259***	0.220***	0.003
	(4.69)	(−0.50)	(11.35)	(3.06)	(1.14)
OEA/A	−0.804**	0.842***	−0.047	0.435**	−0.018**
	(−2.02)	(2.57)	(−0.63)	(2.03)	(−2.08)
MS	0.025	0.019	−0.004*	−0.007	0.0008***
	(1.63)	(1.72)	(−1.77)	(−0.77)	(5.27)
GDP	−0.046	−0.052**	0.022***	−0.034**	0.0003
	(−1.57)	(−2.09)	(3.86)	(−2.21)	(0.44)
INF	0.484	−0.306	0.423	0.088	0.046
	(0.25)	(−0.19)	(1.12)	(0.09)	(0.82)
Constant	−0.178	0.352	0.349***	0.716**	0.027***
	(−0.36)	(0.91)	(4.16)	(2.51)	(3.35)
R^2	0.124	0.324	0.633	0.108	0.418
N	300	300	300	299	283

Notes: 1. Significance levels of 1 percent, 5 percent, and 10 percent indicated by ***, **, and *, respectively.
2.. Asymptotic standard errors in parentheses.

who also found profitability indicators to be positively correlated with the presence of foreign banks. The results differ from those of some other previous studies, however, such as those by Claessens et al. (2001) and Unite and Sullivan (2003), which suggest that there is a negative relationship between profitability and the presence of foreign banks. These differences in the findings may be due to varying levels of competition found in different countries. Lensink and Hermes (2004) point out that, in developing countries, the banking sector is normally less competitive and domestic banks are able to increase their profits in order to offset the increased costs of learning new banking practices from foreign banks. Therefore, the impact of foreign banks on profitability may also depend on the level of competition within the domestic banking sector. As China is still a developing country, its banking sector has huge potential to grow and expand further. Competition in the Chinese banking sector tends not to be very fierce and domestic banks still have the market power to control pricing and earn abnormal profits.

In addition, the extent of foreign bank penetration could influence the nature of its effects. Where there is a higher level of foreign bank penetration, the benefits gained from the adoption of modern practices from foreign banks will be negated by the competitive pressure exerted by foreign banks entering the banking sector. Conversely, where the level of foreign bank penetration is low, the efficiency gained by domestic banks via the foreign banks (either as a result of the latter demonstrating their services or actually introducing them to the domestic banks) will outweigh the competitive pressure caused by the presence of foreign banks. This is the case for the Chinese banking sector. The market share of foreign banks accounts for only around 2 percent over the sample period, indicating that the extent of foreign bank penetration is relatively limited. Thus, there is a positive relationship between the presence of foreign banks and both net profit margin and return on assets.

6.5.2 Efficiency analysis

In our analysis, we find that the presence of foreign banks is negatively related to the efficiency ratio, which indicates that foreign banks have improved the efficiency of the Chinese banking sector. This result is consistent with the findings of Claessens et al. (2001), Unite and Sullivan (2003) and Manlagñit (2011). It can be explained by the fact that, with the foreign banks, new banking practices and technology are brought into the local market. By adopting these modern methods, the domestic banks can increase their efficiency. Moreover, when foreign banks become strategic investors or form partnerships with local banks, the corporate governance of the local banks is likely to improve, resulting in even greater efficiency. It is worth noting that this finding regarding the improved efficiency of domestic banks also lends support to the profitability analysis presented earlier. As they are operating more efficiently, banks are able to generate more income using the same level of resources. In other words, the more efficient the banks are, the greater profitability they can achieve. Thus, the presence of foreign banks has improved both the profitability and the efficiency of the Chinese banking sector.

6.5.3 Analysis of non-interest-generating activities

Our results show a positive but insignificant relationship between the presence of foreign banks and other operating income. This indicates that the presence of foreign banks does not stimulate local banking, or force the local market, to develop or place a greater emphasis on non-lending activities such as consultancy, brokerage or credit card business. This finding does not correspond to our expectation that new products or services introduced by the foreign banks and/or increased competition will force local banks to develop other sources of income. A possible explanation for this could be that the Chinese banking sector is far from saturated. Although there has been increased penetration by foreign banks, the traditional interest-based lending business is still a fruitful source of income. Therefore, the motivation for increasing the proportion of non-lending business is likely to be relatively low.

6.5.4 Risk analysis

From Table 6.3, we can see that there is also no significant relationship between the presence of foreign banks and the loan loss reserve ratio. This indicates that the presence of foreign banks may not cause a deterioration in the quality of loans and increase the risk levels incurred by the Chinese banking sector. The findings do not support Barajas et al.'s (2000) argument that, as the presence of foreign banks increases, high-quality customers may switch to foreign banks, reducing the loan quality of local banks. This finding could again be due to the less competitive environment within the Chinese banking sector. The proportion of foreign banks in China is still relatively small and they have not yet established an extensive branch network. Moreover, the Chinese banking market is still expanding and is large enough to absorb new entrants. Therefore, the quality of loans offered by domestic banks will not significantly deteriorate if high-quality customers choose to switch to foreign banks.

6.5.5 Analysis of control variables

As well as analyzing the impact of foreign banks, we also investigate some control variables with the potential to influence a bank's performance. In terms of the effect on the net interest margin, we find that the coefficient associated with non-interest expenses is positive and significant. This indicates that spending more money on improving the quality of services, such as investing in staff training and upgrading equipment in order to attract more profitable customers, could increase profit margins. A negative relationship is found between other earning assets and the net interest margin, possibly because investment and securities do not directly generate interest income, which may therefore suppress the net interest margin. In terms of the effect on ROA, both the coefficients of the equity ratio and the total loan ratio are negative and significant. There may be several reasons for this finding. First, the cost of equity is typically more expensive than deposits, and therefore increasing equity may also significantly increase the total costs. Moreover, the high level of equity may constrain banks from engaging in risky business, which could decrease the returns. By contrast, banks with a higher level of non-interest earning assets are associated with a higher ROA, which indicates that non-interest-generating activities may produce higher business returns, boosting banks' profits.

The equity ratio, non-interest expense ratio and GDP growth rate all have a significantly positive effect on the efficiency ratio according to our results. This suggests that increasing the capital adequacy ratio and non-interest expenses may improve the efficiency of the Chinese banking sector and increase GDP growth, thereby creating a favorable economic environment, which in turn increases banking efficiency. Looking at the dependent variable of non-interest income, a significant negative relationship with the equity ratio is found, and this may be due to equity holders acting as monitors, thereby constraining banks to focus on traditional interest-lending activities, which in turn lowers their non-interest income. Similarly, a high level of interest-based lending activities (loans) could suppress non-lending activities and reduce the non-interest income. As expected, a significant positive relationship between non-earning assets and non-interest income is found. Finally, we find that there is a significant negative relationship between the loan loss reserve ratio and the equity ratio and non-interest earning assets. These results may imply that a higher equity ratio could reduce banks' risk levels and improve the quality of their loans. In addition, a bank engaging in non-lending activities could diversify the risk level of its interest-lending activities.

6.6 Conclusion

The main goal of this chapter was to add to the literature relating to the entry of foreign banks into the Chinese banking sector. Our study investigates the impact of the presence of foreign banks on the profitability, efficiency, risk levels and non-lending activities of the Chinese banking sector post-WTO entry, from 2002 until 2010. We find that the presence of foreign banks has increased the profitability of Chinese banks, and this may be attributed to domestic banks adopting the modern practices of foreign banks. We also find that foreign banks have had a positive impact on the efficiency of the Chinese banking sector. This indicates that Chinese banks have successfully acquired management skills and advanced technology from foreign banks. However, our findings show that the presence of foreign banks has had no significant impact on the risk levels and non-interest lending activities of domestic banks.

Overall, the presence of foreign banks is positively facilitating the development of the Chinese banking sector. Therefore, policy makers should keep the Chinese market open and continue to develop an effective platform to encourage more foreign banks to enter the market. The remaining geographical restrictions, as well as those on business scope, should be fully removed and foreign banks should be treated the same as domestic banks by the regulatory and supervisory authorities. In addition, the Chinese government should encourage domestic banks to form partnerships with foreign banks. Through co-operation, local banks will be able to learn superior practices from the foreign banks and, ultimately, this will help to speed up the development of the Chinese banking sector.

Finally, it is worth noting that the observed positive effects may have occurred mainly because foreign banks currently have a relatively small presence in the Chinese banking sector. As the penetration of foreign banks continues to increase, this positive influence may be outweighed by negative impacts, such as an increased level of risk for the local banking sector. Therefore, further research could explore what the optimal level of foreign bank penetration should be.

Notes

1. They are the Industrial & Commercial Bank of China (ICBC), the China Construction Bank (CCB), the Bank of China (BOC) and the Agricultural Bank of China (ABC).
2. Nevertheless, the CBRC requests that foreign banks must be locally incorporated as legal entities before they can conduct local currency business for Chinese citizens.

References

ACFB. 2003–2011. *Almanac of China's Finance and Banking*, China's Financial Publishing House, Beijing.

Barajas, A., Steiner, R. and Salazar, N. 2000. The impact of liberalization and foreign investment in Colombia's financial sector. *Journal of Development Economics*, 63: 157–196.

Berger, A.N. 1995. The profit-structure relationship in banking – tests of market-power and efficient-structure hypotheses. *Journal of Money, Credit and Banking*, 27: 404–431.

Berger, A.N., Hasan, I. and Zhou, M. 2009. Bank ownership and efficiency in China: what will happen in the world's largest nation? *Journal of Banking and Finance*, 33: 113–130.

Blomstrom, M. and Kokko, A. 1998. Multinational corporations and spillovers. *Journal of Economic Surveys*, 12: 247–277.

Bonin, J.P., Hasan, I. and Wachtel, P. 2005. Bank performance, efficiency and ownership in transition counties, *Journal of Banking and Finance*, 29: 31–53.

Buch, C.M. 1997. Opening up for foreign banks: how central and eastern Europe can benefit. *Economics of Transition*, 5: 339–366.

Chen, X., Skully, M. and Brown, K. 2005. Banking efficiency in China: application of DEA to pre- and post-deregulation eras: 1993–2000, *China Economic Review*, 16: 229–245.

China Banking Regulatory Commission (CBRC). 2004–2010. *CBRC Annual Report*, CBRC, Beijing.

Claessens, S. and Demirguc-Kunt, A. and Huizinga, H. 2001. How does foreign entry affect domestic banking markets? *Journal of Banking and Finance*, 25: 891–911.

Clarke, G.R.G., Cull, R., D'Amato, L. and Molonari, A. 1999. The effect of foreign entry on Argentina's domestic banking sector, Policy Research Working Paper 2158, The World Bank.

Demirguc-Kunt, A. and Huizinga, H. 1999. Determinants of commercial bank interest margins and profitability, some international evidence. *The World Bank Economic Review*, 13: 379–408.

Denizer, C. 1999. Foreign entry in Turkey's banking sector, Policy Research Working Paper 2462, The World Bank.

Drakos, K. 2003. Assessing the success of reform in transition banking 10 years later: an interest margins analysis, *Journal of Policy Modeling*, 25: 309–317.

Fries, S. and Taci, A. 2005. Cost efficiency of banks in transition: evidence from 289 banks in 15 post-communist countries, *Journal of Banking and Finance*, 29: 55–81.

Grigorian, D.A. and Manole, V. 2002. Determinants of commercial bank performance in transition: an application of data envelopment analysis, Policy Research Working Paper 2850, The World Bank.

Hasan, I. and Marton, K. 2003. Development and efficiency of the banking sector in a transitional economy: Hungarian experience. *Journal of Banking and Finance*, 27: 2249–2271.

Hymer, S. H. 1960. The international operation of national firms, a study of direct foreign investment, Doctoral dissertation, Massachusetts Institute of Technology.

Isik, I. and Hassan, M.K. 2002. Technical, scale and allocative efficiencies of Turkish banking industry. *Journal of Banking and Finance*, 26: 719–766.

Lensink, R. and Hermes, N. 2004. The short-term effects of foreign bank entry on domestic bank behavior: does economic development matter?. *Journal of Banking and Finance*, 28: 553–568.

Levine, R. 1996. Foreign banks, financial development, and economic growth. In: Barfield C.E. (ed.), *International Financial Markets: Harmonization Versus Competition*. The AEI Press, Washington, DC.

Manlagñit, M.C. 2011. The economic effects of foreign bank presence: evidence from the Philippines. *Journal of International Money and Finance*, 30: 1180–1194.

Shen, C.H., Lu, C.H. and Wu, M.W. 2009. Impact of foreign bank entry on the performance of Chinese banks. *China and World Economy*, 17: 102–121.

Shepherd, W.G. 1983. *Economies of Scale and Monopoly Profits in Industrial Organization, Antitrust, and Public Policy*, Kluwer Nijhoff, Boston.

Unite, A.A. and Sullivan, M.J. 2003. The effect of foreign entry and ownership structure on the Philippine domestic banking market. *Journal of Banking and Finance*, 27: 2323–2345.

Xu, Y. 2011. Towards a more accurate measure of foreign bank entry and its impact on domestic banking performance: the case of China. *Journal of Banking and Finance*, 35: 886–901.

7
Chinese Executive Compensation: Where Do We Stand?

Martin Conyon and Lerong He

7.1 Introduction[1]

In recent years, scholars have begun to devote significant attention to the systematic examination of Chinese corporate governance given China's tremendous economic growth and development of capital markets (Allen et al., 2005; Conyon and He, 2011; Hu et al., 2010; Peng et al., 2003, 2010). Executive pay is a significant corporate governance issue. The optimal design of compensation contracts helps resolve agency costs associated with the separation of firm ownership from its control. There are several important questions to address. Are Chinese executives paid in the same way as western executives, given China's limited experience with stock markets and governance reform? Are the drivers of executive pay, such as firm performance and size, as important in China as in the west? How does the Chinese state affect the provision of incentives in Chinese firms? These questions are, of course, located in the broader question of whether executive pay will globalize along American lines (Cheffins, 2003).

There are few concrete answers to these important questions as yet. This study synthesizes nascent research on Chinese executive compensation. In addition, it offers new and contemporary empirical evidence on the drivers of CEO pay in China. The existing empirical evidence has appeared only in the last few years (for example, Adithipyangkul et al., 2010; Chen et al., 2010; Conyon and He, 2011; Firth, et al., 2006, 2007; Kato and Long, 2006; Li, et al., 2007). In addition to providing new evidence on the determination of CEO pay, we also provide new evidence on the use of incentive pay such as stock options. This is a central governance issue that has been ignored in prior Chinese executive compensation literature (mainly due to lack of available data). Our study also provides preliminary evidence on some of the potential determinants of option and equity incentives in China.

The remainder of this chapter is organized as follows. Section 2 provides an overview of the Chinese institutional context. Section 3 provides a review of the extant studies on Chinese executive pay. Section 4 provides new results on the trend and determinants of executive pay and equity incentives in China. Section 5 compares executive compensation in China with executive pay in other nations. Section 6 offers some conclusions.

7.2 Institutional context

7.2.1 Capital market growth

Since the late 1970s, China's economy has gradually transformed from a centrally planned system to a more market-oriented one. A series of reforms have been implemented including increased autonomy for state-owned enterprises (SOEs), the opening up of the economy to foreign trade and investment, the development of domestic stock markets, and the rapid growth of the private sector. These have led to significant efficiency gains. Since 1978, China's gross domestic product (GDP) has increased more than tenfold, with an average GDP growth rate of 9.3 percent over 1992 to 2012. In 2010, China's GDP was valued at 5.87 trillion USD, and became the world's second largest economy after the US. The global economic axis is tilting towards China, driven by its scale, scope and manufacturing prowess.

China's equity markets have grown significantly since its start in the early 1990s. There are currently two domestic exchanges in China: the Shanghai and the Shenzhen Stock Exchanges. In 1992 there were only 53 firms listed on the stock exchanges. By 2000, there were 1088 listed firms and the number reached 1718 by 2009. The significance of capital market reforms is reflected in the fact that the combined market capitalization of the Shanghai and Shenzhen Stock Exchanges accounted for 73 percent of China's GDP in 2009, as compared to about 45 percent in 2001 and 18 percent in 2005.

7.2.2 Executive compensation

Historically, Chinese executives have received only cash salaries, bonuses and stipends. Equity compensation in the form of stock options is rare, and has been permissible only since 2005. In addition, Chinese executives receive perks from their companies, but the value of these is frequently difficult to value (Adithipyangkul et al., 2010). Moreover, executives may own shares in their own firms. Conyon and He (2012b) for example document that CEOs own shares at only about 30 percent of publicly traded firms.

Disclosure and regulation of executive pay information is weaker in China compared to the United States and several other western economies such as the United Kingdom. However, the situation is improving over time as capital market reforms deepen and China's economy transitions to secure the benefits of the free-market model. The China Securities Regulatory Commission (CSRC) regulates the disclosure of executive compensation information in publicly traded firms. Early regulation (pre-2001) did not require public firms to disclose information about executive pay in their annual reports (CSRC, 1998). Some firms did on a voluntary basis. From 2001 the CSRC required all public firms to report the aggregated sum of total compensation for the three highest-paid executives. Firms also had to report total pay of the three highest-paid board members (including executive board members). The mix of salary, bonus and other remuneration was not divulged. Also, compensation disclosure was not required for individual executives separately before 2005 (CSRC, 2000, 2002, 2005). The extant Chinese executive pay studies typically use the aggregated cash compensation data from these periods (Conyon and He, 2011; Ding et al., 2010; Firth et al., 2006, 2007, 2010; Kato and Long, 2006; Li, et al., 2007). From 2005 onwards publicly traded firms were required to report each individual board member's and top management's total compensation as the sum of salary, bonus, stipends, and other benefits (CSRC, 2006). Overall, the direction of recent regulatory history suggests more information disclosures about executive pay.

7.2.3 Corporate ownership

China has a highly distinctive pattern of corporate ownership, which has important implications for the configuration of executive pay. Two central features of public firm ownership stand out. First, the Chinese state is a major shareowner in many public firms, with stakes exceeding 40 to 50 percent. Second, the ownership of shares is highly concentrated. Both of these facts contrast markedly to standard diffuse patterns of ownership in Anglo-Saxon economies. In Anglo-Saxon economies the norm is that owners are many, widely dispersed and each own a small fraction of the firm's common equity. This gives rise to the classic separation of ownership and control – and, of course, the moral hazards associated with the agency problem.

Historically, there are three major classes of share ownership in China. First, the Chinese state owns shares, held through such government agencies as the State-owned Assets Supervision and Administration Commission (SASAC). Second, legal entities can own shares, held through state-controlled legal persons, or privately controlled legal persons. Finally, individuals, institutions, and private businesses can own shares. When a state-owned enterprise is listed, only a small proportion of equity is sold to private investors in the initial public offering (IPO) process. The state and parent SOEs still retain sufficient shares in the form of state shares or legal person shares to retain voting control, which typically accounts for two thirds of total shares outstanding. State shares and legal person shares are generally non-tradable (Conyon and He, 2012a).

In January 2004, the State Council issued 'The Guidelines on Promoting Reform, Opening-up, and Steady Development of Capital Markets', which officially launched the stock reform in listed firms to covert non-tradable state-owned and legal person shares to tradable shares. The next salient change occurred in 2005, when the CSRC, SASAC and Ministry of Finance (MOF) jointly promulgated the 'Guidelines for Reforms of Segmented Shares of Listed Companies' (Guidelines), which further specify basic frameworks and key principles, as well as deadlines (set as the end of 2006) of stock structure reforms in listed firms. In this process, owners of tradable shares were allowed to negotiate with owners of non-tradable shares for compensation to offset the dilution effects on tradable shares (Yeh et al., 2009). By the end of 2006, the announced deadline, the restructuring process was basically complete, with the vast majority of listed companies eliminating their non-tradable shares and making their entire equity holdings tradable (Bernardo and Beltratti, 2007).

7.2.4 Executive equity incentives

The introduction of equity incentives is a very recent phenomenon in China. The earliest regulation could be traced back to 2002, when the MOF and Ministry of Science and Technology (MST) jointly promulgated several regulations regarding the grating of stock options in state-owned high-tech companies. These regulations are typically viewed as the first to allow stock-based incentives in SOEs. In the abovementioned Guidelines, listed firms that have completed the stock restructuring reform are allowed to adopt stock-based incentives for their management.

The most salient advancement appeared when the CSRC issued 'The Trial Measures for the Administration of Equity Incentive Schemes of Listed Companies' (Measure) effective on 1 January 2006. This regulation provides detailed requirements regarding equity grants to employees, disclosure standards, pricing methods, and other procedures for the implementation of stock-based incentive plans in listed firms that have successfully completed their restructuring reform. Under this Measure, employees of a listed company, including its senior management, are allowed to receive equity-based incentives from the firm. However, members on the supervisory board and outside independent directors of the board are ineligible. In addition, the Measure also specifies caps related to the percentage of shares eligible for incentive grants. Specifically, the number of shares allocated to an incentive plan may not exceed 10 percent of the company's total shares outstanding. In addition, no more than 1 percent of the company's total shares outstanding may be issued to a single individual, except those approved by shareholders' meeting.

7.2.5 Tax and accounting issues associated with equity payments

The tax and accounting treatment of stock options and other equity payments in China appears somewhat similar to that in western economies. Tax seems to be due at the point of equity sale. Income tax rates in China are progressive. The highest income tax rate is currently 45 percent for *monthly* incomes that are greater than 80,000RMB.[2] The State Administration of Tax has issued Circular 461 to provide guidance to previous Circulars 5 and 35 concerning the individual income tax treatment for employment-related Stock Appreciation Rights (SARs), and Restricted Stock (RS). Expert opinion[3] seems to suggest the following arrangements: income derived from SARs and RS should be taxed as wage/salary according to the calculation method set out in Circular 35. Taxable income for SARs (Circular 461) means that taxable income = (stock price on date of exercise – stock price on date of grant) × number of shares. For restricted stock, taxable income = {[stock price on registration date + stock price on date stock is free to sell) ÷ 2] × number of shares to sell – actual amount paid by RS qualifying person} × number of shares free to sell ÷ total number of RS stock shares authorized.

In terms of information disclosure for firms granting stock options and other equity incentives, 'The Trial Measures for the Administration of Equity Incentive Schemes of Listed Companies' specified that listed firms should disclose the issuance of incentive schemes in a timely manner, including information on the equity incentive plan, equity incentive management measures, the selected option pricing model, and explanations related to the estimation of the fair market value of stock options as well as the prospective earning of the restricted stocks. The accounting treatment of equity incentive plans is later regulated in the 'Accounting Standards for Enterprise, No. 11-Share-based payments' issued by the MOF in February 2006. Since 2007, all listed firms were required to comply with the International Financial Reporting Standards (IFRS).

7.2.6 The board of directors

China operates a two-tier board system consisting of a main board of directors and a supervisory board. Traditionally, the state and other controlling shareholders have huge influence on the appointment of board and supervisory board members. An enduring concern is that state-appointed bureaucrats are ineffective in monitoring management (Hu et al, 2010; Fan et al., 2007). In response to shareholder pressure, China's listed firms have increasingly adopted Anglo-Saxon style internal corporate governance structures (Allen, et al., 2005; Chen et al., 2010). For example, CSRC issued 'Guides to the Establishment of Independent Directors' System' in August 2001, which mandated that at least one third of board members in listed firms should be independent directors. Later, in January 2002, CSRC and the State Economic and Trade Commission (SETC) jointly issued the 'Code of Corporate Governance for Listed Companies in China' (Code) to outline core principles and standards of corporate governance for listed companies in China. This Code provides a series of guiding principles on the proper conduct of the board of directors; on the relationship between the listed company and its controlling shareholders; on the usage of incentive programs by listed companies; and on the requirement of independent directors.

Overall, these new regulations and disclosure rules are implemented to enhance accountability and to regulate the behavior of top management and the board of directors. It is believed that increased quality in internal control and governance standards would provide investors with confidence and ultimately enhance overall quality and reputation of the Chinese capital market, especially in an economy which has had concerns relating to the enforcement of property rights and shareholder protection (Hu et al., 2010; Peng et al., 2003, 2010).

7.3 Chinese executive compensation studies

This section reviews some recent salient studies investigating executive compensation in China. In contrast to the enormous number of studies using US data, there have been relatively few studies investigating the determinants of Chinese executive pay. Studies have looked at two fundamental issues. First, what is the link, if any, between executive pay and firm performance? Second, what is the role of the Chinese state? The first of these questions deals with the economic determinants of executive pay – especially the incentives provided to CEOs to promote firm performance. The second deals with institutions and corporate governance. The emerging evidence suggests that executive pay is, in fact, positively correlated to firm performance. However, there are often caveats that researchers document. In addition it is found that the state plays an important part in the determination of executive pay. In particular, it is frequently found that executive pay is lower in firms that are controlled by the state. However, there does seem to be an increasing interest in executive pay in China (Conyon and He, 2011; Firth et al. 2006; Kato and Long, 2006; Rampling et al., 2011).

Because stock markets are at an earlier stage of evolution in China compared to the United States and some western economies, early studies on executive compensation in China (such as Bai and Xu, 2005; Groves et al., 1995; Mengistae and Xu, 2004) relied on survey data collected from SOEs in the 1980s – a period when stock markets simply did not exist. With the development of capital markets and strengthening of disclosure rules in executive compensation, researchers began to investigate executive compensation in publicly traded firms listed on the Chinese domestic exchanges. However, due to the much weaker disclosure and regulation of CEO pay explained above, the extant Chinese executive pay studies typically use the aggregated cash compensation data for the top three executives and measure top management compensation as the sum of salary, bonus, and stipends (Conyon and He, 2011; Ding et al., 2010; Firth et al., 2006, 2007, 2010; Kato and Long, 2006; Li, et al., 2007). The majority of studies concentrate on (and use data from) the period between 1999 and 2006.

Most of the research on executive compensation in Chinese firms follows the Anglo-American research agenda by grounding research questions in the agency model. Executive and CEO contracts are designed to reduce 'agency' conflicts (Jensen and Meckling, 1976; Jensen and Murphy, 1990) arising from the divergent interests of senior executives (agents) and shareholders (principals) within the firm. Namely, left to their own devices an executive might opportunistically pursue his own interests at the expense of the firm's owners.

Motivated by agency theory, most prior executive compensation research using China's data evaluates the strength of the relationship between firm size and executive pay and then compares this to the correlation between firm performance and compensation. A clear pattern has emerged. There appears to be a robust firm size effect on top executive compensation, consistent with studies in the US context. Studies also find some evidence of pay for performance. The results are not consistent across all studies, however. Some researchers find that accounting measures such as ROA are utilized along with stock returns in executive compensation contract (Buck et al., 2008; Conyon and He, 2011). Other researchers, instead, find that accounting performance measures are utilized instead of stock returns (Firth et al., 2006, 2007; Li et al., 2007; Wang and Xiao, 2011); others note that accounting measures are likewise utilized when rewarding top executives with perquisites but not in the case of stock market measures (Adithipyangkul et al., 2010); and still others find that stock returns are utilized but not accounting measures when related to changes in compensation (Kato and Long, 2006).

Other economic determinants of executive pay are also investigated. In their study, Mengistae and Xu (2004) found that the CEO pay-for-performance link decreased with the variance of performance. A similar result is also documented by Conyon and He (2011) who found a negative impact of firm risk (measured by stock volatility) on both total pay and equity incentives. This result is consistent with the agency theory prediction of an inverse relation between incentives and risk aversion. Mengistae and Xu (2004) also found that the executive pay-for-performance sensitivity increased with the marginal productivity of executive action, which in turn has increased significantly in China's state enterprises following a series of state initiated reforms. Again, this is consistent with the agency theory's incentive principle. Finally, Mengistae and Xu (2004) found little empirical evidence that CEO pay was correlated to relative performance.

In addition, ownership type (mainly the role of the State) and the concentration of corporate ownership have been found to be important in the determination of executive pay. First of all, much of the literature is understandably focused on SOEs, historically the dominant form of business enterprise in China. Chinese SOEs are found to pay less than private firms (Chen et al., 2011; Conyon and He, 2011; Firth et al, 2006, 2007; Lin et al., 2009), and to possess weaker pay-performance linkage than private firms (Conyon and He, 2011; Firth et al., 2007; Kato and Long, 2006). It is also found that firms with dominant SOE shareholders (in contrast to private block-holders or foreign shareholders) are more likely to link executive compensation to accounting profits rather than stock returns (Firth et al, 2006, 2007).

In addition, the extant literature also find that the presence of foreign ownership increases pay level (Chen et al., 2010; Chen et al., 2011; Li et al., 2007) and pay-performance sensitivity (Ding et al., 2010; Firth et al., 2006, 2007). There is also evidence suggesting that higher ownership concentration is associated with lower pay and lower equity incentives (Conyon and He, 2011).

For example, an important study by Kato and Long (2006) examined the link between executive pay and firm performance, together with the role of the state, using a sample of listed firms between 1998 and 2002. Kato and Long (2006, p. 947) find 'statistically significant sensitivities and elasticity of annual cash compensation (salary and bonus) for top executives with respect to share- holder value in China's listed firms. The size of the estimated sensitivities implies that an RMB 1,000 increase in shareholder value yields an RMB 0.045 increase in annual cash compensation, whereas the size of the estimated elasticity suggests that a 10 percent increase in shareholder value results in 1.7 percent increase in annual cash compensation for top executives.' Second, they find that 'the relationship between firm performance and executive compensation is weaker for firms with a higher percentage of government ownership, suggesting that the interests of top executives in firms that are less state-controlled are more in line with those of the shareholders.' In short, economic performance is important in driving CEO pay, but so is the role of institutions such as the Chinese State.

Kato and Long (2006) raise a number of significant issues that remain important, and have implications for subsequent studies of executive compensation using Chinese data. One of the most significant issues, we believe, is that the relative lack of disclosure of all the elements of compensation for each separate executive might lead to false inference when estimating executive compensation models. This is especially the case for managerial perks. Kato and Long assert (2006, p. 960) that: 'According to popular belief in China, the importance of corporate perquisites is another distinctive feature of executive compensation in China. Although anecdotes abound that suggest that perquisites are an important component of total compensation for Chinese executives, there is no empirical evidence on the relative size of these perquisites.' The authors then try to estimate the degree to which perks are important and consequently by how much CEO pay is incorrectly measured. They provide estimates for vehicle usage and housing subsidies. In the context of vehicles, they figure out how much it costs to lease a car that would typically be used by an executive. In the context of houses, they figured out how much it would cost to rent an executive house by interviewing various real estate experts and estimating the subsidy. Perhaps surprisingly, they find that perks account for only somewhere between 15 percent and 32 percent of total pay. They conclude: 'These numbers give a range of the size of executive perks in China, with the lower bound at RMB 17,000, or 15 percent of the total annual compensation for Chinese executives (cash compensation plus perquisites) and the upper bound at 48,000, or 32 percent of total annual compensation.' And 'In short, in China's listed firms cash compensation (salary and bonus) appears to remain the most dominant form of executive compensation'. At the time of their investigation (1998–2002), these authors noted that stock options and restricted stock were not an important part of the executive compensation package, and therefore could be legitimately ignored. However, as we show below, stock options might be becoming a more important feature of the executive pay landscape in China since 2006.

The extant literature also examines the impact of corporate governance structure on executive compensation level and pay-for-performance sensitivity. Unlike studies in western context, which typically find that more effective corporate governance mechanisms help curtail the level of executive pay and strengthen pay-for-performance relationships, evidence in China is mixed and limited. With respect to the pay level, Chen et al. (2010) and Conyon and He (2011) both find that the presence of a compensation committee is associated with a higher level of executive compensation. Similar positive relationships are documented in firms with a higher proportion of independent directors in works by Li et al. (2007), Chen et al. (2011) and Conyon and He (2011). In addition, larger board size, large supervisory board size and leadership duality are all found to be associated with higher levels of executive pay (Chen et al., 2010; Chen et al., 2011; Conyon and He, 2011; Ding et al. 2010).

As far as pay-for-performance incentives, Kato and Long (2006) found that independent directorship and lack of leadership duality do not strengthen the pay-performance linkage using an earlier sample. In contrast, Firth et al. (2007), Conyon and He (2011) documented that a greater percentage of independent directors is correlated with higher pay-performance elasticity, particularly in the case of accounting performance. In addition, leadership duality and supervisory board meeting frequency are also found to affect pay-performance relationships (Ding et al., 2010; Firth et al., 2007). No significant impacts are documented for other board and governance variables.

Overall, the empirical evidence has focused on the link between Chinese executive compensation and firm performance. However, our view is that the available evidence is far from conclusive and the concrete drivers of executive compensation have yet to be established fully.

7.4 Chinese executive pay: further evidence

This section presents further evidence on Chinese executive pay, focusing on three salient issues. First, we present some evidence on the trends in CEO compensation in China's publicly traded firms since the year 2000. Second, we provide evidence on the link between CEO compensation and firm performance. Third, we present new evidence on the use of equity incentives in China's executive compensation contracts.

7.4.1 Data

We use executive compensation, corporate governance and financial data supplied by the GTA. This data source has been used in our recent study of CEO compensation, firm performance, and corporate governance in China (Conyon and He, 2012b). The data source has also been used to examine the tournament model of executive pay in China (Chen et al., 2011). The main advantage of GTA data over some other Chinese data sources (such as SINOFIN) used in most previous studies (for example, Chen et al., 2010; Conyon and He, 2011; Firth et al., 2006, 2007; Kato and Long 2006) is that it provides individual executive's compensation and demographic information as well as up-to-date equity incentives data. Our final database consists of 2177 unique publicly traded firms on the two domestic Chinese exchanges between 2001 and 2010 with a total observation of 14,506 firm years. These firms account for almost all listed firms in China. The near universal coverage of firms helps mitigate any sample selection biases arising from choosing, say, only the largest firms.

Executive compensation is disclosed and measured as the sum of basic salary, bonus, and stipends. We use two measures of executive compensation. First, we report results based on the average of the top three highest-paid executives' compensation, to be consistent with the majority of the prior literature studying Chinese executive compensation. Second, we report results based on individual CEO's compensation, to reduce measurement errors and provide a better picture of CEO compensation. It should be noticed that the title 'Chief Executive Officer' or 'CEO' is not commonly used in China. In this study, we identify the CEO position by the title 'General Manager' or 'President'.[4]

7.4.2 Trends in Chinese executive compensation

7.1.1 Median top executive compensation (RMB)

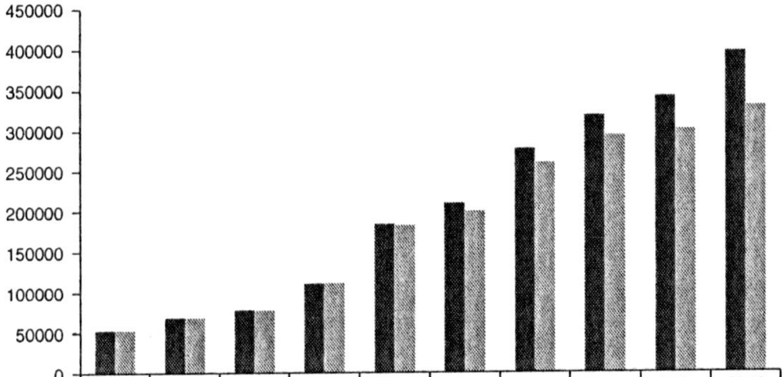

	2001	2002	2003	2004	2005	2006	2007	2008	2009	2010
■ Norminal Comp.	52900	68632	77800	111000	184150	210000	277300	318350	341400	396500
▒ Real Comp.	52900	68457	77244	111057	182137	199937	259291	293380	300343	329384

7.1.2 Median top executive compensation (RMB)

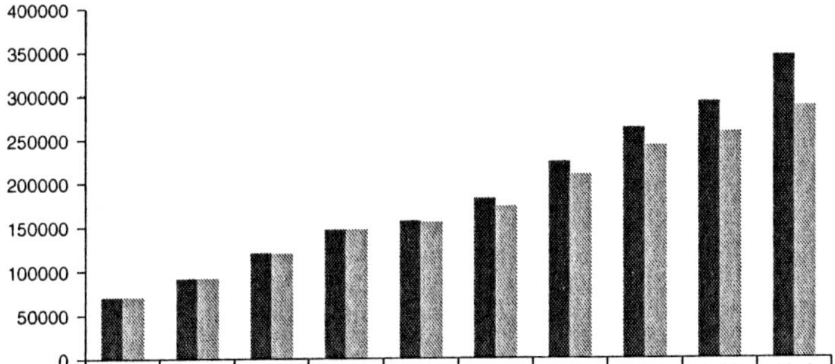

	2001	2002	2003	2004	2005	2006	2007	2008	2009	2010
■ Norminal Comp.	70333	91824	120600	146686	156666	181966	223816	262333	292066	345066
▒ Real Comp.	70333	91590	119739	146761	154954	173247	209280	241756	256942	286656

Figure 7.1 Trends of Chinese top executive compensation

Figures 7.1.1 and 7.1.2 report average Chinese compensation between 2001 and 2010, calculated as the median compensation of all sample firms in a given year. Figure 7.1.1 applies the aggregate data that measure top executive compensation as the average of the three highest-paid executives' annual compensation. Figure 7.1.2 reflects individual compensation of the CEO. It should be noted that individual compensation information is limited for years before 2005 because of a more primitive disclosure requirement explained above. Therefore, only a limited number of firms chose to report individual executive's compensation. As a result, the average numbers in the pre-2005 period may not be representative of all listed firms, and should be viewed with caution.

We also plot Chinese executives' and CEOs' real wage in Figures 7.1.1 and 7.1.2 respectively to prevent the impact of inflation on executive pay. The real compensation is calculated by discounting compensation data using the consumer price inflation (CPI) index reported by National Bureau of Statistics of China. All years are discounted to 2001 level.

Figures 7.1.1 and 7.1.2 indicate that top management compensation increased significantly between 2001 and 2010. Figure 7.1.1 shows that an average executive only earned 70,333 RMB (roughly 10,000 USD) in the year 2001. The nominal compensation is five times higher and reaches 345,066 (roughly 50,000 USD) in 2010. Even after the inflation factor is considered, an average executive's compensation still increases four times to 286,656 RMB (roughly 40,000 USD) in 2011. Figure 7.1.2 reflects a similar trend. An average CEO earned about 52,900 RMB in 2001, and the nominal compensation increased to 396,500 RMB in 2010, with a real compensation level of 329,384 RMB.

An interesting observation is that the reported average CEO compensation is lower than the reported average executive compensation in years with voluntary disclosure of individual executive's compensation (2001–4), while it is higher in years with mandatory disclosure of individual compensation (2005 and after). This suggests that firms with lower executive compensation tended to voluntarily disclose their individual executives' compensation information in the early years.

7.4.3 CEO and employee pay

Another element of executive compensation is the issue of pay equality between the CEO and other non-CEO employees. For example, the media in the US has often argued that CEO compensation is 'excessive' compared with that of an average worker. Indeed, the issue of who receives the product of growth is a much-debated issue. In the US, the most recent report by the Institute for Policy Studies suggests that the ratio between compensation of an average worker and an average CEO was as high as 325-to-1 in 2010 (calculated with S&P500 data), a sharp increase from 263-to-1 in 2009, and 42-to-1 in 1980.[5] Another critique in the US lies in the misalignment between CEO pay increases, average workers' pay increases, and economic performance. For example, the same report indicated that in 2010, the average S&P500 CEO's compensation increased by 27.8 percent over its 2009 level, while an average worker's pay only increased by 3.3 percent over the year before, and the GDP growth rate was roughly 3 percent. As economies grow, and incomes diverge, the distribution of income becomes a very salient issue. We do not expect the situation to be different for China in the future.

We believe that it is difficult to figure out precisely what 'excessive' is. Namely, when trying to understand 'excess' compensation it is important to know what the theoretically right level of pay is. If we knew this, then we could say with a fair degree of accuracy whether executive compensation was excessive or not. We would simply compare it to our benchmark case. The problem, of course, is that it is difficult to get consensus on what the optimal level of pay is – or should be. For example, it is probably always the case that the CEO earns more than the typical employee. However, what is a reasonable multiple? Is twice as much too low? Is 10 times about right? Is 100 times 'excessive'? Or is it 75 times? Often, the answer to this question might depend on personal taste, preferences, or ethical stance. In this sense the answer is somewhat arbitrary. What seems important to us, however, is that the CEO compensation contract provides appropriate incentives to create value. Once wealth is created, then the second question is how it is distributed in society. If it is not created then no one gains. In general, we think that it is important that a CEO's pay should be related to his or her marginal productivity. It is important to note that some economic theories give rise to predictions about the distribution of pay (such as superstar or tournament theories). For example, tournament theories of executive compensation argue that the gap in a person's pay at the current organizational level and the one preceding should increase as the person advances through the organization. Indeed, tournament models argue that optimal compensation should be convex in the organizational hierarchical levels to create option like incentives.

What does CEO pay look like compared to that of the typical worker in China? To examine the issue of compensation growth and pay equality in China, we plot the growth rate of executive compensation in this period with GDP growth rate, as well as the growth rate of average compensation of urban workers. Both GDP growth rate and average compensation of urban workers are obtained from historical data reported by the National Bureau of Statistics of China. Nominal data are used for all of these measures. Figure 7.2 shows that GDP, employee compensation and executive compensation all experienced significant growth within 2002 to 2012. The GDP growth rates remain higher than 9 percent in all

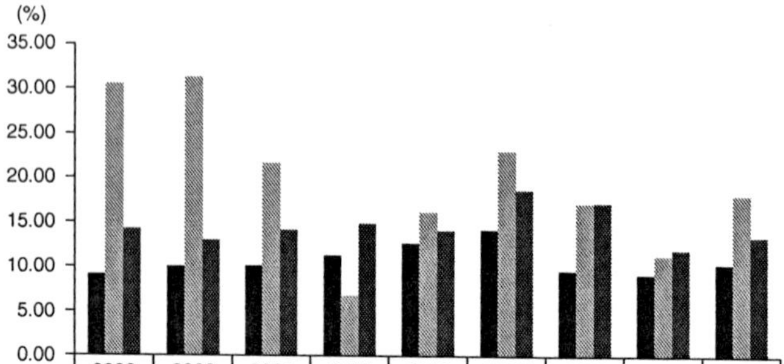

	2002	2003	2004	2005	2006	2007	2008	2009	2010
■ GDP Growth(%)	9.10	10.00	10.10	11.30	12.70	14.20	9.60	9.20	10.40
▒ Executive Comp. Growth(%)	30.56	31.34	21.63	6.80	16.15	23.00	17.21	11.33	18.15
■ Employee Comp. Growth(%)	14.28	13.03	14.13	14.86	14.10	18.72	17.23	12.00	13.47

Figure 7.2 Annual GDP, executive, and employee compensation growth (in %)

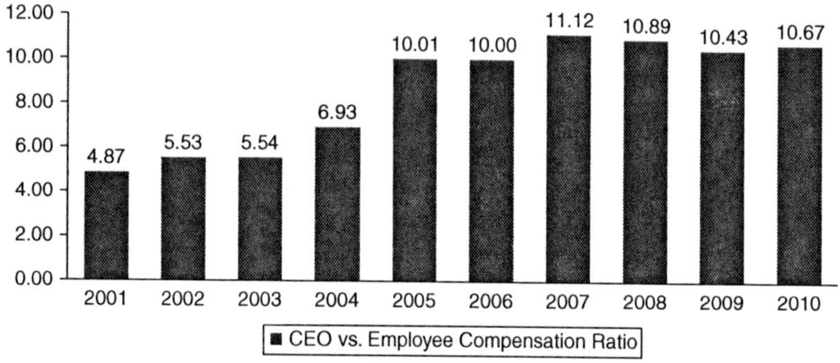

Figure 7.3 CEO vs. employee compensation ratio

these years. An average employee also enjoys two-digit growth in annual compensation yearly, ranging from 13 percent to 18 percent. The growth rate of executive compensation is typically higher than the growth rate of employee compensation, ranging from 7 percent to 30 percent, but is still in line with GDP growth and employee compensation growth. Therefore, the increase in Chinese executive and CEO compensation could be partially attributed to strong economic growth that benefits the whole nation.

We then calculate the CEO versus employee compensation ratio and illustrate our results in Figure 7.3. Figure 7.3 indicates that before 2005 (the mandatory disclosure year for individual CEO compensation), average CEO compensation was roughly 5 to 6 times employee compensation; the ratio increases to about 10 to 11 times after 2005 but remains relatively steady over the years. These results again seem to suggest that CEO and executive compensation growth is in line with employee compensation growth in China.

7.4.4 Pay for performance

As discussed in previous sections, a central research hypothesis in the literature is whether CEO pay is linked to firm performance. In this subsection we provide some further econometric analysis of the pay-for-performance link in China. We use the data described above (Conyon and He, 2012b) to estimate a standard general linear model. The results are presented in Table 7.1. Two columns of results are presented. The first column of data is based on ordinary least squares (OLS) estimates. The second set of results is based on firm fixed effects. In the dataset there are 1710 separate firms, over the time horizon 2005 to 2010.[6] Descriptions of variables are summarized in Appendix 1.

Before discussing the results, we briefly summarize the means of the variables in the sample. Average CEO total pay (salary plus bonus plus stipend) is approximately 438,000 RMB (2005 to 2010). The mean of the log of CEO pay is 12.5. Both stock returns and return on assets are

Table 7.1 CEO pay for performance in China's public firms

	OLS	Fixed Effects
Lag stock returns	0.039***	0.027***
	(0.012)	(0.009)
Lag return on assets	1.587***	0.724***
	(0.111)	(0.122)
Log sales	0.273***	0.227***
	(0.009)	(0.030)
Market to book	0.044***	0.028***
	(0.007)	(0.007)
State owned	–0.064***	0.007
	(0.018)	(0.027)
Constant	6.336***	7.781***
	(0.222)	(0.665)
Observations	8,134	8,134
R-squared	0.412	0.282
Number of firm fixed effects	n.a.	1,710
Region effects	Yes	No
Industry and time effects	Yes	Yes

Source: Based on GTA data (described in Conyon and He, 2012b). The dependent variable is the log of CEO pay (= salary + bonus + stipend).

lagged by one period in order to control for the endogenous variable problem. The data are also winsorized at the top and bottom 2.5 percent levels to obviate any problems associated with outlying variables. The mean of the stock return variable is 0.56, the mean of the return on assets variable is 0.03, the mean of log firm sales is 21.5, the average of the market to book ratio (growth opportunities) is 1.98, and finally the mean of the state-controlled firm dummy variable is 0.45.

It is important to stress that this is the link between current levels of pay and measures of firm performance. This regression approach is standard in the literature. However, we must stress that it does not speak of the perhaps more important question of what incentives the CEO faces to improve performance going forward. In this sense, it is the ownership position that the CEO has in the firm that might be more salient. This said, our regression results show some interesting findings. The OLS results show that CEO pay is correlated to both firm's stock returns and return on assets. The same qualitative result is demonstrated for the fixed effects results. We conclude, therefore, that CEO cash compensation in China is correlated to firm performance. The result is statistically significant after controlling for firm size, growth opportunities, and ownership structure. In common with other studies (Conyon and He, 2011; Firth et al, 2007; Kato and Long, 2006) we find that CEO pay in China is positively correlated to firm size. The estimated elasticity of pay to firm size is in the range of 22.7 percent to 27.3 percent. We also find that CEO pay is lower by approximately 6 percent in state-controlled firms. This result is valid only for the OLS results, and not for the fixed effects estimates. That lower pay in state-controlled firms is to be expected if we think that the quality of management is different in state-controlled firms (Bloom and Van Reenen, 2010, 2012). In addition, the fact that the effect of the state-owned firm on CEO compensation disappears after we control for firm fixed effects adds credence to the interpretation that this variable is capturing unobserved firm heterogenzeity.

7.4.5 The Use of equity incentives in Chinese executive pay contracts

Equity incentives such as stock options are an important component of executive pay in the US and other western countries, because it directly links the wealth of executives with those of shareholders. As described above, the grant of equity incentives is a recent phenomenon in China and is permissible only since 2005. In particular, the disclosure of total executive and CEO compensation data in China excludes the cash value of stock options and other equity incentives, which may

Table 7.2 The prevalence of equity incentives in China

	2005	2006	2007	2008	2009	2010
Number of firms granting equity incentives						
Number of firms	2	32	10	29	24	72
Percentage of all listed firms	0.15%	2.26%	0.65%	1.82%	1.37%	3.42%
Types of equity incentives granted						
Total number of grants	44	2272	345	1302	595	1434
Restricted stocks	44	374	2	241	166	391
Stock options	0	1874	296	1054	429	1026
Stock appreciation rights	0	26	47	7	0	17
Mix of equity incentives grant types						
Only restricted stocks	2	8	2	5	8	16
	(100%)	(25%)	(20%)	(17%)	(33%)	(22%)
Only stock options	0	23	7	22	16	53
	(0%)	(72%)	(70%)	(76%)	(67%)	(74%)
Only appreciation rights	0	0	1	0	0	1
	(0%)	(0%)	(10%)	(0%)	(0%)	(1%)
Mix of types	0	1	0	2	0	2
	(0%)	(3%)	(0%)	(7%)	(0%)	(3%)

partially explain the pay difference between Chinese executives and their western counterparts. Equity incentives (such as stock options and restricted stock) are supremely important as a mechanism to provide individuals with powerful forward looking incentives to create firm value. To shed some light on the role of equity incentives in Chinese executive compensation, we report the use of equity incentives in Chinese listed firms in Table 7.2.

The table indicates that the use of equity incentives such as restricted stocks, stock options, or stock appreciation rights is very rare in China. In 2005, only two firms (0.15 percent of all listed firms) issued equity incentives to executives. The number significantly increases to 32 firms in 2006 but drops again to 10, 29 and 24 firms in year 2007, 2008, and 2009 respectively. The largest usage occurred in 2010, with 72 firms (3.42 percent of total listed firms) issuing equity incentive grants. Overall, these results indicate that equity incentive is rarely used by Chinese listed firms and that the take-up rate has been slow between 2005 and 2010.

We also report the types of equity incentives provided to executives. We find that all 44 grants issued in 2005 were restricted stocks. Stock options gained popularity and became the dominant grant format in the following years. The final part of the table depicts firm level usage of grant types. In 2005, 100 percent of firms used restricted stocks; 72 percent of firms used stock options in 2006, and 25 percent adopted restricted stocks. Similar patterns are observed in the following years, with around 67 percent to 76 percent of firms issuing stock options to their executives; 17 percent to 33 percent of firms used restricted stocks, and the rest used either stock appreciation rights or a mixture of different formats. These results suggest that stock options are the most popular type of incentive grant used in China.

To get a better picture of the role of stock options we provide a simple case study example. The company that we consider is Suning Appliance Company Limited and is one of the largest privately owned electrical appliance retailers in China, headquartered in Nanjing, Jiangsu. As of 31 December 2010, the company had 1311 stores in 231 cities across China. It was listed on the Shenzhen Stock Exchange in 2004 (SZSE: 002024). The following describes CEO compensation and equity incentives of the company in 2010. The CEO is Mr. Jin Ming. Total cash compensation was 800,000 RMB. The number of stock option grants in the year was 3 million. The exercise price of these options was 14.5. Now suppose that these stock options can be valued at 20 percent of the face value of the grant price, not too unusual an assumption. In this case each stock option is worth 14.5 times 0.2, which is equal to 2.9 RMB. This means that the 3 million stock options that were granted are worth approximately 8.7 million RMB. If we now divide the value of the granted options by the value of the total cash compensation received in the same year we arrive at the ratio 10.87. An alternative way to think about this is that stock option pay is approximately 92 percent of total pay, where total pay is made up of stock option pay plus total cash pay. This means that the CEO of Suning Appliance Company receives 10 times more equity compensation than he does cash compensation. We use this particular example for illustrative purposes only and not to claim anything about the general nature of the value of stock option grants in Chinese publicly traded firms. We leave this topic for future research.

What are the potential implications of this finding? First, even though the number of executives receiving stock options is very low in China, an executive's compensation might actually be quite high when it is conditional on receiving a stock option grant.

Second, for those executives who received stock options, executive compensation in previous studies has been mis-measured. As a result, statistical regression models might be biased when investigating the link between pay and performance. This is because the typical way to measure Chinese executive pay only includes cash compensation. As we illustrate above, it should in fact include a measure of the value of granted stock options, or other equity instruments that have been granted during the year. This observation is similar to the measurement problem identified by Kato and Long (2006) and Conyon and He (2011) when they talked about the non-observability of perk compensation.

Consider the following general linear model: $y = \beta_0 + \beta_1 x + \varepsilon$, where y is a true measure of pay equal to the log cash plus bonus plus the value of options granted in the year, x is firm performance and ε is a stochastic error component (mean zero and constant variance). An incorrectly estimated model, due to y being measured with error, will give rise to an endogenous variable problem. Suppose the incorrect dependent variable is $y^* = y - \chi$, where χ is the random error capturing the value of the granted options, so the (wrongly) estimated model becomes $y^* = \beta_0 + \beta_1 x + (\varepsilon + \chi)$. If the included performance term (x) is correlated with the stock options ($cov(x, \chi) > 0$) then in general we would expect β_1 to be biased (if stock options are important in the pay contract and correlated to the other included regression variables). Thus, we think that future research on China should consider the importance of stock options in the pay contract.

7.4.6 Equity contracts: Regression results

To further explore characteristics of firms issuing equity incentives such as stock options, we estimated a logistic regression model with robust standard errors. At this stage we have no strong priors as to what the true determinants of equity grant policies are. Instead, we look at some interesting and rather simple covariates. The dependent variable is a dummy variable equal to 1 if the firm is issuing equity incentives in that given year to its CEO, and 0 otherwise. Because no firms are allowed to issue equity incentives before 2005, we drop firm years before 2005 from the analysis. We include three sets of dependent variables in the analysis: (1) Economic characteristics, including firm accounting performance, firm stock market performance, firm size, stock volatility, market to book value, leverage measured as debt to equity ratio, and firm age; (2) Ownership characteristics, including SOE, foreign ownership, ownership concentration ratio; (3) Board and CEO characteristics, including CEO pay, the existence of a compensation committee, leadership duality, board size, supervisory board size, and independent directors' ratio on the board. In addition, we add industry and regional dummy variables as well as time dummy variables as controls. All dependent variables are lagged one year

Table 7.3 Characteristics of firms issuing equity incentives

	(1)	(2)	(3)	(4)
	coef	se	coef	se
Log CEO pay	0.008***	0.002	0.008***	0.002
Combined CEO & chair	0.010***	0.003	0.010***	0.003
Board size	–0.000	0.001	0.000	0.001
Supervisory board size	–0.002*	0.001	–0.002	0.001
Outsider ratio	0.029	0.020	0.028	0.022
Compensation committee	0.010***	0.004	0.011***	0.004
State owned	–0.019***	0.004	–0.018***	0.004
Largest shareholder	–0.000***	0.000	–0.000**	0.000
Foreign owned	–0.002	0.008	–0.000	0.008
Stock returns	0.008***	0.002	0.008***	0.002
Market to book	0.001	0.001	0.001	0.001
Return on assets	0.001***	0.000	0.001***	0.000
Volatility	–0.030***	0.011	–0.030***	0.011
Debt to equity	–0.001	0.001	–0.002*	0.001
Log sales	0.004**	0.002	0.005***	0.002
Firm age	–0.001***	0.000	–0.001***	0.000
Observations	8,925		8,925	
Region/industry effects	No		Yes	

Dependent variable is 'CEO Granted Equity', which is an indicator variable (1/0) if the CEO is granted stock options, or restricted stock, or share appreciation rights (SARs) during the fiscal year. Robust standard errors in parentheses: * significant at 10%; ** significant at 5%; *** significant at 1%. Marginal effects are reported from the coefficient estimates from a logistic regression. The reported standard errors are robust to heteroskedasticity. Models are estimated over the period 2005 to 2010.

to help establish causality. Measures of these independent and control variables are explained in Appendix 1 in more details.

Table 7.3 reports the results from the logistic regression. We report the economic marginal effects. Column (1) reports the model excluding region and industry effects. Column (3) includes these variables. We find that firms with higher CEO pay and those that combined the posts of CEO and chair are more likely to issue equity incentives. We also find that firms which have adopted a compensation committee are much more likely to issue equity incentives. On the other hand, there is some evidence that the probability of receiving equity incentives is lower in firms with a large supervisory board, although this effect is insignificant in the model containing regional and industry effects. Overall, we find important corporate governance effects on the determination of equity incentive grants in Chinese firms.

We also find important ownership effects on the issuing of equity incentives. We find that state-controlled firms are much less likely to issue equity incentives compared to privately controlled firms. In addition we find that when the largest single shareholder is bigger the firm is much less likely to issue incentives. This seems to be consistent with the prediction of agency theory. The larger the largest shareholder, the stronger the monitoring effects, and the less important the equity incentives will be. We find little evidence that foreign controlled firms are different in terms of their equity incentive policy compared to non-foreign controlled firms.

In terms of firm performance we find that companies with higher stock returns are much more likely to issue equity incentives. There is little effect of growth opportunities, as measured by the market to book ratio. The association between return on assets and the likelihood of equity grants is similarly positive. Consistently with agency theory we find an inverse relation between the firm's stock price volatility and the probability of incentive grants. In general, we find that bigger firms are more likely to issue equity incentives, but older firms are less likely to. Overall, these results are consistent with studies in the US by researchers such as Murphy (1985), Jensen and Murphy (1990), and Core and Guay (1999).

7.5 China CEO pay versus CEO pay internationally

How does CEO pay in China compare to CEO pay internationally? Based on our empirical analysis and extant literature one can conclude that a) the level of CEO pay is significantly lower in China compared to the US and Europe, and b) equity compensation in the form of stock options and restricted stock is much more important in the US and European nations compared to China. However, similarly to the US and Europe, a) CEO pay in China is determined by firm size, and b) CEO pay is related to measures of firm performance, particularly accounting performance. Overall, there are important differences as well as similarities in CEO pay determination between China and the rest of the world.

Table 7.4 is calculated based on the data of Conyon et al. (2012). Table 7.4.1 shows the composition of CEO pay in the US and Europe, and Table 7.4.2 shows the link between pay and performance for the UK, Europe and the US. Table 7.4.1 indicates that US firms on average have higher executive compensation compared to counterparts in Europe. Within European countries, Germany, Ireland, Italy, Switzerland, and the UK have the highest average and median executive pay. All ten countries listed in Table 7.4.1 have much higher CEO pay than China. Table 7.4.1 also provides the average composition of CEO pay in these ten countries. On average, CEOs in Europe receive 50 percent of their total

Table 7.4 International CEO pay

7.4.1 Level and composition of CEO pay

Country	Firms	Total pay: Average (€000s)	Total pay: Median (€000s)	Average composition of total pay: Base salary	Bonus	Equity pay	Other pay
Belgium	28	1,328	884	64%	20%	6%	10%
France	156	1,522	822	60%	21%	15%	4%
Germany	80	2,606	1,739	39%	42%	9%	11%
Ireland	23	2,585	1,375	54%	9%	23%	15%
Italy	46	2,717	2,183	53%	19%	13%	15%
Netherlands	60	1,526	1,166	49%	21%	17%	13%
Sweden	51	1,273	1,055	61%	16%	1%	22%
Switzerland	29	3,636	1,336	57%	17%	12%	14%
UK	419	2,016	1,183	46%	18%	28%	9%
All Europe	892	1,989	1,200	50%	21%	19%	10%
United States	1,426	3,784	2,414	29%	20%	46%	6%

7.4.2 Pay for performance in the US and Europe

		Pay-performance elasticities based on separate regressions for each performance measure			Pay-performance elasticities based on a single regression including all three performance measures		
	firm years	Stockreturn	Sales growth	Change in ROA	Stockreturn	Sales growth	Change in ROA
UK	2,082	0.096***	0.137***	0.641***	0.068**	0.134***	0.619***
Europe	3,894	0.117***	0.067	0.651***	0.100***	0.046	0.602***
US	6,596	0.405***	0.363***	0.784***	0.358***	0.203***	0.506***

Notes: Source Conyon et al (2012). 7.4.1: European data from Boardex and US data from ExecuComp exclude firms with less than €100m in 2008 revenues. CEOs in their first year are excluded. Total compensation defined as the sum of salaries, bonuses, benefits, and grant-date values for stock options, restricted stock, and performance shares. US dollar-denominated data are converted to Euros using the 2008 year-end exchange rate (€1 = $1.3919). 7.4.2: Data are based on first-differences from 2003–8. Pay-performance elasticities are calculated from a regression of ΔLn(CEO pay) on one or all three performance measures; regressions include additional controls for industry (12 dummy variables based on Fama-French industries) and year (dummy variables for 2005 through 2008). For the purposes of these regressions, (Stock Return)t is defined as Ln(1+Shareholder Return) for period t; ΔROA is defined as the year-over-year change in ROA (defined as net income before extraordinary items plus interest divided by average assets over the year); and sales growth is defined as ΔLn(Sales)t. Monetary data are converted to 2008-constant US dollars, adjusted for inflation, and then converted to Euros using the 2008 year-end exchange rate (€1 = $1.3919).

pay in the form of base salaries, 21 percent in bonuses and 19 percent in equity-based pay (including stock options, restricted stock and performance shares). In contrast, the US CEOs receive a much smaller amount of their compensation in the firm of salaries (29 percent) and a much larger amount in equity incentives (46 percent). Compared to China, CEOs in the US and Europe receive a much higher proportion of pay in the form of stock and options. The result is also consistent with Conyon and He (2011) who, after controlling for size, corporate governance, economic factors, and purchasing power, show that CEO pay is higher in the US than in China.

Table 7.4.2 shows the pay-for-performance relation for the US, the UK, and Europe generally. The results show that the pay-for-performance link for European CEOs, taken collectively, is systematically lower than for US CEOs. Table 7.4.2 suggests that increasing shareholder value by 10 percent corresponds to an increase in cash compensation of about 4.1 percent in the US, but only 1.2 percent in Europe. Table 7.4.2 also indicates that each 10 percent growth in sales corresponds to an increase of 3.6 percent in cash compensation for US CEOs, and (an insignificant) 0.7 percent for European CEOs. The pay-for-ROA elasticity is similar across the continents at the level of 0.6, which is also qualitatively similar to the pay-for-performance link in China established in this chapter and other literature such as Conyon and He (2012b).

7.6 Conclusions

The goal of this study was to describe the broad landscape of executive compensation in China. Three domains were included. First, we described the institutional context of executive pay setting in China. Second, we provided a review of salient prior research in the field of Chinese executive compensation. Third, we provided new evidence on the determinants of Chinese executive pay.

The study yielded a number of conclusions. First, our review indicates that there is still limited information available on executive compensation in China compared to the voluminous literature on executive compensation in the US and other developed nations (see reviews by Murphy, 1999, 2012). In particular, the enduring concrete drivers of executive compensation have yet to be established conclusively in China. Although there is a robust firm size effect on top executive compensation, the relationship between executive pay and firm performance is far from consistent, and the positive correlation is typically more widely documented for accounting performance relative to stock return. Conyon and He (2012a) suggested that the lack of information transparency and opaqueness in Chinese stock markets (Jin and Myers, 2006; Morck and Yeung, 2002) make accounting-based measures of firm performance rather than stock market measures more informative to shareholders in evaluating executive performance in China. Overall, these arguments suggest that the studies of Chinese executive compensation would benefit more from integrating Chinese institutional contexts in the investigation.

Second, consistent with the worldwide trend, Chinese executives experienced a significant pay increase over 2000 to 2010. However, China's executives are paid at a much lower base – even after controlling for purchasing power parity, and other exchange rate adjustments. We find that executive compensation growth is in line with the economic growth and is consistent with the growth of employee compensation as well. We also find, using data from 2005 to 2010, that there is a positive correlation between pay and performance, where performance was captured both as a market based and an accounting-based measure.

Third, while equity compensation is widely used in American and other western countries, it is a very recent phenomenon in China. The first equity incentive grants to listed firms' executives only happened in 2005 and the take-up rate has been far from dramatic. Having said this, there are signs that economic and governance factors drive the use of equity compensation in the total CEO pay package. We find that larger firms, firms with better stock market or accounting performance, lower stock volatility, younger firms, privately controlled firms, firms with lower ownership concentration, firms with a compensation committee and a combined leadership position are more likely to offer equity incentives to executives.

China is now the world's second largest economy. Since 1992 its capital markets have grown significantly, both in terms of market valuation, and the number of IPOs and aggregate number of corporate listings. China's macroeconomic performance, relative to similar sized countries, is unrivalled. Against this background we think that there have been relatively few executive compensation studies – especially those that address the issue of equity compensation. Such studies are important to better understand executive incentives to promote economic growth. We hope our study can shed some light on this issue.

Appendix 7.1 Data definition

Executive compensation	=	Log (executive compensation) as the average of top three highest-paid executive's compensation
CEO compensation	=	Log (CEO compensation) as the annual total compensation of CEO. Compensation is the sum of salary, bonus and other pay. The CEO is the 'General Manager' title in the GTA dataset. If not the 'General Manager' then we manually checked all firms for the identity of the most senior executive team manager who was assigned the title CEO
Granted equity	=	1 if there is a grant of equity incentives (stock options, restricted stock, or share appreciation rights) to the CEO in the given fiscal year, and 0 otherwise
Return on assets	=	Return on assets calculated as earnings before interest and tax divided by total assets
Stock returns	=	Annualized stock returns derived using monthly return data
Firm size	=	Log value of total assets
Volatility	=	Past three year stock returns volatility calculated as rolling average
Market to book	=	Market value of shares divided by total assets
Debt to equity	=	Debt to equity ratio calculated as total liabilities divided by total assets
State owned	=	1 if the ultimate owner of the firm is the state
Foreign owned	=	1 if the ultimate owner of the firm is a foreign institution
Largest shareholder	=	The percentage ownership of the largest shareholder
Combined CEO & chair	=	1 if the CEO is also the chairperson of the board, 0 otherwise
Board size	=	The number of directors on the board
Supervisory board size	=	The number of directors on the supervisory board
Outsider ratio	=	The proportion of independent directors on the board
Compensation committee	=	1 if the firm has adopted a compensation committee, 0 otherwise
Industry dummies	=	Based on 22 CSRC classifications of industries: 1: Agriculture and fishery; 2: Mining; 30: Manufacturing-food/beverage; 31: Manufacturing-Textiles; 32: Manufacturing-Furniture; 33: Manufacturing-Paper/Printing; 34: Manufacturing-Petroleum; 35: Manufacturing-Electronic; 36: Manufacturing-Metal/Non-metal; 37: Manufacturing-Machines; 38:

Continued

Appendix 7.1 Continued

		Manufacturing-Pharmaceutical; 39: Manufacturing: others; 4: Electricity, water and other energy manufacturing and supply; 5: Construction; 6: Transportation and logistics; 7: Information technology; 8: Wholesales and retails; 9: Finance and insurance; 10: Real estate; 11: Service; 12: Communication; 13: Others
Regional dummies	=	Based on 31 regions in China, including 4 direct-controlled municipalities and 27 provinces. The 4 direct-controlled municipalities are: Beijing, Shanghai, Tianjin and Chongqing. The 27 mainland provinces (excluding Taiwan, Hong Kong and Macau) are Anhui, Fujian, Gansu, Guangdong, Guangxi, Guizhou, Hainan, Hebei, Heilongjiang, Henan, Hubei, Hunan, Jiangsu, Jiangxi, Jilin, Liaoning, Neimeng (Inner Mongolia), Ningxia, Qinghai, Saanxi, Shandong, Shanxi, Sichuan, Xizang (Tibet), Xinjiang, Yunnan, Zhejiang

Notes

1. This chapter draws upon our joint research on corporate governance in China. Further details are contained in Conyon and He (2011, 2012a, 2012b). We are grateful to Douglas Cumming, Alessandra Guariglia, Wenxuan Hou, and Edward Lee for the opportunity to contribute to this volume. Martin Conyon gratefully acknowledges the support of the Center for Human Resources at the Wharton School, University of Pennsylvania.
2. http://www.sjgrand.cn/china-s-new-individual-income-tax-rates (accessed April 2012).
3. http://www.china-briefing.com/news/2009/09/11/china-tax-issues-concerning-employee-stock-options.html (Accessed April 2012).
4. These two titles capture most CEOs. We also manually checked other titles such as 'Administrative President', 'Executive President' in cases where current CEO compensation data was missing.
5. Critics of CEO compensation have assembled such data. Source: Executive excess 2011: The Massive CEO Rewards for Tax Dodging. Institute for Policy Studies. Downloaded from http://www.ips-dc.org/reports/executive_Excess_2011_the_massive_ceo_rewards_for_tax_dodging.
6. We choose to exclude CEO compensation data before 2005 because pre-2005 disclosure rules did not require listed firms to report individual executive's compensation. We also required firms to have a minimum two years of consecutive data.

References

Adithipyangkul, P., Alon, I. and Zhang, T. 2011. Executive perks: compensation and corporate performance in China. *Asia Pacific Journal of Management*, 28: 401–425.

Allen, F., Qian, J. and Qian, M. J. 2005. 'Law, finance, and economic growth in China. *Journal of Financial Economics,* 77: 57–116.

Bai, C.E. and Xu L, L. 2005. Incentives for CEOs with multitasks: evidence from Chinese state-owned enterprises. *Journal of Comparative Economics,* 33(3): 517–539.

Beltratti, A. and Bortolotti, B. 2007. The nontradable share reform in the Chinese stock market, FEEM Working Paper No. 131.06. Social Science Research Network. Available at SSRN: http://ssrn.com/abstract=944412.

Bloom, N., Genakos, C., Sadun, R., Van Reenen, J. 2012. Management practices across firms and countries. *Academy of Management Perspectives,* 26(1): 12–32.

Bloom, N. and Van Reenen, J. 2010. Why do management practices differ across firms and countries?. *Journal of Economic Perspectives,* 24 (1): 203–224.

Buck, T., Liu, X. and Skovoroda, R. 2008. Top executive pay and firm performance in China. *Journal of International Business Studies,* 39 (5): 833–850.

Cheffins, B. 2003. Will executive pay globalize along American lines?. *Corporate Governance: An International Review,* 11(1): 8–24.

Chen, J.J., Liu, X. and Li, W. 2010. The effect of insider control and global benchmarks on Chinese executive compensation. *Corporate Governance: An International Review,* 18(2): 107–123.

Chen, J., Ezzamel, M. and Cai, Z. 2011. Managerial power theory, tournament theory and executive pay in China. *Journal of Corporate Finance,* 4: 1176–1199.

Conyon, M. and He, L. 2011. Executive compensation and corporate governance in China. *Journal of Corporate Finance,* 4: 1158–1175.

Conyon, M. and He, L. 2012a. CEO turnover in China: the role of market-based and accounting performance measures. *European Journal of Finance,* forthcoming.

Conyon M. and He, L. 2012b. CEO compensation and corporate governance in China. *Corporate Governance: An International Review,* forthcoming.

Conyon, M. J., Fernandes, N., Ferreira, M. A., Pedro, M. and Murphy, K. 2012. The executive compensation controversy: a transatlantic analysis. In: Boeri T., Lucifora, C. and Murphy, K. (eds), *Productivity, Profits and Pay,* Oxford University Press, NY.

Core, J. and Guay, W. 1999. The use of equity grants to manage optimal equity incentive levels. *Journal of Accounting and Economics,* 28 (2): 151–184.

CSRC. 1998. Guidelines on contents and formats of information disclosure of annual report for listed companies – 1998 version, China Securities Regulatory Commission.

CSRC. 2000. Guidelines on contents and formats of information disclosure of annual report for listed companies guidelines on contents and formats of information disclosure of annual report for listed companies – 2000 version, China Securities Regulatory Commission.

CSRC. 2001. Guidelines for introducing independent directors to the board of directors of listed companies, China Securities Regulatory Commission.

CSRC. 2002. Code of corporate governance for listed companies in China, China Securities Regulatory Commission.

CSRC. 2002. Guidelines on contents and formats of information disclosure of annual report for listed companies – 2002 version, China Securities Regulatory Commission.

CSRC. 2005. Regulation for the stock options grants in public firms, China Securities Regulatory Commission.

CSRC. 2005. Guidelines on contents and formats of information disclosure of annual report for listed companies – 2005 version, China Securities Regulatory Commission.

CSRC. 2006. Guidelines on contents and formats of information disclosure of annual report for listed companies – 2007 version, China Securities Regulatory Commission.

Ding, Z., Ahktar, S., Ge, G. 2006. 'Organizational differences in managerial compensation and benefits of Chinese firms. *International Journal of Human Resource Management*, 17 (4): 693–715.

Ding, S., Wu, Z., Li, Y., Jia, C. 2010. Executive compensation, supervisory board, and China's governance reform: a legal approach perspective. *Review of Quantitative Finance and Accounting*, 35 (4): 445–471.

Firth, M., Fung, P. and Rui, O. 2006. Corporate performance and CEO compensation in China. *Journal of Corporate Finance*, 13: 693–714.

Firth, M., Fung, P. and Rui, O. 2007. How ownership and corporate governance influence chief executive pay in China's listed firms. *Journal of Business Research*, 60 (7): 776–785.

Firth, M., Leung, T. and Rui, O. 2010. Justifying top management pay in a transitional economy. *Journal of Empirical Finance*, 17: 852–866.

Groves, T., Hong, Y., McMillan, J. and Naughton, B. 1995. China's evolving managerial labor market. *Journal of Political Economy*, 103 (4): 873–892.

Hu, H.W., Tam, O. K. and Tan, M. G. 2010. Internal governance mechanisms and firm performance in China. *Asia Pacific Journal of Management*, 27 (4): 727–749.

Jensen, M. C. and Meckling, W. H. 1976. Theory of firm – managerial behavior, agency costs and ownership structure. *Journal of Financial Economics*, 3 (4): 305–360.

Jensen, M. C. and Murphy, K. J. 1990. Performance pay and top-management incentives. *Journal of Political Economy*, 98 (2): 225–264.

Jensen, M.C. and Warner, J. B. 1988. The distribution of power among corporate managers, shareholders, and directors. *Journal of Financial Economics*, 20: 3–24.

Jin L. and Myers, S. 2006. R2 around the world: new theory and new tests. *Journal of Financial Economics*, 79: 257–292.

Kato, T. K. and Long, C. X. 2006. Executive compensation, firm performance, and corporate governance in China: evidence from firms listed in the Shanghai and Shenzhen stock exchanges. *Economic Development and Cultural Change*, 54 (4): 945–983.

Li, D., Moshirian, F., Nguyen, P. and Tan, L. 2007. Corporate governance or globalization: what determines CEO compensation in China?. *Research in International Business and Finance*, 21: 32–49.

Mengistae, T. and Xu, L. X. C. 2004. Agency theory and executive compensation: the case of Chinese state-owned enterprises. *Journal of Labor Economics*, 22 (3): 615–637.

Morck, R., Yeung, B. and Yu, W. 2000. The information content of stock markets: why do emerging markets have synchronous stock price movements?. *Journal of Financial Economics*, 58: 215–260.

Murphy, K. J. 1985. Corporate performance and managerial remuneration – an empirical analysis. *Journal of Accounting and Economics*, 7: 11–42.

Murphy, K. J. 1999. Executive compensation. In: Ashenfelter O. and Card D. (ed.), *Handbook of Labor Economics*, Vol. 3b, Elsevier Science, North Holland.

Murphy, K. J. 2012. Executive compensation: where we are, and how we got there' in Constantinides, G., Harris, M. and Stulz, R. (eds), *Handbook of the Economics of Finance*, forthcoming, Elsevier Science, North Holland.

Peng, M. W. 2003. 'Institutional transitions and strategic choices. *Academy of Management Review*, 28: 275–296.

Peng, M., Li, Y., Xie, Y. and Xu, W. 2010. CEO duality, organizational slack and firm performance in China. *Asia Pacific Journal of Management*, 27(4): 611–624.

Rampling, P. N., Eddie, I. A. and Liu, J. 2011. Executive remuneration in China: a literature review, Available at SSRN: http://ssrn.com/abstract=1945558.

Wang, K. and Xiao, X. 2011. Controlling shareholders' tunneling and executive compensation: evidence from China. *Journal of Accounting and Public Policy*, 30: 89–100.

Yeh, Y., Shu, P., Lee, T. and Su, Y. 2009. Non-tradable share reform and corporate governance in the Chinese stock market. *Corporate Governance: An International Review*, 17 (4): 457–475.

8
Independent Directors and Corporate Performance in China

Hanzhang Jiao, Yizhe Dong, Wenxuan Hou, and Edward Lee

8.1 Introduction

Guidelines issued by the China Securities Regulatory Commission (CSRC) require companies to appoint independent directors to their boards. According to the *Guidelines about Establishing an Independent Director System in Listed Companies*, ever since 2002, it has been a requirement to have at least two independent directors. This rule was amended in 2003, requiring at least one third of board members to be independent. Thus, independent directors play an important part in China's corporate governance reform.[1] In western developed countries, former and current executives are the main sources of independent directors. In China, however, people of varying backgrounds, including academics and politicians, are often appointed. Since independent directors are pivotal to a firm's governance, the main objective of this study is to explore whether the background of an independent director has any association with the performance of the firm they work for.

In this study, we classify independent directors into seven groups according to occupation and experience: academics, accountants, politicians, legal professionals, financial professionals, overseas returnees, and others. Academics account for the largest proportion (37.63 percent), followed by accountants (17.14 percent) and politicians (12.27 percent). This indicates that individuals with a higher level of education, an accountancy background or political connections are highly valued by Chinese firms. Our main analysis focuses on examining the association between the characteristics of independent directors and firm performance. Specifically, we focus on operating performance measured by return on assets (ROA) and productivity measured by the ratio of sales to number of employees (SEMP). In further analysis, we examine whether the political connections of the Chief Executive Officer (CEO) or board chairperson affect a firm's preference over independent directors' characteristics.

Our findings are as follows. First, firms with academics or accountants as independent directors are associated with higher productivity. Second, firms with politicians or financial professionals as independent directors are associated with lower operating performance. Further analysis reveals that firms with a politically connected chairperson are less likely to hire accountants, bankers or overseas returnees as independent directors. Firms with more concentrated ownership are more likely to hire accountants or politicians and less likely to hire lawyers.

The implications of these findings are as follows. First, the association between independent directors and firm performance in China varies depending on the background of the former. This suggests that the expertise and experience of independent directors may potentially affect the operations of a firm. Second, future corporate governance reforms in China should not only focus on the degree of board independence but also on the expertise of board members.

This chapter is organized as follows: Section 2 reviews the literature. Section 3 describes the research methodology and sample. Section 4 reports the findings. Section 5 concludes.

8.2 Literature review

8.2.1 Strengths and weaknesses of independent directors

Independent directors are expected to contribute to a company's governance by facilitating the alignment of managerial and shareholder interests within an agency framework. The monitoring hypothesis (Demsetz and Lehn, 1985; Gillian, Hartzell, and Starks, 2004; Lehn, Patro, and Zhao, 2004; Raheja, 2004; Coles, Daniel, and Naveen, 2006; Linck, Netter, and Yang, 2005; Harris and Raviv, 2008) suggests that independent directors support executives in making investment decisions and ensure that the executives' performance is effectively scrutinized. For instance, some studies in both the US (Beasley, 1996; Dechow, Sloan, and Sweeney, 1996) and the UK (Pope, Peasnell and Young, 2001) demonstrate that the presence of more independent directors on a board may decrease the probability that the company will engage in financial statement fraud.

Fama (1980) and Fama and Jensen (1983) also argue that independent directors not only enhance the effectiveness of the board but also reduce the probability of top management colluding in order to expropriate benefits at the expense of shareholders' interests. Independent directors safeguard effective governance by selecting, rewarding and sanctioning managers on behalf of shareholders. Weisbach (1988) finds that the proportion of independent directors has a marginally significant positive association with the likelihood of CEO dismissal in the US. Dahya, McConnell, and Travolos (2002) find a higher CEO turnover in UK companies that comply with the board composition recommendation of the Cadbury Committee. Thus, the effectiveness of independent directors depends on their degree of independence from the management.

Additionally, the expertise hypothesis (Fama and Jensen, 1983; Brickley and James, 1987; Bhagat and Black, 1999; Agrawal and Knoeber, 2001; Lehn, Patro, and Zhao, 2004; Coles, Daniel and Naveen, 2005) suggests that independent directors play an important role in formulating business strategy, by contributing their expertise in problem solving, knowledge of technologies and markets that may be unfamiliar to inside directors. The reputation hypothesis (Fama and Jensen, 1983) suggests that the human capital of an independent director relies largely on their performance. Although independent directors receive lower remuneration than their insider counterparts, their incentives are driven by reputation and career concerns. If a company is discovered to have been behaving against shareholder interests, then the human capital of both the full-time internal managers and the independent directors alike will be devalued.

However, the functioning of independent directors in the corporate governance mechanism can be compromised in many ways. The entrenchment hypothesis (Morck, Shleifer, and Vishny, 1988; Holthausen and Larcker, 1993; Yermack, 1996; Bhagat and Black, 2001) suggests that independent directors may not act in the best interests of shareholders due to ownership stakes, personal relationships with the CEO, and other ways in which they are beholden to the company. In the UK, Dedman (2003) finds no association between the proportion of independent directors on a board and the likelihood of a poorly performing CEO being dismissed.

Klein (1998), Bhagat and Black (1999), and Raheja (2004) suggest that independent directors may not have the information, time and commitment of inside directors. Gilson and Kraakman (1991) and Black (1990) posit that independent directors should be not only independent but also accountable if they are to effectively look after shareholder interests. Agrawal and Knoeber (1996) argue that additional independent directors are often enlisted because of their political connections, causing board independence to be correlated with the degree of political constraint facing a company. Klein (1998) suggests that independent directors add value only if they are deployed in appropriate committees but finds little evidence of this in large US companies.

8.2.2 Independent directors and corporate performance

Contemporary literature evaluates whether or not independent directors provide net benefits to their companies from two angles, how the market reacts to the appointment of an independent director and how independent directors affect corporate performance. In terms of market reaction, the evidence in the US and UK appears to be inconsistent. In the US, Rosenstein and Wyatt (1990) show positive market reaction to announcements of independent director appointments and Brickley, Coles, and Terry (1994) show a positive relationship between market reaction to the adoption of poison pills and the fraction of independent directors. However, UK studies such as Fox and Opong (1999) and Lin, Pope, and Young (2003) show that the market does not react to announcements of independent director appointments.

In terms of corporate performance too, no consensus is established in the empirical literature. While some studies document a pro-intuitive positive relationship between director independence and corporate performance, others find no association or even a negative one. The US study by Baysinger and Butler (1985) finds that the proportion of independent directors on a board has a mild effect on financial performance measured by the return on equity but there exists a point of diminishing marginal benefits as board independence continues to increase. They argue that the ratio of independent directors to inside directors required to achieve satisfactory financial performance is well below the level advocated by corporate governance reformers. In the UK, though, Ezzamel and Watson (1993) show that independent directors are positively associated with profitability.

Hermalin and Weisbach (1991) find no relationship between board composition and corporate performance as measured by Tobin's Q, however. Bhagat and Black (1999, 2001) also find no evidence that greater board independence enhances performance and argue that the conventional wisdom advocating this particular corporate governance feature is not well supported. Among Fortune 500 companies, Kesner (1987) finds a negative relationship between board independence and the return to investors. Fosberg (1989) finds significant underperformance in the sales-to-asset ratio among companies with fewer insider directors. Using Tobin's Q as a performance indicator, US studies such as Yermack (1996) and Agrawal and Knoeber (1996) and UK studies such as Dedman, Lim, and Lin (2006) document a significantly negative relationship with the degree of board independence. Klein (1998) also finds a negative correlation between changes in the market value of equity and the portion of independent directors.

8.2.3 Limitations of existing studies

Based on a meta-analysis of 54 empirical studies of board composition and 31 empirical studies of board leadership structure and their relationship to financial performance, Dalton, Daily, Ellstrand, and Johnson (1998) conclude that there is little evidence of a systematic association between governance structure and firm performance. They suggest that the true population relationship across the studies included in their meta-analysis is close to zero. Taken together with the discussion in the previous section, it can be concluded that previous empirical studies fail to provide consistent and convincing results on the association between board quality and corporate performance.

To explain this lack of coherence across the empirical evidence, the literature provides the following arguments. First, if each board were optimally weighted between independent directors and inside directors, then such a relation would not be found in equilibrium (Hermalin and Weisbach, 1991; Agrawal and Knoeber, 1996). In this case, the cross-sectional variation in board composition would not reflect good or bad choices but differences in the underlying environments in which the companies operate. This would not necessarily mean that independent directors were ineffective.

Second, Hermalin and Weisbach (1991) suggest that companies may reduce their agency problems to approximately the same residual level, which is all that is required to ensure good performance. Thus, mechanisms used to reduce agency problems – such as board composition – will be uncorrelated with performance. In other words, an independent board may reduce agency costs, but it is not possible to infer this by looking at corporate performance.

Third, Denis (2001) suggests that the relationship between board independence and performance may be endogenous. Weaker companies are more likely both to reform their governance structure and to have poorer performance. However, the empirical evidence relating to this argument is also mixed. Studies such as Weisbach (1988), Hermalin and Weisbach (1991), and Bhagat and Black (2001) find that increases in board independence are preceded by poorer performance. On the other hand, Klein (1998) shows that past performance does not influence board composition, while Denise and Sarin (1999) show that companies that increase their proportion of independent directors tended to have higher stock returns in the previous year instead.

Finally, Dalton, Daily, Ellstrand, and Johnson (1998) point out problems with the performance indicators commonly applied in contemporary studies. They argue that financial accounting measures are prone to manipulation, may undervalue assets systematically, and are subject to distortions due to accounting regulations. Hambriek and Finkelstein (1995) argue that financial accounting measures 'may be seen as more fully under management control'. Although market-based returns are not affected by these biases, they are easily influenced by forces beyond management control. Fama (1998) also suggests that empirical studies of long-run returns suffer from measurement and model specification issues.

8.3 Research design

8.3.1 Data source

To carry out our empirical analyses, we randomly sample 214 Chinese firms listed on the Shenzhen Exchange. We manually collect the backgrounds of the CEOs, chairpersons of the board, and independent directors of these firms between 2002 and 2010. Our sample comprises of 1227 firm-year observations. The data required for our analyses are obtained from three sources: SINA Finance (http://finance.sina.com.cn/), Datastream/Worldscope, and GTA/China Stock Market and Accounting Research (CSMAR).

8.3.2 Classification of independent directors

We categorize independent directors into seven types based on their background as listed earlier (broadly consistent with Liao et al., 2009). First, those who are university professors and researchers at institutions such as the Chinese Academy of Science are classified as academics. Second, those who are Certified Public Accountants (CPA) are classified as accountants. Third, those with a background in government, including retired bureaucrats, former executives of state-owned enterprises, and members of the National People's Congress are classified as politicians. Fourth, those who are qualified solicitors or judges are classified as legal professionals. Fifth, those with a background in banks, security companies or other financial institutions are classified as financial professionals. Sixth, people who have international work and study experience or who are visiting scholars from foreign universities are all classified as overseas returnees. Finally, those who are executives of other firms or have engineering or other specialized professional backgrounds are classified as others.

8.3.3 Regression analyses

To examine the association between subsequent firm performance and background of independent directors, we implement ordinary least squares (OLS) regression analyses based on the following equation:

$$\begin{aligned} Perf_{i,t+1} = {} & \alpha_0 + \alpha_1 ACAD_{i,t} + \alpha_2 ACCT_{i,t} + \alpha_3 POLIT_{i,t} \\ & + \alpha_4 FIN_{i,t} + \alpha_5 LEGAL_{i,t} + \alpha_6 OSEAS_{i,t} \\ & + \alpha_7 OTHER_{i,t} + \sum_{j=1}^{12} \alpha_{j+7} CTRL_{j,i,t} + \varepsilon_{i,t} \end{aligned} \tag{1}$$

where, for firm i in year t, $Perf_{i,t+1}$ is the following year's performance measured either as *ROA* or *SEMP*; $ACAD_{i,t}$, $ACCT_{i,t}$, $POLIT_{i,t}$, $FIN_{i,t}$, $LEGAL_{i,t}$, $OSEAS_{i,t}$, and $OTHER_{i,t}$ are equal to 1 if the firm has any independent directors who are academics, accountants, politicians, finance professionals, legal professionals, overseas returnees, or others, respectively, and 0 otherwise; $CTRL_{j,i,t}$ is a set of control variables that includes an indicator for the board chairperson being politically connected (has previously worked in government or the military) (*PChair*), the CEO being politically connected (*PCEO*), the proportion of independent directors on the board (*BIndep*), the number of independent directors (*NumIndep*), the total number of board members (*BSize*), firm size measured as log sales (*FSize*), firm leverage measured as total liabilities to total assets (*LEV*), ownership concentration measured as the proportion of shares held by the largest shareholders (*OwnCon*), the number of board meetings (*BMeet*), the number of shareholder meetings (*SHMeet*), and the number of supervisory board meetings (*SBMeet*) per year, and the number of supervisory board members (*SBSize*).

To examine whether a politically connected CEO or board chairperson influences a firm's preference for certain independent director characteristics, we implement the following logistic regression:

$$Indep_{i,t} = \beta_0 + \beta_1 PChair_{i,t} + \beta_2 CEO_{i,t} + \sum_{k=1}^{6} \beta_{k+7}\, CTRL_{k,i,t} + \varepsilon_{i,t} \tag{2}$$

where, for firm i in year t, $Indep_{i,t}$ represents in turn the seven independent director characteristics respectively measured by *ACAD*, *ACCT*, *POLIT*, *FIN*, *LEGAL*, *OSEAS*, or *OTHER* (that is, this regression is run seven times using seven different variables as the dependent variables); *PChair* and *PCEO* are indicators as defined previously; $CTRL_{j,i,t}$ is a reduced set of control variables consisting of *BIndep, NumIndep, BSize, FSize, LEV,* and *OwnCon,* as defined earlier.

8.4 Empirical findings

Table 8.1 presents the distribution of the independent directors across the different characteristics. The independent directors were recruited by the 214 sampled firms between 2002 and 2009. PChair = 1 (PChair = 0) indicates a board chairperson that is (is not) politically connected. PCEO = 1 (PCEO = 0) indicates a CEO that is (is not) politically connected. The chairperson and CEO are classified as politically connected if they have previously worked in central/local government or in the military.

In Table 8.1 the full sample of independent directors, academics account for over one third and accountants close to one fifth. Legal professionals, finance professionals and politicians each account for about one tenth of the sample. Boards with a politically connected chairperson appear to hire fewer academics, accountants, legal and finance professionals and overseas returnees. Such boards instead hire substantially more politicians as independent directors. Boards with a politically connected CEO hire marginally more academics, legal professionals and politicians. These patterns suggest that the political connections of CEOs and board chairpersons may influence the type of independent director appointed.

Table 8.2 presents summary statistics of the variables we use in our analyses. *ROA* is return on assets. *SEMP* is the ratio of sales to number of employees. *ACAD, ACCT, LEGAL, FIN, POLIT, OSEAS* and *OTHER* are dummy variables that equal 1 if the firm has an independent director

Table 8.1 Sample description

	Academic	Accountant	Legal	Finance	Politician	Overseas	Other
Full sample	37.63%	17.14%	9.21%	8.30%	12.27%	5.52%	9.93%
By Chair							
PChair = 1	34.98%	12.96%	8.23%	5.97%	22.22%	4.12%	11.52%
PChair = 0	38.40%	18.26%	9.48%	8.87%	9.67%	5.81%	9.50%
By CEO							
PCEO = 1	39.30%	15.40%	9.56%	7.50%	13.62%	3.61%	11.01%
PCEO = 0	36.61%	18.25%	8.96%	8.79%	11.45%	6.72%	9.21%

Table 8.2 Summary statistics

	Obs	Mean	Std dev	Min	Max
ROA	1227	6.50%	6.79%	–38.83%	42.25%
SEMP	1227	5.81	0.45	4.32	7.58
ACAD	1227	0.77	0.42	0	4
ACCT	1227	0.60	0.49	0	2
LEGAL	1227	0.33	0.47	0	2
FIN	1227	0.27	0.44	0	3
POLIT	1227	0.36	0.48	0	3
OSEAS	1227	0.18	0.38	0	4
OTHER	1227	0.38	0.46	0	2
PChair	1227	0.39	0.49	0	1
PCEO	1227	0.21	0.41	0	1
BSize	1227	9.32	1.88	5	18
NumIndep	1227	3.29	0.74	2	8
BIndep	1227	0.36	0.06	0.11	0.71
FSize	1227	8.85	0.50	7.33	10.74
LEV	1227	28.52%	19.49%	0.30%	90.02%
OwnCon	1227	37.10%	14.97%	7.93%	90.87%
BMeeting	1227	8.50	3.22	2.00	33
SHMeeting	1227	2.91	1.42	1	10
SBMeeting	1227	4.55	1.68	1	12
SBSize	1227	3.85	1.27	2	9

who was or is an academic, accountant, legal professional, financial professional, or politician, or is an overseas returnee, or has some other background, respectively, and 0 otherwise. *PChair* is 1 if the firm has a politically connected (previously worked in government or the military) chairperson and 0 otherwise. *PCEO* is 1 for a politically connected (previously worked in government or the military) *CEO* and 0 otherwise. *BSize* is the number of members on the board of directors. *NumIndep* is the number of independent directors. *BIndep* is the proportion of independent directors. *FSize* is firm size measured as the log of total sales. *LEV* is leverage measured as total debts to total assets. *OwnCon* is ownership concentration measured as the proportion of shares held by the largest shareholders. *BMeet* is the number of meetings of the board of directors per year. *SHMeet* is the number of shareholder meetings per year. SBMeet is the number of supervisory board meetings per year. *SBSize* is the number of supervisory board

Table 8.2 shows that over three quarters of the firms have academics and nearly two thirds have accountants as independent directors. About 39 percent of the firms have a politically connected chairperson on the board of directors and about 21 percent have a politically connected CEO.

This suggests that firms are more likely to be influenced by the political connections of their board chairperson than their CEO. On average, the firms in our sample have over nine members on their boards of directors, with nearly one third of them classified as independent, and their boards typically meet more than eight times per year. In contrast, the supervisory boards on average have just under four members and meet less than five times per year. Thus, the boards of directors appear to be more active than the supervisory boards.

Table 8.3 presents the results of our regression analysis of the association between independent director characteristics and firm performance and productivity in the following year. All variables are defined as above. Significance at the 10%, 5%, and 1% levels is indicated by *, ** and ***, respectively. Notice that the coefficients of *FIN* and *POLIT* are both significantly negative. This indicates that firms that hire independent directors with financial or political background are associated with lower profitability. One possible reason for this observation is that

Table 8.3 Independent director characteristics and firm performance

Dependent variable	ROA		SEMP	
ACAD	–0.0042	(0.442)	0.1099	(0.002)***
ACCT	0.0046	(0.296)	0.0305	(0.066)*
LEGAL	0.0010	(0.822)	0.0305	(0.291)
FIN	–0.0083	(0.096)*	–0.0372	(0.242)
POLIT	–0.0119	(0.008)***	0.0067	(0.815)
OSEAS	0.0021	(0.697)	0.0542	(0.111)
OTHER	–0.0039	(0.406)	0.0246	(0.418)
PChair	0.0001	(0.991)	–0.0082	(0.784)
PCEO	–0.0028	(0.621)	0.0031	(0.9314)
BIndep	–0.0477	(0.703)	–0.4161	(0.605)
NumIndep	0.0166	(0.202)	0.0427	(0.609)
BSize	–0.0032	(0.485)	–0.0278	(0.349)
FSize	0.0185	(0.000)***	0.3485	(0.000)***
LEV	–0.1119	(0.000)***	0.0692	(0.364)
OwnCon	–0.0137	(0.324)	–0.0233	(0.794)
BMeeting	–0.0019	(0.014)**	0.0086	(0.071)*
SHMeeting	–0.0009	(0.562)	–0.0078	(0.449)
SBMeeting	0.040	(0.004)***	0.0092	(0.294)
SBSize	0.0040	(0.019)**	0.0005	(0.965)
Constant	–0.0827	(0.168)	2.7379	(0.000)***
Firms	214		214	
Obs	1227		1227	
R^2	0.1373		0.1867	

independent directors with such backgrounds may facilitate the acquisition of capital from banks or the government, which in turn encourages excessive investment into lower Net Present Value (NPV) projects. Another possible reason is that operating performance is persistent and firms that underperform try to hire independent directors with financial and political backgrounds to help boost their capital acquisition. Turning to productivity, notice that the coefficients pertaining to *ACAD* and *ACCT* are both significantly positive. This indicates that firms that hire independent directors with academic and accountancy backgrounds are associated with higher productivity, as measured by the sales to employees ratio. One possible reason for this finding is that the expertise of academics and accountants improves the decisions of the firms that hire them. An alternative reason could be that firms with higher performance are more willing to hire academics and accountants as independent directors.

Table 8.4 presents the results of the regression analysis looking at the association between independent director characteristics and the

Table 8.4 Determinants of independent director characteristics

Dependent variable	*ACAD*	*ACCT*	*LEGAL*	*FIN*	*POLIT*	*OSEAS*
PCEO	–0.2592	0.2076	0.1018	–0.1017	0.0004	–0.1316
	(0.204)	(0.242)	(0.572)	(0.615)	(0.998)	(0.590)
PChair	0.2627	–0.3931	0.0082	–0.3570	0.2305	–0.5414
	(0.130)	(0.007)***	(0.957)	(0.030)**	(0.125)	(0.006)***
NumIndep	0.2494	–0.3924	0.2068	0.9546	0.5883	–0.3394
	(0.606)	(0.360)	(0.626)	(0.065)*	(0.169)	(0.497)
BIndep	–0.0837	3.7940	–2.0049	–5.7277	–3.8253	4.2260
	(0.986)	(0.357)	(0.633)	(0.252)	(0.362)	(0.388)
BSize	0.0338	0.1586	0.0909	–0.1703	–0.0344	0.1536
	(0.844)	(0.306)	(0.548)	(0.363)	(0.822)	(0.395)
FSize	0.0451	–0.0976	–0.1939	–0.5276	0.0258	0.3665
	(0.784)	(0.499)	(0.1917)	(0.001)***	(0.859)	(0.039)**
LEV	–0.6944	0.5286	0.1127	1.3171	–0.2186	0.1832
	(0.094)*	(0.152)	(0.764)	(0.001)***	(0.560)	(0.689)
OwnCon	–0.4334	1.3550	–1.4432	–0.5851	1.3888	0.8139
	(0.380)	(0.003)***	(0.002)***	(0.228)	(0.002)***	(0.130)
Constant	0.0265	–0.7125	0.7302	4.1546	–1.6247	–6.7437
	(0.990)	(0.711)	(0.709)	(0.064)*	(0.401)	(0.004)***
Firm	214	214	214	214	214	214
Obs	1227	1227	1227	1227	1227	1227
R^2	0.0134	0.0154	0.0253	0.0363	0.0280	0.0247

presence of a politically connected CEO or board chairperson. All variables are defined as above. Significance at the 10%, 5%, and 1% levels is indicated by *,** and ***, respectively. Notice that the coefficient of *PCEO* is insignificant across all seven dependent variables. This indicates that there are no observable associations between having a politically connected CEO and the type of independent directors hired. However, *PChair* is significantly negative when the dependent variable is *ACCT, FIN,* or *OSEAS*. This suggests that firms with a politically connected chairperson of their board of directors are less likely to have accountants, finance professionals, and overseas returnees as independent directors. Politically connected chairs may be more capable (due to their background) of gaining financial support from the government, which would in turn reduce the need to hire accountants or finance professionals. Firms with politically connected chairs are also more likely to be well-established state-owned enterprises, which would require less input from overseas returnees relative to newly established younger firms in high growth industries. These findings are robust to controls of the following board characteristics: the number of independent directors, board independence, board size, firm size, leverage and ownership concentration.

8.5 Conclusion

Independent directors play two important roles for firms. First, they bolster their internal corporate governance mechanisms by providing more impartial monitoring of executives. Second, their experience and background could provide firms with useful access to external resources and expertise. In this study, we show a significant association between certain types of independent directors and firm performance in China. This implies that future reforms in China should not only regulate the number of independent directors but also set guidelines as to their characteristics. We further show that the preference for certain types of independent directors is affected by the political connectedness of the chairperson of the board. This implies that future reforms in China should also consider the influence the chairperson has on the monitoring efficiency and the quality of the board of directors.

Notes

1. See Clarke (2006) for further discussion of the institutional background regarding independent directors in China.

References

Agrawal, A. and Knoeber, C. 1996. Firm performance and mechanisms to control agency problems between managers and shareholders. *Journal of Financial and Quantitative Analysis*, 31: 377–397.

Baysinger, B. and Butler, H. 1985. Corporate governance and the board of directors: performance effects of changes in board composition. *Journal of Law, Economics, and Organization*, 1: 101–124.

Beasley, M. 1996. An empirical analysis of the relation between the board of director composition and financial statement fraud. *The Accounting Review*, 71: 443–465.

Bhagat, S. and Black, B. 1999. The uncertain relationship between board composition and firm performance. *Business Lawyer*, Vol. : 921–963.

Bhagat, S. and Black, B. 2001. The non-correlation between board independence and long term firm performance. *Journal of Corporate Law*, 27: 231–273.

Black, B. 1990. Shareholder passivity reexamined. *Michigan Law Review*, 89: 520–608.

Brickley, J. and James, C. 1987. The takeover market, corporate board composition, ownership structure: the case of banking. *Journal of Law and Economics*, 30: 161–180.

Brickley, J., Coles, J. and Terry, R. 1994. Outside directors and the adoption of poison pills. *Journal of Financial Economics*, 35: 371–390.

Clarke, D. 2006. The independent director in Chinese corporate governance. *Delaware Journal of Corporate Law*, 31: 125–228.

Coles, J., Daniel, N. and Naveen, L. 2006. Boards: does one size fit all? *Journal of Financial Economics*, 87: 329–356.

Dalton, D., Daily, C., Ellstrand, A. and Johnson, J. 1998. Meta-analytic reviews of board composition, leadership structure, and financial performance. *Strategic Management Journal*, 19: 269–290.

Dahya, J., McConnell, J. and Travlos, N. 2002. The Cadbury Committee, Corporate performance and top management turnover. *Journal of Finance*, 57: 461–483.

Dechow, P., Sloan, R. and Sweeney, A. 1996. Causes and consequences of earnings manipulation: an analysis of firms subject to enforcement action by the SEC. *Contemporary Accounting Research*, 13: 1–36.

Dedman, E. 2003. Executive turnover in UK firms: the impact of Cadbury. *Accounting and Business Research*, 33: 33–50.

Dedman, E., Lim, S. and Lin, S. 2006. Board reforms and their impact on firm performance: an empirical analysis of the higgs recommendations, Working Paper (University of Manchester).

Demsetz, H. and Lehn, K. 1985. The structure of corporate ownership: causes and consequences. *Journal of Political Economy*, 33: 3–53.

Denis, D. 2001. Twenty-five years of corporate governance research and counting. *Review of Financial Economics*, 10: 191–212.

Denis, D. and Sarin, A. 1999. Ownership and board structure in publicly traded corporations. *Journal of Financial Economics*, 52: 187–223.

Ezzamel, M. and Watson, R. 1993. Organisational form, ownership structure, and corporate performance: a contextual empirical analysis of UK companies. *British Journal of Management*, 4: 161–176.

Fama, E. and Jensen, M. 1983. Separation of ownership and control. *Journal of Law and Economics*, 26: 301–326.

Fama, E. 1980. Agency problems and the theory of the firm. *Journal of Political Economy*, 88: 715–732.

Fama, E. 1998. Market efficiency, long-run returns, and behavioural finance. *Journal of Financial Economics*, 49: 283–306.

Fosberg, R. 1989. Outside directors and managerial monitoring. *Akron Business and Economic Review*, 20: 24–32.

Fox, A. and Opong, K. 1999. The impact of board changes on shareholder wealth: some UK evidence. *Corporate Governance: An International Review*, 7: 385–396.

Gillian, S., Hartzell, J. and Starks, L. 2004. Explaining corporate governance: boards, bylaws, and charter provisions, Working Paper (University of Texas).

Gilson, R. and Kraakman, R. 1991. Reinventing the outside director: an agenda for institutional investors. *Stanford Law Review*, 43: 863–906.

Hambriek, D. and Finkelstein, S. 1995. The effects of ownership structure on conditions at the top: the case of CEO pay raises. *Strategic Management Journal*, 16: 176–193.

Harris, M. and Raviv, A. 2008. A theory of board control and size. *Review of Financial Studies*, 21: 1797–1832.

Hermalin, B. and Weisbach, M. 1991. The effects of board composition and direct incentives on firm performance. *Financial Management*, 20: 101–112.

Holthausen, R. and Larcker, D. 1993. Board of directors, ownership structure, and CEO compensation, Working Paper (University of Pennsylvania).

Kesner, I. 1987. Directors stock ownership and organisational performance: an investigation of Fortune 500 companies. *Journal of Management*, 13: 499–508.

Klein, A. 1998. Affiliated directors: puppets of management or effective directors?, Working Paper (New York University).

Lehn, K., Patro, S. and Zhao, M. 2009. Determinants of the size and structures of corporate boards: 1935–2000. *Financial Management*, 38: 747–780.

Liao, J., Young, M. and Sun, Q. 2009. Independent directors' characteristics and performance: evidence from China, Working Paper (Massey University).

Lin, S., Pope, P. and Young, S. 2003. Stock market reaction to the appointment of outsider directors. *Journal of Business, Finance and Accounting*, 30: 351–382.

Linck, J., Netter, J. and Yang, T. 2005. The determinants of board structure. *Journal of Financial Economics*, 27: 308–328.

Morck, R., Shleifer, A. and Vishny, R. 1988. Management ownership and market valuation: an empirical analysis. *Journal of Financial Economics*, 20: 293–315.

Pope, P., Peasnell, K. and Young, S. 2001. The characteristics of firms subject to adverse rulings by the financial reporting review panel. *Accounting and Business Research*, 31: 291–311.

Raheja, C. 2004. Determinant of board size and composition: a theory of corporate boards. *Journal of Financial and Quantitative Analysis*, 2005, 40: 283–306.

Rosenstein, S. and Wyatt, J. 1990. Outside directors, board independence and shareholder wealth. *Journal of Financial Economics*, 26: 175–191.

Weisbach, M. 1988. Outside directors and CEO turnover. *Journal of Financial Economics*, 20: 431–460.

Yermack, D. 1996. Higher market valuation of companies with a small board of directors. *Journal of Financial Economics*, 40: 185–212.

Index

Printed and bound in the United States of America